CIVIL WAR FIREARMS

CIVIL WAR FIREARMS

*Their Historical Background,
Tactical Use and Modern
Collecting and Shooting*

Joseph G. Bilby

COMBINED BOOKS
Pennsylvania

Library of Congress Cataloging-in-Publication Data

Bilby, Joseph G.
    Civil War Firearms : their historical background, tactical use and modern collecting
and shooting
        / Joseph G. Bilby.
            p. cm.
        Includes bibliographical references and index.
        ISBN 0-938289-79-9
            1. United States—Armed Forces—Firearms—History—19th century.
        2. United States—History—Civil War, 1861-1865—Equipment and supplies.
        I. Title.
        UD383.B55   1996   96-33314
        623.4'42'097309034—dc20   CIP

Printed in the United States of America.

This book is dedicated to the men and women
of the North-South Skirmish Association

Yesterday, Today, and Tomorrow

Contents

Acknowledgments

This book had its origins in a series of columns written for *The Civil War News*. I would like to take this opportunity to thank Peter and Kathryn Jorgensen of *The Civil War News* for giving me the venue to write that column and all the readers of that publication for their encouragement and constructive criticism over the years.

I would also like to thank someone I've never met. Ken Baumann, whose *Arming the Suckers* is a pioneering work which opened up sources of Illinois soldier commentary on firearms that would have taken years of research to plumb.

No work such as this can be the sole product of one individual. I have been fortunate to have a number of people lend a hand over the course of my research and writing. Bill Goble, Inspector General of the North-South Skirmish Association (N-SSA) gave continued encouragement and, more important, research advice. Bill also introduced me to Bill Adams, whose expertise in British and Confederate arms saved me from a number of errors. Bill's continuing research, along with that of Paul Davies and Earl J. Coates, all N-SSA members, will revolutionize much of the Civil War firearms knowledge we now accept as gospel.

I would also like to thank a number of other people who have supplied me with valuable research material, encouraged, and, on occasion argued with me—all to my benefit: Donald Bates, Tony Beck, Tom Berwick, John Bilby, Earl J. Coates,Tom Conroy, Jerry Decius, Steve DesMarais, Frank and Dave Dworak, Fred Everson, Robert F. Fisch, Neal Friedenthal, Harry Gaul, Steve Garratano, Jim Heayn, Charles R. Howard, John Huelskamp, John Jenkins, Tom Kelley, John Kuhl, Ben Maryniak, Dr. David Martin, Michael J. McAfee, Joe McAvoy, Andy Megill, Steve Meserve, Dennis Murphy, "Red" Meinecke, Rob Myers, Bill Nolze, Bill Osborne, Seward Osborne, Brian Pohanka, Harry Roach, John Rountree, Maurice A. Scully, Jr., Phil and Ed Seiss, Charles Smithgall, Dr. Richard Stein, Bud and Steve Wheeler, Ian Whitewood, Bob Wierski, and Charles Worman.

If I have forgotten anyone, please forgive me. Any errors in this book, are, of course, my own.

There has never been another book quite like this, and it is hoped that it will prove of interest and value to historians, Civil War "buffs" and shooters alike.

Joseph G. Bilby
Wall Township, NJ, 1996

Introduction

According to conventional wisdom, the Civil War was the first "modern" war. This contention is based on, among other things, the use of the telegraph for communications and trains for transporting troops by both sides, as well as intelligence gathering through aerial observation (from balloons) and mass production of the sinews of war by the Union. Another factor often used to buttress the modernity argument is the widespread use of long-range rifled artillery and small arms and the introduction of breech loading and repeating rifles.

As is often the case with broad historical generalizations, things are often not as they first appear, particularly in the case of small arms. While it is true that the rifle-musket became the standard infantry arm for both Union and Confederate infantrymen in the Civil War, it is less well-known that these "modern" weapons were not general issue until the war's mid-point.

As late as the battle of Gettysburg, July 1, 2 and 3, 1863, 10.5% of the regiments in the Army of the Potomac, the best-equipped Federal army, were still armed, in whole or in part, with obsolete smoothbore muskets. Except for their percussion ignition, these guns differed little in ballistic capability from the weapons shouldered by those Yankee soldiers' grandfathers in the Revolution and the War of 1812. Smoothbores were common issue in Confederate ranks and in both armies west of the Appalachians well into 1864.

Many analysts attribute the heavy casualties suffered in Civil War battles to the fact that commanders failed to recognize the extended range of the new rifle-musket and used the tactics of earlier conflicts fought with smoothbore muskets, including the Revolution and the Napoleonic struggles of the early part of the nineteenth century. The rifle-musket's potential combat range of up to 900 yards far exceeded the 100 yard practical range of the smoothbore and could, theoretically, inflict large losses on dense attacking formations at long range.

Upon closer examination, however, it is clear that the potential long-range accuracy of the rifle-musket mattered little, particularly in the first half of the conflict. Not only did many soldiers not carry them, but officers, including those commanding men with rifled firearms, routinely had their men hold fire until the advancing enemy was well within the effective range of the older smoothbore. In fact, the smoothbore, with its multi-projectile "buck-and-ball" load of a large round ball and three buckshot, may well have proved more effective than the rifle-musket at usual combat ranges. Interestingly, despite popular belief, casualties in Civil War battles were not proportionately heavier than those suffered in the great smoothbore battles of the Napoleonic era.

A more radical Civil War firearms innovation than the rifling of a musket barrel and introduction of the long-range "minie ball" was the introduction of breech-loading arms, both single shot and repeating. Single-shot breech loaders were most evident in the ranks of cavalry units, where even conservative ordnance officers, who felt muzzle loaders the best arms for infantry, supported their use since they were easier to reload on horseback.

Single-shot breech-loading carbines, many of which failed to stand up to the rigors of field service, fired various "patent" paper, cardboard and metallic cartridges, usually ignited by an external percussion cap. Ammunition for these weapons, which varied according to type, was often in short supply. In addition, even when ammunition was plentiful, most of these "patent" guns, with the notable exception of the Sharps, lacked the range and accuracy of the rifle-musket.

Although carbines had a higher rate of fire than infantry muzzle loaders, cavalrymen armed with breech loaders rarely engaged in sustained firefights with infantry soldiers carrying muzzle loaders. Dismounted cavalrymen, who deployed as a matter of course in a thin "skirmish" formation with every fourth man detached to hold horses, could not stand up to the massed, if slower, rates of fire of infantry formations.

The Sharps, which combined reliability and sturdiness with superior accuracy, was the best of the breechloading single-shot carbines. It was also issued in a rifle version for infantry service. Although the Sharps rifle gained an excellent reputation for long-range accuracy and rapidity of fire in the hands of Berdan's sharpshooters and other troops, it was never in service in enough numbers to affect the course of the war. The Sharps was much more complicated to manufacture than the rifle-musket, and large scale production of Sharps rifles would have deprived the cavalry of needed carbines.

Repeating carbines and rifles firing self-contained cartridges fed from a multi-shot magazine were the most technologically advanced small arms used in the Civil War. The combat effect of these guns, primarily the Henry and Spencer, has been exaggerated as well. There is no evidence that repeaters ever turned the tide in a major battle and their record in smaller actions is mixed. The propensity for soldiers armed with repeaters to shoot away all their ammunition was noted on several occasions and, like the single-shot breech loaders, the Spencer and Henry were essentially short range weapons.

John Singleton Mosby's guerrillas used six shot revolvers (each of Mosby's men carried several handguns) with great effectiveness against Spencer-armed Federal horsemen. The revolver, which predated the rifle-musket, breech loader and repeating rifle alike, was the one Civil War weapon that completely lived up to its reputation. In a close range melee, nothing proved better.

A large part of the blame for the failure of rifle-muskets, breech loaders and repeaters to live up to their technological potential lies with the men who carried them and the men who, in turn, led them. Mosby and his Partisan Rangers were unique in recognizing the capabilities and limitations of their weapons. Most soldiers, sharpshooters on both sides excepted, armed with rifle-muskets, breech loaders, repeaters and revolvers knew little of ballistics or even basic marksmanship techniques— and never learned otherwise. Although they drilled relentlessly, Civil War soldiers rarely practiced shooting, and junior and senior officers generally knew little about firearms. When men did fire their weapons in training it was most likely in the form of what is called in today's military "familiarization firing."

A noted exception of this sorry state of affairs was Confederate Major General Patrick Cleburne. Cleburne, an Irish-born veteran of the British army, trained his infantrymen in range estimation and target practice at various distances up to and including 800 yards. The Irish-born general also established a sharpshooter detachment, armed with long-range British-made Whitworth rifles, which made life dangerous for artillery-men and Yankee officers within 1,500 yards of Confederate lines.

Cleburne's sharpshooters and other special units like Berdan's sharp-shooters and the sharpshooter battalions of the Army of Northern Virginia to the contrary, there is little doubt that modern shooters of original and reproduction Civil War guns, most notably those of the North-South Skirmish Association (N-SSA) are, on average, far better and more knowledgeable shots than their Civil War forbears. Beginning in the early 1950s, the N-SSA retrieved the lost art of shooting Civil War rifle-muskets and has, in the intervening years, added the full spectrum of period small arms to its competition schedule. In the process, much has been learned regarding the actual potential of these weapons. The study of Civil War small arms by actually firing them can best be classified as "empirical history." Unfortunately, many of the lessons learned on the rifle range have not been available to the Civil War academic community.

This work covers the basic types of Civil War infantry and cavalry small arms, including smoothbore muskets, rifle-muskets, sharpshooter weapons, breechloading carbines, repeating rifles and revolvers and their development and tactical use in United States and Confederate service. Each chapter is devoted to a specific type of weapon, and considers both its historical employment and use in modern target practice and "empirical history" study. Needless to say, neither the publisher, myself or those who I have consulted can take responsibility for any firearms experimentation over which we have no control. The loads and experiments detailed herein worked in the particular firearms used for us; we cannot recommend them to others.

CHAPTER I

Smoothbores

The attack rippled down the line, leaving trampled cornfields and burning farmhouses in its wake. In among the broken stalks of a harvest that would never be gleaned lay scattered the bodies of the fallen. It was September 17, 1862, and before the sun went down along the banks of Antietam Creek more than 4,000 men would be dead.

It was late morning now and much of the killing and maiming was still to come. The men of Brigadier General Thomas F. Meagher's Irish Brigade of the First Division of the Army of the Potomac's II Corps dropped their excess equipment and double-quicked across the Roulette farm towards a sunken lane full of Rebels. After dismantling a fence under artillery fire and brushing aside retreating Yankees, the Irishmen pushed forward rapidly, attempting to close the distance between them and the enemy. The closer Meagher's men got, the more effective their .69-caliber smoothbore muskets, loaded with "buck-and-ball" cartridges, would be.

Before reaching the main Confederate position, the brigade encountered Colonel Carnot Posey's Mississippi brigade, which had left the relative security of the road to pursue a retreating Union regiment. The Irishmen leveled their muskets and blasted Posey's men with buckshot and bullets, shooting the Sixteenth Mississippi Infantry to shreds and routing the rest of Posey's command. Pushing within thirty yards of the Grayback line, the Irish Brigade slugged it out in a standup fight. The Irish took heavy casualties, but held their formation until they ran out of ammunition. Then, in a parade-ground maneuver, they gave way to fresh troops, who cleared out the surviving Rebels.

The Confederate corpses littering what came to be called "Bloody Lane" at Antietam were mute testimony to the efficiency of Civil War infantry weapons. Many, if not most of them had been laid low by the Irish Brigade's buck and ball. Interestingly, combination loads of buckshot and round balls and the smoothbore muskets which fired them, were, by all official standards, obsolete before the outbreak of the war.

In the centuries prior to 1861, however, smoothbored weapons had a long and honored history. Although rifled shoulder arms were available in Central Europe by the sixteenth century, smoothbores, which were cheaper to manufacture and could be reloaded more rapidly, were favored for military use. A well-bored eighteenth-century musket was capable of reasonable accuracy on man-sized targets up to fifty yards, and volley fire was effective on large formations up to a hundred yards or so.

A British government test conducted in 1846 found the maximum range of a smoothbore musket with a muzzle elevation of five degrees to be "about 650 yards, the point-blank range being 75 yards." After establishing range parameters, the ordnance testers then fired a smoothbore at "a target 11 ft. 6 in. high by 6 ft. wide." Ten shots fired at this target at a range of 250 yards all missed, while five hit the same target at 150 yards. At 200 yards the board found that it was necessary to aim five and a half feet above a target to come anywhere near it. Although an American calculation indicated that a ball fired from a smoothbore musket retained "sufficient force to pass through a pine board 1 in. thick" at 500 yards, the British board concluded that "as a general rule, musketry fire should not be made at a distance exceeding 150 yards and certainly not exceeding 200 yards, as at and beyond that range it would be a mere waste of ammunition to do so." With these facts in mind, infantry tactics of the time were based on the short-range and relatively rapid fire of the smoothbore.[1]

Within its range limitations, the smoothbore musket was an awesome weapon. At the battle of Austerlitz in 1805, the defeated Austro-Russian Army lost 27,000 men killed, wounded and missing out of a total strength of 85,700. At Borodino, in 1812, Napoleon lost 30,000 of his 130,000 men while his Russian opponents suffered 40,000 casualties from a total force of 120,800 men. These losses, largely inflicted by smoothbore muskets and artillery, are quite comparable to those suffered in most Civil War

This pre-war militiaman was a member of the 8th Massachusetts Militia. Like many state militiamen, he is armed with a Model 1842 smoothbore musket, which was very effective at close range with the deadly buck-and-ball load of three buckshot and a .64- or .65- caliber ball. *(USAMHI)*

battles which, after 1862, were primarily fought with the more accurate rifle-musket. One analysis of smoothbore battles versus pre-Civil War fights in which both sides possessed more accurate rifle-muskets suggested that casualty percentages in the earlier battles were considerably higher: "At Waterloo, French, 0.36, Allies 0.31. At Magenta, June 4, 1859, French, 0.07, Austrians, 0.08."[2]

Although loading a single-round ball seems to have been standard procedure in the early days of the musket, some people stuffed more than one projectile down the barrels of their smoothbores early on. Samuel de Champlain loaded four balls in his arquebus before encountering Iroquois Indians on the shores of the lake which bears his name in 1609. The French explorer's matchlock musket laid several Indians low with one shot.

Men of the 27th New York Infantry in 1861. Like many regiments raised that year, these soldiers are armed with smoothbore muskets, in this case U.S. Model 1842s. *(Seward Osborne Collection)*

Although Champlain used full-sized balls, by the time of the American Revolution it was common practice to load smaller buckshot, averaging around .30-caliber, along with a musket ball in the paper cartridges used in .69- and .75-caliber muskets. The number of buckshot per cartridge varied, and, in the 1775 American attack on Quebec, General Henry Dearborn carried a musket "charged with a ball and Ten Buckshott." In October of 1777, General George Washington recommended that his men deliver their first volley with a load of "one musket ball and four or eight buckshott, according to the strength of their pieces." In October 1777, Washington ordered that "buckshot are to be put into all cartridges which shall hereafter be made." Some Revolutionary War cartridges were purchased from contractors, while others were made up by the soldiers themselves. Maryland issued troops bullet molds casting both buckshot and musket balls.[3]

Single-ball, buckshot-and-ball, and straight buckshot loads of from twelve to fifteen pellets remained part of the American military ammunition inventory after the Revolution. Those men on the Lewis and Clark expedition who carried muskets were issued one hundred balls and two pounds of buckshot each and cartridges loaded with both buckshot and ball were standard issue during the War of 1812. Single-ball loads for the .69-caliber United States musket fired undersized .64-caliber projectiles to facilitate quick loading, at the expense of accuracy. The addition of buckshot made a hit more likely.

Men of the 8th New York State Militia photographed in July 1861 prior to the battle of Bull Run. The New Yorkers are armed with Model 1842 rifled muskets. Originally manufactured as smoothbores, these guns were rifled and had long-range rear sights mounted in the 1850s. *(Michael McAfee)*

As the nineteenth century progressed, firearms theorists in both America and Europe demonstrated that the accuracy of the smoothbore musket could be improved by increasing the size of the ball and decreasing the weight and improving the quality of the powder charge. In the 1840s the diameter of the American musket ball was increased to .65 and the gun's powder charge reduced from 130 to 110 grains. Although accuracy improved somewhat, most military men continued to rely on multiple projectiles to improve combat hit ratios.

Due to the limited effective range of straight buckshot loads, they were largely used as guard cartridges, and buck and ball became the military's favored combat round. Between 1835 and 1840, three times as many buck-and-ball cartridges, loaded with a standard musket ball and three buckshot, were issued as single ball loads by the United States Ordnance Department.

Civilian shooters, especially eastern deer hunters who stalked their quarry in deep woods where ranges were short, also saw advantages in multi-ball loads. According to Ned Roberts, a New Hampshire hunter loaded his "smoothbore rifle" with buckshot in the 1840s because: "When a feller has ter shoot nigh dark, or in a hurry, he hes a better chance ter hit with the smoothbore loaded with buckshot than with a rifle thet hes but one ball." Muskets loaded with buck and ball and buckshot were favored for close in work and defense of forts by many civilian frontiersmen.[4]

It was that "better chance ter hit" that inspired French military writers in the 1830s to extol the American-style buck-and-ball load. The French were predisposed towards loading multiple projectiles, and Marshal Bugeaud had advocated double-ball loading in the musket as early as the Napoleonic Wars. As the French expanded their colonial empire in North Africa, they encountered Arab guerrillas who wouldn't stand in compact formations to get shot, and adopted the American buck-and-ball load in the belief that they had a better chance to tag their elusive adversaries with multi-shot musketry. Only one other European country, Denmark, ever issued a multi-ball load.

Eventually, however, the French developed the conical-expanding "minie" bullet, which allowed rifled weapons to be loaded as fast as smoothbores, and discarded buck and ball. The Americans followed the French lead this time and, in 1855, adopted a .58-caliber "rifle-musket" firing an improved version of the minie ball. The new rifled arms were slow in getting to the troops, however, and to fill the gap, some Model

A Federal infantryman, probably from the western armies, with an imported smoothbore musket. Imported and obsolete guns were common in the west through the end of the war. *(Michael J. McAfee)*

1842 percussion ignition .69-caliber smoothbores were rifled. Minie-style bullets were supplied for these guns and the .54-caliber Model 1841 round-ball rifles in service. Within a few years no regular United States army troops were carrying smoothbore muskets. Although many of the old flintlock smoothbores in state militia arsenals were converted to the percussion-ignition system in the 1850s, most remained unrifled.

The droves of recruits who flocked to Federal and Confederate colors at the outbreak of the Civil War clamored for .58-caliber rifle-muskets, the most modern muzzle-loading arms available. Supplies of these guns, were, however, limited. Of the 503,000 shoulder arms held in Federal and Northern state arsenals at the outbreak of war, 400,000 were .69-caliber smoothbores, and 100,000 of the 135,000 small arms either seized or held by Southern states were smoothbores as well. The unrifled arms

A collection of foreign arms which saw service in America. Top to Bottom: *British India pattern .75-caliber Brown Bess musket.* Recent archeological evidence proves this arm was in use in America at the time of the American Revolution. Some may have been in service early in the Civil War; *British .71-caliber Minie rifle.* Saw extensive service in the Crimea. Some are believed to have been imported by the Confederacy; *three of the Enfield family (rifle-musket, rifle and carbine).* The most common foreign arms used in America during the Civil War; *British .70-caliber Sea Service smoothbore musket.* Some of these guns were imported by the Confederacy; *Austrian .54-caliber Jaeger rifle.* Note the high front sight installed for modern short range shooting; *Austrian .71-caliber Model 1849 naval or marine rifle.* Also known as the Garibaldi rifle due to supposed use by the Italian revolutionary's troops. The Union imported 10,000. *(Bill Goble)*

included Model 1816/1822 Springfield flintlock muskets, the same weapons converted to the percussion system by various means and Model 1842 muskets originally issued as percussion guns. Available rifled firearms in 1861 were largely converted smoothbores and older weapons like the Model 1841 rifle.

Although a trickle of imported weapons, both rifled and smoothbore, which became a flood in 1862, eased the overall firearms shortage on both sides by the end of the year, the majority of Union and Confederate regiments raised in the first year of the war carried U.S. pattern .69-caliber smoothbore muskets, primarily Model 1842s and converted flintlocks. Among the arms captured by Federal troops following their February, 1862 victory at Roanoke Island were large numbers of flintlock muskets. Some Confederates, especially those in the western armies, carried flintlocks as late as the April 1862 battle of Shiloh.

New Jersey militiamen were highly annoyed when the Federal government gave them bright-finished smoothbores—which they would have to polish assiduously for inspections—in exchange for their browned state-issue smoothbore weapons rather than rifle-muskets. Other units reacted more violently, and, in the case of the Seventy-ninth New York, a smoothbore exchange for more smoothbores contributed to a mini-mutiny which had to be suppressed by regular army troops. In 1862, New Jersey recruits vandalized their smoothbores in the vain hope that they would be replaced by rifled arms. One Illinois newspaper dismissed smoothbores as "fit for nothing but drill."[5]

Given the opportunity, many men ditched their smoothbore muskets —often on the battlefield. Soldiers of the Eighth Illinois Infantry were "armed with the American Smooth-bore muskets...until after Shiloh battle, when a large number of the muskets were exchanged for Enfield and other rifles gathered from the field."[6]

Distaste for smoothbore arms was not universal, however. A veteran of the Twentieth Illinois recalled that "although the boys were not very pleased" with the smoothbores they were issued in 1861, "they proved a very efficient and deadly weapon, and some of them were carried all through the service." Brigadier General Thomas F. Meagher, commander of the Irish Brigade, one of the best units in the Union army, specifically requested smoothbore muskets for his men because he thought much of the brigade's fighting "would be at very close quarters." William O'Grady of the Irish Brigade's Eighty-eighth New York Infantry recalled after the war, however, that "sometimes our short-range weapons were a disadvantage."[7]

Many officers, assuming that most fights would take place at seventy-five yards or less, however, agreed with Meagher. As late as 1863, Colonel George L. Willard of the 125th New York flatly stated that "under certain circumstances, the arms formerly employed [smoothbores] were more effective than the new ones, particularly, when at close quarters." According to Willard, the necessity to change sight settings during the

The N-SSA in 1996. The 69th New York color guard wears a mixture of fatigue blouses, New York State coats and frock coats, as was common in the field. Flags are embroidered silk reproductions of the regiment's original first-issue flags. *(Ron Da Silva)*

course of combat, especially when infantrymen faced a fast-closing cavalry charge, was too confusing for average troops. He believed infantrymen would do better to hold their fire until the horsemen were close and then deliver a decimating volley of buck and ball.[8]

In fact, throughout the Civil War, cavalrymen were generally very reluctant to charge infantry armed with anything, but Meagher and Willard might not have been too far off the mark. British military historian Paddy Griffith has asserted that the types of small arms used by opponents in most Civil War battles mattered little because the tactics (or lack of same) employed by officers on both sides led to essentially short-range firefights in which the accuracy of the individual or his weapon were largely irrelevant. If this is true, then the .69-caliber smoothbore may have had an advantage over the rifle-musket in most fights, as a buck-and-ball load gave the shooter four chances to kill or disable his enemy.

Most authorities thought buck-and-ball effective up to a hundred yards, which Griffith states was the average distance of a firefight during the first two years of the war. In a test conducted in Texas in 1855, soldiers firing .69-caliber buck and ball at a six-by-eighteen-foot target a hundred yards away scored as many hits with their Model 1842 smoothbore muskets as a company armed with .54-caliber Model 1841 rifles firing patched round balls when each group fired a specified number of rounds. Although the lethality of buckshot at that distance can be fairly questioned, a wound does not have to be fatal to be tactically effective. In most cases, a wounded man will quickly leave the immediate scene of battle and may require one or more others to help him off.

Due to a lack of surgical antisepsis, minor wounds during the Civil War often proved fatal or disabling far out of proportion to the initial damage they caused. Lieutenant Joseph McDanolds of the Seventh New Jersey was put out of action by a buckshot wound at Chancellorsville. McDanolds was "shot in the head—the ball entering on the left side between the scalp and the skull, and ploughing from the back to the front, coming out near the temple. Had it been a minie ball, it would inevitably have crashed through his skull, and probably caused instant death." The lieutenant had to return home on furlough to recover. A soldier from the Fifteenth New Jersey Infantry suffered multiple buckshot wounds in his right hand at the battle of Salem Church on May 3, 1863. Four balls were extracted by army surgeons, but the man was invalided home, where his local doctor found a fifth shot, flattened out to nearly an inch in diameter, in his wrist. He subsequently received a disability discharge.[9]

By mid-1862 some soldiers had modified their previously dim view of the smoothbore. After surveying the slaughter his regiment wreaked with buck and ball at the battle of Williamsburg in 1862, a New Jersey infantryman wrote: "At times, rifles would have been preferable, but as a general thing we did well with our smoothbores, as buckshot *tells* at short ranges." With rifle-muskets still in short supply, many new regiments raised that year, including the Eleventh New Jersey, Twelfth New Hampshire and Twelfth Rhode Island, were issued a mix of smoothbores and rifles, with the latter arms going to companies designated for skirmishing duty. This policy coincided with Colonel Willard's belief that *"at short ranges, the buck and ball cartridge is certainly more effective, and it is susceptible of proof, that it is a grave error, to adopt for an army, rifled, to the entire exclusion of the smoothbored arms."*[10]

Some outfits were still issued only smoothbores, however. The 116th Pennsylvania, which joined General Meagher's Irish Brigade after the battle of Antietam, was armed, no doubt to the general's delight, entirely with "the 'old pattern musket' that was loaded with a ball,-caliber .69 and three buckshot." In contrast to the policy in most units, however, the men of the 116th actually held "frequent target practice down by the riverbank, where the boys fired away at imaginary Confederates and filled trees full of buck and ball."[11]

Beyond 100 yards or so, it is doubtful that many of the trees the Pennsylvanians plinked at suffered serious injury. In 1861, some men from the Fourteenth Illinois fired 160 shots from their converted flintlock smoothbores at a barrel 180 yards away. They only hit it three times. When the 116th was recruited up to strength prior to the campaign of 1864, though, all the regiment's new men were issued smoothbores as well. It should be noted however, that the Irish Brigade's Twenty-eighth Massachusetts was always armed with rifle-muskets. The men of the Twenty-eighth were often detailed to skirmishing and flank-guard details.

Despite the smoothbore musket's lack of long-range accuracy, many outfits were happy without rifles in the ranks. The men of the Twelfth New Jersey gladly turned in their initial issue of Austrian rifle-muskets for Model 1842 smoothbores. The Jerseyans of the Twelfth developed a sentimental attachment for their muskets, keeping them even when rifle-muskets became generally available. One soldier thought his 1842 was "as handsome a gun as was ever made." The Twelfth had its finest hour at Gettysburg. While waiting for Pickett's Charge, the Jerseymen tore open buck-and-ball cartridges and loaded their versatile smoothbores with massive charges of buckshot, with which they riddled the left flank of the Confederate attack. The Twelfth's Gettysburg monument, passed by thousands of no-doubt puzzled tourists every year, is a column surmounted by a huge round ball and three proportionately oversized buckshot, mute testimony to the reverence the men of the outfit retained for their obsolete but effective guns. Some of the regiment's South Jersey farmboys proudly carried their smoothbores through to Appomattox.[12]

Close in, there was no arguing with the effectiveness of buck and ball. The Yankees of the Ninth New York Heavy Artillery, fighting as infantry, used their "old smoothbore muskets, with canister loads" to "make havoc in the Rebel ranks" in a fighting withdrawal at Monocacy, Maryland on July 9, 1864, and even the ambivalent Captain O'Grady of the Eighty-eighth New York recalled that "the splendid volleys of the [Irish] Brigade were conspicuous and effective," at Fair Oaks, Virginia in 1862 and concluded that the Bloody Lane fight proved "the efficacy of buck-and-ball at close quarters."[13]

The Irishmen and the Jerseyans of the Twelfth were not the only Federals still shouldering smoothbores at Gettysburg. Of the 242 Union infantry regiments that fought there, twenty-six, or 10.5%, were armed in whole or in part with various models of unrifled small arms. Although statistics are unavailable for their Rebel opponents, the number was probably at least as high. In the west, soldiers of both sides were less well-equipped than their eastern brethren. One study revealed that 44% of the men in the Confederate Army of Tennessee were armed with smoothbore muskets in April of 1863. Almost a year later, 11% of the men in this army were still carrying smoothbores.[14]

Some smoothbores carried by Confederates to Gettysburg were used against them. Soldiers of the Sixty-ninth Pennsylvania, a Philadelphia Irish unit manning the Union center, were armed with a mixture of Springfield and Enfield rifle-muskets and rifled .69-caliber muskets. The day before Pickett's Charge, the Sixty-ninth picked up a number of .69-caliber smoothbore muskets and a quantity of buck-and-ball ammunition left scattered around their position. Like the Jerseyans of the Twelfth, the Irishmen of the Sixty-ninth "abstracted the buckshot from

Harper's Ferry Armory during the Civil War. Burned by retreating Yankees and looted by advancing Confederates in 1861, Harper's Ferry never produced another weapon. *(USAMHI)*

the ammunition and reloaded the spare guns putting 12 to the load, and almost every man had from two to five guns that were not used until Pickett got within fifty yards of the wall." John Buckley of the Sixty-ninth's Company K recalled years afterward that "the slaughter was terrible, to which fact the ground literally covered with the enemy's dead bore ample testimony."[15]

As the soldiers of the Twelfth New Jersey and Sixty-ninth Pennsylvania discovered, a distinct advantage of the smoothbore musket was its ability to, within range limitations, handle a variety of loads tailored to a specific situation. Yet another advantage was the gun's ability to shoot the .64-caliber musket balls which were used to fill artillery spherical case shells. Newly recruited volunteers of the Tenth Minnesota Infantry defending Fort Ridgely, Minnesota from attacking Sioux warriors in 1862 ran out of fixed ammunition for their smoothbore muskets. Guided by the veteran ordnance sergeant in charge of the post, the recruits rolled their own cartridges with loose buckshot and balls extracted from spherical case rounds and managed to hold out until relief arrived. The Indians the Minnesotans faced were largely armed with double-barreled shotguns, which were as versatile in digesting varied ammunition as the smoothbore musket and offered two quick shots as well. The shotgun was also used for military purposes further east, and, as historian Stephen Z. Starr noted: "A shotgun loaded with 'buck and ball'...was not a weapon to be despised."[16]

More than not despised, the sporting double-barreled shotgun became a necessary and in some cases a preferred smoothbore weapon for some Rebel soldiers. During a critical early-war weapons shortage when Confederate officers urged volunteers to bring their own guns and bought sporting arms on the open market to arm recruits, many ended up with double-barreled shotguns. Lieutenant Samuel T. Foster noted that the combined infantry/dismounted cavalry Texas brigade he served in at Arkansas Post was armed in early 1863 with Enfield rifle-muskets, Mississippi rifles, smoothbore muskets and "...double-barrel shotguns—The muskets and shotguns use the Buck-and-ball Cartridge, that is an ounce ball and three buckshot."[17]

The men of two companies of the Third Texas Cavalry bought shotguns to arm themselves in 1861, and one wag suggested that his regiment of "Texas Mounted Rifles," part of the Texas Brigade which invaded New Mexico under the command of Brigade General Henry H. Sibley in 1862, should more properly be designated "Texas Mounted

Shotguns." Missouri Rebels in 1861 were described as mostly "armed with shotguns or squirrel rifles; some had the old flintlock muskets." The shotgun remained a vital part of the Rebel arsenal well into 1862. On October 26th of that year, Confederate General Theophilus Holmes reported to Richmond that not only were many of his men totally unarmed, but a "large part of the remainder have only the shot-guns and rifles of the country."[18]

At close range, in a quick fight, shotguns were quite effective. Cornered Missouri guerrillas under William C. Quantrill shot their way to freedom after Quantrill ordered "'Shotguns to the front'" and "six, loaded heavily with buckshot, were borne there." The guerrillas rushed their Yankee opponents with shotguns and revolvers blazing, and most managed to escape.[19]

Some commanders specified shotguns for their commands. Benjamin F. Terry, a Texan who raised "Terry's Texas Rangers" in 1861, advised his recruiting officers to recruit men who could furnish a shotgun and pair of revolvers each. Recruits could either sell their arms to the Confederate government or lease them to the government for one dollar a month. More from availability than desire, Rebel infantrymen involved in a fight at Ivy Mountain, Kentucky in 1861 were armed almost entirely with shotguns and squirrel rifles.

Most Rebel soldiers who carried shotguns for any lengthy period of time were cavalrymen. One self-styled military pundit, Reverend Peter W. McDaniel, however, recognizing that "as the North has in her borders large establishments engaged in manufacturing arms of the most approved type," and the South "having not the time or facilities to acquire them," advocated that infantry outfits be equipped not only "with large homemade Bowey [sic] Knives" but with "our common double-barreled shotguns loaded with buckshot." McDaniel also believed that his shotgun and "Bowey" equipped soldiers should supplement their personal arsenals with "similar instruments to John Brown's Pikes."[20]

Although McDaniel was not the only pike enthusiast in the early days of the Confederacy, he was no doubt one of the first. Even Robert E. Lee considered the possibility of pike use early in the war, but by 1862, with an ample supply of captured and imported firearms supplemented by a small but steady domestic production, the idea quickly faded.

Although pikes faded from the scene early on, the fascination with multi-ball loads that the smoothbore handled so well was noted even by rifle-musket enthusiasts. The Federal government purchased a quantity of cartridges loaded with the .58-caliber "Shaler" sectional bullet. The Shaler was a three-part nested slug of conical design, intended to replicate the multiple-hit capability of the smoothbore with longer range potential. Although ingenious, these rounds "did not meet with favor when tried in the field." In 1862, Confederate ordnance chief Josiah Gorgas detailed Captain John W. Mallet to, among other things, prepare straight buckshot cartridges for the Enfield rifle-musket, although Federal ordnance people had abandoned similar efforts prior to the war. Despite these efforts, the .69-caliber smoothbore with buck-and-ball remained king of the hill in short-range encounters.[21]

Interestingly, a development which might have increased the smoothbore's versatility and range with single projectiles was disregarded. In late 1861 an inventor named W. B. Chace approached Abraham Lincoln with a new bullet designed to extend the effective range of the smoothbore musket. During a demonstration firing over the Potomac, the president witnessed "the projectile... fired alternately, with the ordinary round-ball cartridges, from the same smooth-bore musket, at the same elevation, and the projectile carried a full third, or more, farther upon the water of the Potomac than the round ball." Although Lincoln recommended further testing of the Chace bullet, and a test was apparently held, Union Ordnance chief Brigadier General James W. Ripley, who felt most new small-arms inventions were frivolous, apparently "lost" the report.[22]

Just what the configuration of the Chace bullet was has gone unrecorded. There is, however, a good possibility that the design was not original to Chace. In an attempt to improve the effective range of the musket, the Imperial Russian government, which maintained a close relationship with the master gunmakers of Liege, Belgium, throughout the nineteenth century, adopted the Belgian designed "Nessler" ball in the 1850s. The 464-grain Nessler bullet was "cylindrospherical in form" and "hollow at the base to make it expand and had a projecting point in the bottom of the cavity."[23]

Although the Nessler projectile allegedly extended the effective range of the smoothbore out to 300 or 400 yards, it never caught on in western Europe or the United States, where development of rifled arms took precedence. The Nessler bullet was considered for use in .69-caliber U.S. rifled muskets, as it gave far less recoil than the standard minie ball. It was not adopted, however.

Even without the Chace/Nessler slug, however, at the usual Civil

Australian gunsmith Allan Vaishon's conversion of a reproduction Charleville musket to the percussion system, following a French pattern. Many older muskets, converted to percussion, were imported during the first year of the Civil War. Reenactors interested in an accurate portrayal of a unit armed with conversion guns may either have a flintlock custom converted or buy the new Dixie Gun Works conversion of the U.S. Model 1816/1822 musket. *(Dick Stein)*

War combat ranges the smoothbore armed soldier was not as disadvantaged as he seems in retrospect in an accuracy-obsessed modern age. Accuracy is a relative thing, and many Civil War soldiers felt their smoothbores were accurate enough for the job at hand. With most officers ordering their men to hold fire until the enemy was well within 100 yards, at least in the early years of the war, the musket's inferiority to the rifle-musket was largely moot.

In order to test this premise I conducted an experiment in March of 1991. Although the lack of identical powder and cartridge paper prevents the exact replication of 1860s ammunition, it is possible to get a general idea of the effectiveness of buck-and-ball using modern materials. Four shooters brought their own muskets, including a .75-caliber "Brown Bess" and .69-caliber Charleville, both flintlock Navy Arms replicas, an original .69-caliber U.S. Model 1816 converted from flintlock to percussion and an original Prussian made .70 (approximately)-caliber musket

Dixie Gun Works reproduction Model 1816/1822 .69-caliber flintlock smooth-bore musket converted to the percussion ignition system. Large numbers of converted flintlocks were issued by both sides during the first year of the war. Dixie used the drum-and-bolster method of conversion. *(Dixie Gun Works)*

imported by the Union during the war. The shooters, Steve Garratano, Jim Heayn, Maurice A. "Bud" Scully and Steve Wheeler were members of the North-South Skirmish Association's (N-SSA) Sixty-ninth New York State Volunteer Infantry and/or the Monmouth County, New Jersey Rifle and Pistol Club, on whose range the experiment was conducted.

Original Civil War .69-caliber cartridges were loaded with 110 grains of musket powder behind a .64-caliber ball and three buckshot. They were loaded by biting off the end of the paper and ramming powder, ball, paper and buckshot down the muzzle. Cartridge paper filled up the "windage" or clearance between the diameter of the undersized ball and the .69 barrel, providing some of the benefits of a patch. Due to the impossibility of exactly duplicating the gunpowder and paper available in the 1860s and the danger of a "cook off" from the smoldering remains of a paper cartridge in a barrel, the loads used in the test varied somewhat from original cartridges.[24]

In the modern experiment, the .69-caliber guns were loaded with .662 round balls behind fifty grains of Goex FFFG black powder (for cleaner shooting than the original FFG musket powder) while the .75-caliber was stoked with eighty grains of Goex FFG and a .729 round ball. The round balls were loaded without a patch and followed down the muzzle by three #0 buckshot, .320 in diameter, wrapped tightly in bond paper held together by clear tape. The paper wrapping on the buckshot performed, to a degree, the "windage" reduction role of original paper cartridges. Plastic tubes and paper used to hold powder were discarded in the loading process. Although these loads worked well in the muskets used in the experiment, neither I nor the shooters assume any responsibility for their use in arms over which we have no control.

Both small and large targets were used. First, six full twelve-ounce cans of seltzer water were strung on a frame at fifty yards. Averaging 2.5 shots each, the shooters quickly cleared the cans from the frame. Next, two full-size police silhouette targets were mounted on four-by-four-foot backers. Two men fired five shots each at each target, scoring eighteen hits (eight balls and ten buckshot) on one and thirteen hits (six balls and seven buckshot) on the other. Misses riddled the cardboard target backers and would have caused a number of casualties in a close two-rank-deep Civil War infantry formation.

Interestingly, in a second test, paper cartridges prepared to more closely approximate the original buck-and-ball rounds, with .64-caliber balls and loaded in the original manner by Neal Friedenthal of the N-SSA Fifteenth New Jersey Volunteer Infantry, so fouled an original Model 1842 musket that it was unloadable after a few rounds. This experience was reflected in a report from the Fifty-seventh Illinois Infantry during the Civil War: "...the old altered flint-lock muskets of the regiment became fouled after a few rounds rendering it impossible to get a load down, though many of the men, in their efforts to drive the charges home, after getting them started, drove the rammers against the trunks of trees." A smoothbore-armed New Jersey infantryman wrote following the battle of Williamsburg: "after we had fired about twenty rounds, our guns were so dirty that we had to punch the ball in by sticking our rammers against trees." The lack of lubrication in smoothbore cartridges was, no doubt, responsible for the problem.[25]

All things considered, however, the evidence, both historical and modern, is fairly conclusive. Buck and ball was (and is) a devastating load in a smoothbore musket at fifty yards, and dangerous to dense formations out to a hundred. Although the pace of technological change growing out of and following the Civil War quickly made buck-and-ball cartridges and the guns that fired them ordnance curios, they blazed a fearsome trail across American military history. "At very close quarters," nothing proved better.

Skirmisher Bob Wierski of the 11th New Jersey takes aim with the author's original Model 1842 musket. The musket's original barrel was badly pitted inside, and probably unsafe to fire. It was replaced for shooting purposes with a discarded sawed-off original barrel which was lengthened and relined by R.A. Hoyt. The 1842 was one of the most common guns issued to volunteers in the early war period, and a favorite close-range weapon when loaded with the buck-and-ball cartridge. *(Joseph Bilby)*

Collecting and Shooting Smoothbores Today

In its effort to establish competitions featuring as many types of Civil War firearms as possible, the N-SSA instituted a smoothbore musket competition in 1992. N-SSA smoothbore targets are shot at fifty yards, using the one-hundred-yard rifle-musket target. More original arms are seen among the ranks of smoothbore shooters than any other category of N-SSA competition, save, perhaps, carbine.

When smoothbore competition was initiated, the only approved reproduction smoothbore available was the Dixie Gun Works reproduction of the U.S. Model 1816 flintlock, a gun used in large numbers in the first year of the war, especially in Rebel ranks. A skillful gunsmith could no doubt convert one of these guns to percussion in the manner of the

Phil Seiss of S&S Firearms with a Belgian-made .58-caliber Saxon rifle-musket. Although clunky in comparison to American or British models, the Saxon rifle-musket was classified as a first-class arm by American ordnance officers. *(Joseph Bilby)*

1850s or 1860s, but such an arm would no doubt void any Dixie warranties and would have to be inspected by the N-SSA Small Arms committee before it could be used in competition. Dixie introduced a percussion conversion of the 1816, using the drum and nipple process, in early 1996. It was subsequently approved for N-SSA use. The Armi-Sport company released a reproduction of the U.S. Model 1842 in 1996 as well.

Custom barrelmaker Dan Whitacre makes a new reproduction barrel for the U.S. Model 1842 musket. Another highly respected barrelmaker, R. J. Hoyt, will reline a pitted original barrel and even extend and line a barrel which was cut down for use as a single-shot shotgun in the long ago. Enough reproduction parts, including stocks, are available so that a shooter can make his own Model 1842 if he possesses an original lock.

Original flintlock smoothbores fired a 412-grain round ball backed by 130 grains of musket powder. Ten grains of this powder was the priming charge, while 120 grains went down the muzzle to propel the ball. Improvements in powder quality and the fact that a priming charge

All firearms used in N-SSA competition must pass inspection by the organization's Small Arms Committee. Here a member of the committee, custom Civil War gunmaker Gary Vikar, checks the dimensions of a gun submitted for approval. *(Joseph Bilby)*

was no longer necessary after the advent of the percussion system resulted in a decrease of the charge to 110 grains.

While original-style paper cartridges are allowable in N-SSA competition, providing they are inspected and accepted by the organization's inspector general, most shooters use a more modern, easily assembled cartridge. Ammunition for modern N-SSA smoothbore competition is limited to a single round ball, which is usually loaded over the powder charge in a plastic or cardboard tube.

As in the old days, skirmishers have found that the closer a ball is in diameter to the musket's bore diameter the more accurately the gun will shoot. It is generally true as well that a smaller powder charge than used in the original load contributes to more bearable recoil and accuracy. Sixty to seventy grains of FFG powder, which works better on the whole than FFFG in large bore-guns, is a good starting place. It should be noted that some shooters believe that a heavier powder charge is more accurate. N-SSA regulations specify that whatever the charge, it should not exceed the original army load.

Bullet molds are available from manufacturers like Rapine or through dealers like the Regimental Quartermaster or S&S Firearms. Before investing in a mold, however, a prospective smoothbore shooter may

Charles Peterkin's "Berwyn Blue Bellies" take the line at the first "North South Shoot" held at Muirkirk, MD, May 28, 1950. Muskets are all originals, as is much of the equipment. Uniforms are catch-as-catch-can with original post-war headgear. Bayonet scabbards are for post-war .45-70 rifles. *(N-SSA)*

want to try different diameter balls to determine which size gives him the best compromise between easy loading and accuracy. Swaged lead balls are available in different diameters from October Country and other muzzle-loading supply houses.

Original guns should be checked by a competent gunsmith before firing. Original muzzle loaders are often found loaded! In addition, the ravages of age and abuse often leave a pitted and weakened barrel which may not stand the stress of firing. Pitted barrels may also provide a safe harbor for a smoldering bit of residue which will ignite the next powder charge dumped down the barrel, resulting in an unpleasant "cook off."

Whether original or reproduction, the barrel of a smoothbore should be thoroughly cleaned to remove all traces of oil before firing. Oil in the barrel will "kill" a charge, leaving the shooter with the problem of extracting it. After cleaning and before firing, check once more to verify whether or not the gun is loaded. While this may seem unnecessary, it helps ingrain good safety habits. Drop the ramrod down the barrel. If you hear a metallic ring rather than a thud and the ramrod goes down as far inside the barrel as it does when held alongside the outside of the barrel, the piece is unloaded and safe to load.

Before actually loading, point the musket in a safe direction, cap it and fire it down range. The explosion of the caps will clear any remaining oil and debris out of the nipple channel and serves as a final check to assure the gun is unloaded. Then point the musket at the ground in front of you and snap another cap. If the grass or dirt in front of the muzzle is disturbed, the nipple channel is clear. With a flintlock, fire off a pan of priming powder down range before loading.

To load, remove the ball from the cartridge tube and, keeping the muzzle away from your face, pour the powder charge out of the tube down the muzzle. Grasp the ball between thumb and forefinger and then insert it in the muzzle in a sliding motion, making sure to keep the fingers from directly crossing the muzzle. Take the ramrod between thumb and forefinger and ram the ball down on top of the powder charge. Then raise the musket to the "ready" position, at waist level with muzzle pointing safely down range, thumb the hammer to half cock and place a musket cap over the nipple. Bring the musket to your shoulder, fully cock the hammer, aim and fire.

The procedure for loading and firing flintlock muskets is the same, except for priming. To prime a flintlock, push the frizzen forward, uncovering the pan, then bring the hammer to half cock. Place priming powder in the pan and close it. The military used coarse musket powder from the cartridge for priming and almost any powder will do in a pinch, but FFFFG works best. It is unnecessary to fill the pan with powder. A small amount, placed *away* from the touchhole in the side of the barrel, is sufficient. After priming, close the frizzen, point the musket down range and fire, burning any residual oil out of the touchhole. Although original army drill required the soldier to prime his gun before loading the main charge down the muzzle, this is considered an unsafe practice today and is forbidden in N-SSA competition. With a flintlock, load first, then prime.

Most smoothbores (some German muskets imported during the Civil War being notable exceptions) have no rear sight. The shooter's eye is the musket's rear sight. For this reason, a smoothbore shooter should place his cheek on the same spot on the buttstock for each and every

Jack Rawls' "Norfolk Long Rifles" represented the Confederates at Muirkirk. *(N-SSA)*

shot, providing consistency of aim. A piece of tape applied to the stock may prove helpful. Elevation and, to some degree, windage corrections, may be made by filing or moving the front sight, which, in the case of U.S. and French-style guns, is attached to the front barrel band. In order to avoid damaging the historical value of original guns, it is advisable to buy a reproduction front band for smoothbore shooting. The band can be fitted with a high front sight which may be filed down or moved left or right using a propane torch and solder.

Unlike the minie ball fired in the rifle-musket, a round ball has no grooves to hold lubricant which softens powder fouling. Without lubricant, a tight-fitting ball will quickly become difficult to ram home. The fouling problem can be mitigated by cleaning between shots, but N-SSA rules forbid this practice. An easy way to provide lubricant while smoothbore shooting is to encase the ball in a lubricated cloth patch when loading. Since patches were not used in smoothbore musket loads by the military during the Civil War, however, the practice is not allowable in N-SSA competition.

A lubricated, less-than-bore diameter ball is necessary to limit fouling during an N-SSA shooting string of five to ten shots. One way to lubricate a round ball is to insert the ball in the soft plastic cartridge tube, depress it a quarter inch below the top of the tube and spoon melted bullet lubricant (a vegetable shortening and beeswax mix is popular) on top of the ball. This process creates a lubricant "plug" on one end of the ball. Load the ball with the lubricant on top of the powder.

Another convenient way to apply lubricant to a round ball is to take a small square of aluminum foil and deposit a spoonful of lubricant in the center of the foil. Place the musket ball on the lubricant, then fold up the foil around the ball and twist it shut. Insert the ball into a cartridge tube, twist up. The ball is removed easily from the tube by the twist, then inserted, twist up, in the bore. Not only does this method provide lubrication to keep fouling soft, but the foil also acts as a patch to help center the ball in the barrel, providing better accuracy.

Although not allowed in N-SSA competition, a smoothbore experimenter may wish to shoot some short "wadcutter" minie balls cast in a Rapine mold. The Rapine bullets probably come as close to replicating the Chace/Nessler design as anything around today. They also have the advantage of grease grooves, which may be filled with lubricant.

The smoothbore musket has a long and distinguished history. Within its limitations, it is still a useful and versatile sporting arm. For the real feel of the early years of the Civil War, shoot a smoothbore!

CHAPTER II

The Rifle-Musket

American soldiers were armed with rifles, as well as smoothbore
muskets, even before the official birth of the United States army.
Spiral grooves cut in the rifle barrel's interior spun and stabilized a
round-ball projectile and gave it far more range and accuracy than the
same type of projectile fired from a smoothbore musket. Strange as it
may seem to many Americans, nurtured on stories of Revolutionary
riflemen, Europeans invented the rifle before there were colonies on this
side of the Atlantic and were the first to issue rifles to their troops. Rifled
arms saw limited use in the hands of seventeenth-century French
dragoons and eighteenth century German *Jaegers*.

Many Americans, in fact, were totally ignorant of the rifle and its
capabilities at the outbreak of the Revolution. John Adams commented
with surprise on the accuracy of "a peculiar kind of musket, called a
rifle" carried by Virginians and Pennsylvanians who joined the New
England militia force besieging Boston in 1775. Although sharpshooting
riflemen subsequently contributed to America's struggle for inde-
pendence on a number of fields, most notably Kings Mountain (where
Americans fought each other), the overall tactical importance of early
American riflemen has often been grossly exaggerated.[1]

General George Washington, a more perceptive analyst of his army's
needs than latter day commentators, actually rearmed some rifle units
with smoothbore muskets. Contrary to song and story, well-served
artillery was far more of a factor in Andrew Jackson's 1815 victory at

New Orleans than rifle-wielding Kentucky militiamen, most of whom arrived at the Crescent City ill-clothed, barefoot and unarmed.

Although most early-nineteenth-century officers believed that the smoothbore musket was the ideal weapon for infantrymen, the rifle remained a limited-issue weapon in the American army following 1815, since it was useful for a number of special tasks, including skirmishing and sniping. Accurate on man-sized targets up to and somewhat beyond 200 yards, the rifle was loaded with a measured powder charge and an under-bore-size round ball encased in a greased patch which engaged the rifling. Although prepared cartridges including patched balls were sometimes provided for riflemen, the rifle had a slower rate of fire than the comparatively inaccurate smoothbore musket and was not usually fitted for a bayonet.[2]

The musket, which had dominated the battlefields of the world for two centuries, was easily loaded with a paper cartridge containing an undersized ball, (often supplemented by buckshot or a second ball) capable of relatively rapid fire and equipped with a bayonet. Every general dreamed of sweeping his enemy from the field with a successful bayonet charge. To be successful, it should be noted, soldiers charging with fixed bayonets did not have to (and most often didn't) close with their opponents. The simple sight of cold steel advancing was usually enough to put a less disciplined enemy to flight.

Thoughtful military men on both sides of the Atlantic did, however, realize that a number of advantages would accrue from marrying the rapid-fire feature of a musket with the inherent accuracy of a rifle. In the years after the downfall of Napoleon Bonaparte, French army officers proved the axiom that innovation often follows in the wake of defeat. Although the French copied the American "buck-and-ball" (one musket ball and three buckshot) smoothbore load to temporarily improve small-arms hit ratios, and one French general advocated loading muskets with two balls, they concentrated their research and development efforts on inventing a rifle/musket hybrid, which would use the new percussion-ignition method. The percussion system, which substituted a copper cap filled with explosive material for the flint and steel firing mechanism of the flintlock musket, was developed in the early nineteenth century and, by 1830, was in fairly common use on sporting arms.

In the 1830s a French infantry captain named Delvigne developed a method of loading a rifled gun in which an undersized-unpatched round ball was rammed down the gun's barrel and then "upset" to a larger diameter against the rim of a chambered breech by thumping it several times with a heavy ramrod. On firing, the expanded ball engaged the rifling. Delvigne-system guns were carried to Algeria by the *Tirailleurs de Vincennes* in 1840. Armed with the new rifles, the *Tirailleurs* gave a good account of themselves, and one reportedly dropped a mounted Arab at a distance of 600 meters. Variations in ramming pressure, along with powder fouling buildup and occasional lead fragments lodging on the chamber rim, led, however, to inconsistent accuracy in the Delvigne rifles.

After further experiments the chamber rim was replaced as an expansion device with the *tige*, a one and a half inch spike projecting from the gun's breechplug face into the barrel. The *a tige*, or "pillar breech," rifles, invented by a Colonel Thouvenin, were field tested with round-ball ammunition in North African colonial fighting in 1846. Accuracy was satisfactory, but the *tige* itself proved susceptible to damage and corrosion and complicated cleaning the breech area as well.

Captain Claude-Etienne Minie, Inspector of Musketry at the Vincennes Military School, assisted Colonel Thouvenin with the design of a solid-based conical bullet which improved the accuracy and range of the *tige* rifles. Thousands of flintlock smoothbore Model 1822 muskets were subsequently converted to percussion-ignition, rifled and fitted with *tige* breechplugs. Many were still in use at the time of the Crimean War.

With the principle of the conical bullet now firmly established, Captain Minie sought to remove the Thouvenin system's main problem, the *tige* itself. Following through on earlier experiments by Delvigne, Minie developed an under-bore-size bullet with a tapered iron plug in its hollow base. The new conical ball needed no special chamber rim or spike to expand it, and was upset into the rifling by the force of the exploding propellant charge, which drove the plug into the soft lead.

The invention of progressive depth rifling, which decreased in depth towards the muzzle, by Minie's colleague Tamasier, enabled the expanded "minie ball" to get a good bite into the rifling on firing and swaged it a bit as it spun down the barrel. Tamasier added grooves around the circumference of the minie bullet, on the theory that, like the feathers on an arrow, they would stabilize the slug as it zipped through the air. Although this theory was most likely incorrect, the Tamasier grooves did provide convenient receptacles for lubricant which kept powder fouling soft and permitted more shots to be fired between cleanings.

These early-war Yankee infantrymen are armed with Pattern 1853 Enfield rifle-muskets of the second-type, made from 1855 to 1858 in Britain. Second-type Enfields have their barrel bands held by band springs rather than screws. Weapons of this type were also made in the United States by Robbins & Lawrence of Windsor, VT, for the British army during the Crimean War. These guns may have been imported from Britain or may have been overruns from the Robbins & Lawrence British contract. *(LC)*

In the years following 1815, the French filled the role of occasional ally and potential adversary to their former enemies across the English channel. Throughout their research, the Gallic small-arms reformers had to buck older officers who believed the smoothbore flintlock was the ultimate military weapon and that the round ball was the only fit projectile for a firearm. Despite the opposition of many senior commanders, however, new firearms and tactical ideas gained more of an audience in France than Britain.

Although the British, drawing from their American experience, deployed riflemen as skirmishers during the Peninsular campaign in Spain and at Waterloo, most British officers displayed little small-arms creativity in the post-Napoleonic period. Those who did were actively discouraged. Rifle enthusiast Captain John Norton experimented with a hollow-base cylindrical bullet similar to Minie's eventual design as early as the 1820s. Norton discovered that the bullet would shoot accurately in the Baker rifle, then the issue weapon for British riflemen, but was rebuffed by the ordnance establishment. The Duke of Wellington, who headed the British military, generally believed that the .75-caliber smoothbore "Brown Bess" would serve his old soldiers' grandsons as well as she had them. Eventually, however, the duke was forced to concede that the percussion system was the wave of the foreseeable future. The British army adopted a percussion smoothbore musket in 1842. In his last years in office the victor of Waterloo reluctantly agreed to trials of Captain Minie's new projectile.

With the passing of the Iron Duke in 1852, British soldiers took a more serious look at French small-arms developments. The Minie trials of 1850 proved successful and resulted in the adoption of an interim

A fully-equipped Union infantryman poses with his Enfield P53 rifle-musket. The Enfield was second only to the Springfield in numbers issued to the Union army. *(Michael J. McAfee)*

Private George Thompson of the Fifteenth New Jersey Infantry poses proudly with his newly-issued Enfield rifle-musket. Although his commanding officer, Colonel William Penrose, detested his men's Enfields, many of the men felt the British-made guns were more effective than Springfields at long range. *(John Kuhl Collection)*

design, the .70-caliber "Minie rifle." The Minie rifle replaced both the standard percussion smoothbore Model 1842 musket and the Brunswick rifle, a round-ball gun which had succeeded the Baker in British service. In a concession to the ghost of Wellington, the new weapon's bore diameter was set at .702 so that undersized round-ball ammunition designed for the .75-caliber smoothbore could be fired in the new guns in a pinch. In the event, however, the old-style balls were only usable in a Minie rifle with a clean barrel. It was nearly impossible to ram them down a barrel fouled with powder residue. In actual combat, ammunition interchangeability proved a non-issue.

Many, including artists who have portrayed the conflict, believe the .577-caliber P53 Enfield, the Minie rifle's successor in British service, was the weapon of Her Majesty Queen Victoria's troops in the Crimean War of 1854-1856. Such was not the case. Although the first Enfields were delivered to the British army in the spring of 1854, three of the four divisions sent to the Crimea in that year carried Minie rifles; the remaining division was armed with smoothbores. Supplies of new P53 Enfields did not arrive at Sevastopol until after most of the fighting was over, and were issued to the smoothbore-armed troops. The British army fought the Crimean War largely armed with the big-bore Minie rifle.

Sergeant Daniel Bush, Company D, 10th Rhode Island Volunteer Infantry, is armed with a two-band Enfield rifle and a non-commissioned officer's sword. Although the British army reserved rifles for sergeants and members of rifle regiments, there was no such issue pattern in the American army. *(Michael J. McAfee)*

The Minie rifle was sighted to 900 yards, and the British were quick to take advantage of the gun's long-range capability in the rolling, open Crimean terrain. At Alma, the British "Light Division" advanced firing at will on the enemy, wreaking havoc on Russian formations at ranges up to 400 yards.

On October 25, 1854, the Russian garrison of Sevastopol mounted a reconnaissance in force against the besieging British picket line. As the smoothbore-armed Russians advanced in dense column formations, the well-disciplined British regulars fell back firing, each picket force holding until its flanks were threatened. When the day was done and the enemy retreated, the pickets had inflicted far more casualties than they had suffered. The deadly .70-caliber Minie rifles, firing a projectile with great penetration power, even at long range, often killed or wounded several Russians per shot.

British infantrymen continued to use their rifled arms to good effect during the remainder of the siege. One young lieutenant, who viewed the war as a new type of sport, reported that he had hit three Russians out of thirty-five shots fired at a distance of around 800 yards. An Irishman in the Rifle Brigade took 600-yard pot shots at enemy soldiers running to the latrine, averring that, even if he missed, it "would be as good as a dose of opening medicine" for the terrified Russians.[3]

The soldiers who used their new arms so effectively in the Crimea were pretty much self-taught marksmen. This was not to be the case in the future, however. The increasingly professional British army established its School of Musketry at Hythe in 1853. As in many such matters,

Although the regiment of this Enfield-armed Yankee is unknown, his short jacket and SNY belt buckle identify him as a member of a New York outfit. *(Michael J. McAfee)*

the British were following the lead of the French reformers, who had been the first to use the new conical projectiles and had already established their own marksmanship institute, the *Ecole de Tir*. Hythe is located on the Kent coast, where miles of beaches provided space for ranges, allowing study of the effect and accuracy of long-distance small-arms fire.

Officers and men were detailed from their regiments to attend courses at Hythe and then returned as instructors to their outfits. Since British regiments operated on the battalion system, with the depot battalion personnel serving as replacement training cadre, recruits were exposed to far more instruction than in the American system, where an infantry recruit was posted almost directly to his tactical unit.

Long-range rifle-musket work was taken seriously at Hythe, with emphasis on correct trigger pull or squeeze, range estimation and various firing positions. Standing or "offhand" was stressed as the most likely combat position, but kneeling, which the soldier could drop into quickly and provided a steadier firing platform, was also strongly emphasized.

The British recruit was introduced gradually to his weapon, progressing from dry firing through snapping percussion caps to live fire. The standard British army target in the 1850s was a six-by-two-foot cast-iron plate. At longer ranges a number of these targets were linked together to simulate the space occupied by an enemy unit. Soldiers fired at ranges up to 900 yards, when available space permitted.

Following its brief but distinguished service, the Minie rifle was replaced by the P53 Enfield rifle-musket. Although the P53 spawned a family of .577-caliber guns, the most important was the rifle-musket, a weapon with the weight, barrel length and bayonet reach of a musket, yet rifled for greater long-range accuracy. The Enfield version of Claude Minie's projectile was a long, heavy .568 diameter bullet with the standard cast-iron plug inserted in its hollow base. When British ordnance people discovered that the minie-style plug was not only unnecessary to assure proper expansion, but occasionally drove through the bullet with unpleasant results, it was replaced by a boxwood or clay plug, which served to protect the bullet base from damage in transportation.

Lubrication for the smooth-bodied Enfield "Pritchett" slug was provided by the greased paper in which it was encased. The thickness of the paper also acted as a patch, compensating for the difference

Sergeant Sigourrey Wales, of the 4th Battalion Rifles, Massachusetts Volunteer Militia, poses in 1860 or 1861 with a U.S. Model 1841 Mississippi rifle. His rifle is in the original .54-caliber with fixed rear sight and not fitted for a bayonet.
(Michael J. McAfee)

between bore and bullet diameter. Improved powder led to more efficient combustion and a consequent reduction in bullet diameter to .550. An original Enfield smooth-sided slug fired without paper patching is too undersized for accurate shooting and will invariably "keyhole" or hit the target sideways, if it hits at all. Properly patched with lubricated paper, however, the Pritchett bullet proved remarkably accurate at extreme long range. It swabbed fouling from the Enfield's bore as well, and it is reported that one P53 was fired 16,000 times without cleaning!

Although not comparable in size, training or global responsibilities with the French or British armies, the American military kept close tabs on European developments. United States army weapons and uniforms were largely patterned on French models and drill manuals attributed to American authors were mainly plagiarizations of French editions. Brevet Major Peter V. Hagner visited France in 1848-1849 and reported extensively on small-arms developments. Efforts to develop a rifle-musket began on his return, and in 1853-1854, Colonel Benjamin Huger tested foreign muskets and a variety of experimental .54 and .69-caliber U.S.

arms modified to use solid *a tige* bullets and hollow-based minie-style slugs.

Although France was in the forefront of mid-nineteenth century military matters, James H. Burton of Harper's Ferry Armory introduced some design changes in what was coming to be called the "minie ball." Like the British, Burton dispensed with Minie's iron base plug, but he deepened and widened the conical ball's base cavity to insure that pressure from the exploding powder charge would expand the slug. Most of the billions of bullets (except those imported by the Confederacy from Britain) fired during the Civil War are technically "Burton balls," not "minie balls." In the popular imagination they became, however, and remain, "minie balls." Unlike the British slug, Burton's bullet used Tamasier-style grooves to hold lubrication rather than a greased-paper patch.[4]

Although Europeans were far ahead of Americans in firearms development, arms production methods were much further advanced on this side of the Atlantic. In the early 1850s, British officers visited the Springfield and Harper's Ferry Armories to study the American arms industry and purchase stock-shaping and lock-making machinery. They then hired Master Armorer Burton to supervise production at the British government armory at Enfield.

Before the end of 1854, American troops armed with the .54-caliber U.S. Model 1841 "Mississippi" rifle (which had previously fired a patched round ball) were issued cartridges loaded with .54-caliber minie balls. While experiments directed towards the development of a whole new series of small arms progressed, some 1841s were fitted with long-range adjustable sights and sent to the frontier, where they replaced smoothbore muskets in the hands of infantrymen.[5]

The .69-caliber Burton bullet proved more accurate than the .54 in the army's tests, but the recoil from rifled Model 1842 muskets was deemed severe. In an attempt to compromise between the accuracy of the larger caliber and tolerable kick of the smaller, the ordnance department chose .58-caliber for the new family of firearms adopted in 1855. Although the 1855 models included a short, heavy-barreled rifle, a carbine and a large single-shot pistol-carbine with detachable stock, these arms were eventually dropped from production.

The centerpiece of the development program was the forty-inch barreled rifle-musket. The Model 1855 was fitted with a Maynard primer magazine integral with its lock. Maynard primers were loaded into the magazine on a roll similar to that used in a modern child's cap gun. A cap was fed onto the gun's nipple (which could also be used with regular musket caps) every time its hammer was cocked. The Maynard primers proved unreliable in bad weather, however, and the magazine was omitted from the Model 1861 rifle-musket lock. Private Philip H. Smith, issued the Model 1861 early in the Civil War, believed the new gun was "a far superior rifle altogether." Smith thought "tape locks is played out, some likes them the best but I can't see the edge. I have used them both and I know." Hammer, barrel-band and ramrod configurations underwent minor changes throughout the .58-caliber Springfield rifle-musket series, which included the Model 1863 and 1864 (also known as 1863 "second type") guns. Ordnance officers saw no significant difference among these weapons, however, and lumped them in the same category on their returns.[6]

While Springfield and Harper's Ferry Armories were tooling up for the new models, a number of Model 1842 .69-caliber muskets were rifled, fitted with long-range sights, and issued as *rifled* muskets. Frontier soldiers put up with the heavier recoil of the 1842 because of the gun's

Private Andrew J. Herrick, Company A, 6th Massachusetts Militia, poses with a Model 1855 rifle-musket. The first rifled arm adopted for general infantry issue, most, if not all, Model 1855s saw use in the Civil War. The 6th was a militia outfit which served for 100 days in 1861. Most of that time was spent guarding Union lines of communication in Maryland. The regiment became famous for its fight with a mob of Southern sympathizers in Baltimore, where it lost four men killed. *(USAMHI)*

Sergeant Graham Moffet, Company H, 28th New York Infantry, holds a Model 1841 Mississippi rifle, probably rebored to .58-caliber and issued with a sword bayonet. Model 1841s were originally issued in .54-caliber without bayonets. Many were converted after 1855. The 28th New York served from 1861 to 1863 and fought at the battles of Cedar Mountain, Second Manassas, Antietam and Chancellorsville. *(USAMHI)*

accuracy edge over the Model 1841 rifle. The Model 1841's deep-cut rifling, designed for patched round balls, may have allowed gas blow-by, and consequent inferior accuracy.

In another modernization effort, earlier model flintlock guns were converted to percussion ignition, rifled and fitted with new "patent breeches" and Maynard primer locks at Philadelphia's Frankford arsenal. Many, if not most, of these conversions were issued to various states for militia use; New Jersey received several thousand in 1857. Some Model 1841 rifles were rebored, rerifled and resighted for the new .58-caliber ammunition. All of these arms would see extensive service in the Civil War.

The .58-caliber Model 1855 rifle-musket, which began to reach the field in 1857, had a three-groove barrel cut with progressive depth rifling. Springfield Armory specifications allowed a bore dimension range from .580 to .5825. The rifle-musket's paper cartridge contained sixty grains of musket powder and a .5775 diameter hollow- based bullet lubricated with tallow and beeswax. To load the Model 1855, a soldier had to bite off the end of the cartridge, pour the powder down the muzzle of his gun, discard the excess paper, ram the lubricated bullet down on the powder charge and place a percussion cap on the nipple. The Model 1855 was expected to shoot ten consecutive rounds into a four-inch bull's eye at 100 yards.

At the outbreak of the Civil War, most regular army soldiers were armed with Model 1855 guns, and a few had been distributed to the militia. Supplies of rifled arms were limited, however, and the majority were obsolescent Model 1841 rifles in both .54 and .58-calibers and .69-caliber rifled smoothbores. Chief of Ordnance Ripley tried to restrict issuance of .58-caliber rifle-muskets to regular army units and three year volunteers, but his reserve supply was exhausted by August of 1861. Ripley's Confederate counterpart, Major Josiah Gorgas, had only 1,765 rifle-muskets at his disposal. One Confederate ordnance officer recalled after the war that the South had only "some 12,000 or 15,000 rifles" of all types on hand at the beginning of the conflict.[7]

This soldier of the 29th Regiment, National Guard of the State of New York, is armed with the infantry standard of the war, the U.S. Model 1861 rifle-musket. This photograph dates from 1864-1866.
(Michael J. McAfee)

As the demand reached a crescendo, Ripley's attempts to control the trickle of Model 1861 rifle-muskets reaching his bureau from Springfield Armory, the only domestic source of new rifle-muskets since the Confederates seized the Harper's Ferry Armory, were constantly undermined by politicians and officers determined to use all available means and influence to secure .58-caliber Springfields for their regiments. Along with spiffy foreign drills, natty uniforms and racy names, shiny new rifle-muskets became status symbols to the enthusiastic Yankee volunteers.

Secretary of War Simon Cameron, a Pennsylvanian, tried to funnel as many new rifled arms as possible to his home state's units. Governor Charles Olden of New Jersey lobbied Ripley for Springfields for the Ninth New Jersey Infantry. Perhaps because the Ninth was recruited as a sharpshooter regiment, the Chief of Ordnance relented and had a supply of new weapons shipped straight from Springfield Armory to Trenton to arm the unit. The flamboyant and politically connected Brigadier General Philip Kearny managed to requisition enough rifle-muskets to arm several selected companies of his First New Jersey Brigade. The lucky Jersey riflemen became the brigade's elite "light battalion."

The obvious answer to the rifle-musket shortage, Union and Confederate, was to increase domestic production, an easier task in the industrialized North. The Federal Ordnance Department quickly contracted with a number of private firms to produce the Model 1861. Unfortunately, some of these entities were mere paper companies, while still others depended on the same sub-contractors for most of their parts. Many of these firms did not furnish firearms for several years, if ever. By late 1863, however, the situation had stabilized and contractors began to deliver an increasing number of new arms, supplementing a vastly expanded Springfield Armory operation.[8]

Some Southern states bought excellent firearms from Northern manufacturers, including Colt, Maynard and Whitney, right up to the outbreak of hostilities, when the Federal government clamped down on the trade. With the exception of Richmond Armory, and to some degree Fayetteville Armory, both outfitted with machines and tooling captured at Harper's Ferry, Rebel rifle-musket makers never did get their production untracked. Although Richmond, the crown jewel of the Confederate ordnance department, shipped 323,231 "Infantry arms" between 1861 and 1865, they were "chiefly arms from battle fields repaired" rather than new guns. Southern private contractors produced small numbers of guns of varying quality, but made more of a contribution to the modern collector's market then they ever did to the Rebel war effort[9].

With large-scale arms production in its infancy in the North and not a significant factor at all in the South for the first two years of the conflict, both sides initially depended largely on obsolete weapons already in storage and guns purchased from private dealers.

Although there were more muskets in Northern arsenals than Southern, many were, as a newspaper noted, "next to useless." Governor Olden of New Jersey informed his legislature that "there may be about 3,000 stand of arms in tolerable good condition for use in the hands of the militia, and about 4,000 stand of arms in the arsenal with flintlocks." New Jersey Quartermaster General Lewis Perrine soon contracted with private firms, including Hewes and Phillips of Newark, to convert flintlock muskets to percussion ignition and rifle them. Employees at the state arsenal in Trenton were soon converting more smoothbores. Ammunition supplies were low as well. Perrine had to send an officer to a New York City gun store to buy cartridges for New Jersey militiamen leaving Trenton for the defense of Washington. Things were slow to improve. Several months later a Jersey volunteer performed guard duty with "an old Harper's Ferry musket without a lock...in citizen's dress."[10]

Things were worse in the west, where both Federal and Confederate commanders scrambled for small arms. Yankee sharpshooters of the Sixty-sixth Illinois were armed with sporting rifles purchased from a local gun dealer. Desperate Trans-Mississippi Rebel commanders like General Ben McCulloch bought guns from private individuals and gun stores and requested recruits to bring their personal weapons with them when they enlisted. Many "country" or hunting rifles purchased by Rebel officers from citizens were rebored to at least an approximation of the standard .58-caliber by local gunsmiths or state arsenal workers. Cherokee Indian volunteers for Thomas' Legion, a western North Carolina outfit, were originally "armed with small 'squirrel' rifles some of which had been boured [sic] out so as to admit a larger bullit [sic]. They were all percussion locks and no fine ammunition [cartridges] but loose powder."[11]

Although most flintlock smoothbore muskets were phased out of Confederate service in the months following Shiloh, flint-ignition hunting rifles were still in use by some Rebel Indian soldiers as late as 1864. Captain George W. Grayson of the Second Creek Regiment was injured

Three members of the 22nd Regiment, National Guard of the State of New York, pose behind their stacked Enfield rifles equipped with sword bayonets.
(Michael J. McAfee)

at the battle of Cabin Creek that year when one of his men fired "a long flintlock squirrel rifle with which he was armed at the enemy, holding it in his excitement only a few inches away from the left side of my face." Flint fragments and the blast from the gun's touchhole temporarily blinded Grayson.[12]

The Confederate government quickly realized that it would need far more firearms than would be available through domestic purchase, confiscation, capture or contracting, and dispatched Caleb Huse to Europe to buy arms in April, 1861. By the time the first Federal arms buyers, spurred by the shock of losing the battle of Bull Run, had crossed the Atlantic, Huse had negotiated long-term contracts with several of the best Enfield manufacturers in Great Britain. Largely due to his efforts, the P53 would become the standard Southern infantry weapon. Josiah Gorgas specified the Enfield caliber of .577 as standard for Confederate manufactured weapons and James Burton, who had defected to the Confederacy with the outbreak of war, acquired plans to build an armory to replicate the British rifle-musket in the South.

The first Union overseas arms agent appointed, Colonel George L. Schuyler, had little technical knowledge of small arms, which, when the inspector detailed to accompany him fell ill, severely hampered his acquisition of first-class guns. Schuyler also had to compete not only with Rebel arms buyers like Huse, but with other Yankees appointed by Federal and state governments as well as private contractors like Herman Boker & Company. In many cases Union agents bid not only against their Confederate competitors, but against each other, driving up the eventual price of the guns they sought to buy.

The largest number of small arms imported by the American belligerents during the course of the Civil War were Enfield-style rifle-muskets. These guns varied a bit in barrel band and ramrod style, but were generic P53 rifle-muskets. Smaller numbers of the shorter-barreled Enfield rifles and still shorter carbines or "musketoons" were also imported. Although guns made at the British government small-arms factory at Enfield were not sold to either side, private British contractors were free to sell Enfields to anyone. Since Caleb Huse contracted for most of the London Armory's run of "machine-made" Enfields with interchangeable parts, most (but not all) Federally purchased rifle-muskets were of the "hand-made" variety produced by Birmingham makers. The "hand made" guns were assembled from parts forwarded to a consortium from a number of small contractors, some British and others Belgian, and each with his own machining tolerances—or lack of them. The resultant lack of interchangeability of parts is evident in surviving specimens.

The overall quality of hand made Enfields varied. The soldiers of the Thirty-fifth Massachusetts Infantry were issued British rifle-muskets with nipples which were excessively hardened. When a hammer fell on one of these brittle nipples, it shattered, leaving a broken stump still screwed into the gun. Without field access to the nineteenth-century equivalent of an "easy-out," the weapon became useless. Soldiers of the Tenth Illinois were issued Enfields whose mainsprings were "too weak to 'snap caps.'"[13]

Like the Bay State foot soldiers of the Thirty-fifth, the men of the Fifteenth New Jersey were less than delighted with their Enfields. Following the May 3, 1863 battle of Salem Church, the Fifteenth's Colonel William Penrose informed VI Army Corps commander Major General John Sedgwick that he believed the Enfields "now in the hands of the men of this regiment" were "refuse ones being purchased in a foreign country by the Government in the early part of the War and [have] evidently never passed inspection." According to Penrose, "the various parts of the pieces are badly finished and when a part from any cause is broken or lost it is with difficulty that another can be found to replace it."[14]

More important than parts finish or breakage were the problems the men of the Fifteenth had with their Enfields at Salem Church. After a few rounds the Jerseyans found it difficult to ram minie balls down the barrels of their weapons. Some soldiers had to push their ramrods against trees to seat the bullets in their guns. Although Colonel Penrose opined that his men's loading difficulties were due to lead deposits caused by "imperfections in the grooving" of the barrels, and this is possible, the problems were most likely caused by powder fouling coupled with undersized bores and/or oversized bullets. Enfields came in two bore diameter sizes, the British .577 standard (twenty-five-gauge) and the American .58-caliber (twenty-four-gauge), the latter specifically intended for the American export market. Although ammunition originally intended for Springfields could be fired in .577 barrels, fouling buildup made loading difficult after a few shots.[15]

Similar situations occurred in the Confederate army. One Rebel brigade at Chickamauga was armed with Enfields in both bore sizes. Following the fight an ordnance officer wrote that "caliber No. .57 was loose and never choked the guns, while the No. .58, after the first few rounds, was found too large, and frequently choking the guns to that extent that they could not be forced down, thereby creating some uneasiness among the men using that number of ammunition."[16]

Some Southern-made cartridges were over bore size for either Enfield caliber. This situation surfaced time and again in the Confederacy, largely due to improper gauges and poor production control. Oversized ammunition became such a problem that at one point a Rebel ordnance officer reported that a general in the Army of Northern Virginia informed him that "the men have repeatedly sought Miss.[issippi] rifle ammunition (cal. .54) for their Enfield rifles and rifled muskets (cal. .577 and .58)"[17]

Company C, 110th Pennsylvania Infantry, in a picture taken in the spring of 1863. Like many Union and Confederate infantry outfits, Company C has a mix of small arms, including Springfields and Enfields. The non-commissioned officer standing next to the officer is armed with a Model 1855 Springfield rifle-musket with patch box. *(USAMHI)*

Although Colonel Penrose's plea for Springfields to replace his Enfields was ignored, the aftermath of the battle of Gettysburg presented him with a solution to his small-arms problems. The colonel marched his men down to the Wheatfield, which was littered with the weapons of the fallen. The Jerseymen stacked their Enfields and replaced them with Springfield-style guns, including a few Richmond rifle-muskets. Sergeant Lucien Voorhees of the Fifteenth assured the home folks that the Richmond-made guns would be used against their former owners "as chance proffers."[18]

Not all Yankee soldiers preferred Springfields over Enfields, however. When the men of Colonel Henry O. Ryerson's Tenth New Jersey Infantry turned in their Enfields for Springfields in the spring of 1864, many of the new guns' mainsprings broke after they were cocked a few times. Regretting the exchange, Ryerson quixotically decided to "rely on the bayonet" in the upcoming campaign. He did not survive it.[19]

Although there were complaints, the Enfield was generally regarded as highly as the Springfield by soldiers and was considered a "first class" firearm by the Ordnance Department. A soldier in the Forty-fifth Illinois proudly announced that his "regiment is armed throughout with the Enfield 'rifle with sabre bayonet' which is probably as good an arm as any in the country." After the capture of Arkansas Post in 1863, Carlos Colby and his comrades of the Ninety-seventh Illinois eagerly "threw away their old guns, [smoothbore muskets] and took Enfield rifles captured from the enemy." Not all of the men in the Fifteenth New Jersey were glad to exchange their Enfields for Springfields, and the regimental historian remembered that "numbers of our soldiers had learned to love the old Enfields, to which they had grown accustomed, and with which they fancied they could shoot farther, and with more certainty of aim."[20]

With their own limited domestic production capacity, and the generally better quality of their Enfields, Confederate infantrymen appreci-

This Zouave of the 23rd Pennsylvania (Birney's Zouaves) is armed with an Austrian Lorenz. *(Michael J. McAfee)*

ated the British-made guns perhaps more than any Yankees. The soldiers of the Twentieth Tennessee, "a body of men that appreciated a good thing" were delighted when they received new Enfields to replace their "old flintlocks, squirrel rifles and shotguns" on the eve of the battle of Shiloh. Colonel Basil W. Duke of the Second Kentucky (Confederate) Cavalry noted that Enfields were "unequalled weapons (the right arms for soldiers who want to fight)." Noted cavalry commanders John Hunt Morgan and Nathan Bedford Forrest preferred the shorter "rifle" version of the Enfield. Morgan and Forrest felt that the rifle was easier to carry on horseback than the rifle-musket yet more accurate than the still shorter Enfield carbine. This "medium Enfield" was the favorite weapon of the men of Morgan's 2nd Kentucky (Confederate) Cavalry "because of its ease of handling on and off horseback."[21]

Another common imported rifle-musket was the Austrian Lorenz, both in its original .54-caliber and rebored to various approximations of .58-caliber. The Lorenz, introduced into Austrian service in 1854, was a sound weapon well regarded in Europe. Both Yankee and Rebel buyers eagerly snapped up Lorenz-style rifle-muskets; the Union recorded purchases of 226,924 and the Confederacy bought at least 100,000. Lorenz guns were acquired from several sources; the Hapsburg armories in Vienna and private arms makers in Vienna and Ferlach. There were three styles of Austrian rear sights; a non-adjustable "block," an adjustable leaf and, on a short "Jaeger" rifle designed for sharpshooters, a leaf which slid in a track not unlike that used by the U.S. M-1 Garand of World War II fame. Some of the Jaeger guns were fitted with the *tige* breech.

Although Captain Silas Crispin, who inspected Lorenz rifle-muskets imported for the Union by Boker, described them in general as "fair arms in workmanship and finish, and in weight and caliber according more nearly with our established model than any other arms of Continental manufacture," Lorenz quality apparently varied. Crispin was impressed by one lot of Austrian rifle-muskets, "finished in some respects, in imitation of the Enfield rifle..." as "somewhat superior, in every respect" to other lots of Lorenzes.[22]

Rebel Lorenz shipments apparently varied as well. Although Caleb Huse scored an initial coup with a large purchase of excellent rifle-muskets from the Vienna arsenal, he also bought Austrian arms from other sources. Unfortunately, not all of these guns were as good as Huse's initial purchase. In 1863, Major Smith Stansbury, a Confederate inspector

A soldier on guard at a fort outside Washington salutes with an Austrian Lorenz rifle-musket with quadrangular bayonet. The most common imported arm after the Enfield, the Lorenz was liked by many, and condemned by many as well. Quality of Lorenz guns, apparently dependent upon where in the Hapsburg lands they were made, appears to have varied. *(USAMHI)*

in Bermuda, classified a shipment of Austrian weapons as "a lot of trash, in horrible condition." After a thorough inspection and cleaning, however, most of these apparently well-used guns were found to be satisfactory. The bulk of them seem to have ended up serving in the Army of Tennessee and forces further west.[23]

Some Austrian gun dealers no doubt took advantage of the warring Americans' need for firearms and deep pockets to fob off guns of inferior quality. Among these may have been weapons rejected by the Austrian government or culled from some Balkan battlefield or the recent war in northern Italy, as well as copies of the Lorenz made elsewhere.

Exterior finish on the Lorenz rifle-muskets varied, with some guns blued, others browned and still others polished bright. A large number of Lorenz guns were rebored, both in Europe and America, in an attempt to make them conform to the standard .58-caliber. These conversions were more or less successful, with actual calibers noted as varying from .577, .57, and .58 to .59. Lorenz rifle-muskets were widely issued and there is archeological evidence of their use as far west as Glorietta Pass,

Private Simon Creamer of the Twelfth New Jersey with his Austrian rifle-musket. Soon after this picture was taken, the men of the Twelfth turned in their Austrian guns for U.S. Model 1842 smoothbore muskets, which they preferred. Austrian guns varied in quality, and the men of the 104th Pennsylvania and Fifth New Jersey were quite fond of theirs.
(John Kuhl Collection)

New Mexico, site of an April, 1862 battle between Union and Confederate forces.

The Lorenz was well-regarded by some troops to whom it was issued, including those of the Fifth New Jersey and 104th Pennsylvania. Private Alfred Bellard of the Fifth praised his .54-caliber Lorenz for being "short, light and very easily cleaned," while Quartermaster James D. Hendrie of the 104th believed his outfit's Austrian guns to be "very superior weapons, although not so well finished as the American arms." The 104th's colonel remembered his regiment's guns as "rough but good and reliable." The men of the 23rd Pennsylvania were delighted to trade in their .69-caliber rifled muskets for Austrian arms, which they found to be "most efficient firearms." An Illinois officer regarded the Lorenz as: "although a little heavy, a fine piece for service." Leander Stillwell of the Sixty-first Illinois considered his .54 Lorenz "a wicked shooter." Stillwell

Zouave with a Lorenz rifle. These Austrian guns, in original .54 and rebored .58, were, after the Enfield, the most common foreign arms in service in both armies. *(USAMHI)*

and his comrades "were glad to get the Austrians, and were quite proud of them." The Suckers of the Sixty-first carried their Lorenz rifle-muskets until June of 1863, when they exchanged them for Springfields.[24]

Other Yanks were not as enthusiastic. In 1863, a Union inspecting officer condemned the Austrian weapons of the Forty-seventh Massachusetts Infantry. Lorenz rifle-muskets issued to western troops in the second year of the war seem to have been decidedly inferior to those issued the previous year. William E. McMillan of the Ninety-fourth Illinois' Company E wrote that his unit's Lorenzes were "not worth much," while the 100th Illinois reported that its rebored .58-caliber Lorenz guns "are roughly and improperly made and cannot be called an effective weapon." The men of the 106th Illinois complained that the .58-caliber Lorenz was "miserably poor" and "rather a poor excuse for a gun" and the 120th Illinois classified its .54 Lorenz guns as "worthless."[25]

The 125th Illinois was issued Austrian rifle-muskets rebored to .58-caliber of "which not over one-half were perfect...many will not explode a cap." The 125th's regimental historian complained that some of the Austrian guns' nipples "were not entirely drilled out," and some could not mount a bayonet without hammering it on. The 130th Illinois reported that "one-third or three-eights of these arms [Austrian] are defective."[26]

Like Colonel Penrose of the Fifteenth New Jersey, Major Robert L. Bodine of the Twenty-sixth Pennsylvania rearmed his regiment on the field at Gettysburg. Bodine's men came to Gettysburg armed "with the Austrian rifle of an inferior quality, and I desired to exchange them for Springfield rifles; which was done without the red tape processes. Quite a number of them were taken from the Rebels." Like the Jerseymen of the Fifteenth, Bodine's men picked up several Rebel-made rifle-muskets along with the Springfields. Apparently unaware of the Confederacy's production facilities at Richmond, Bodine reported that these guns "had gone through the renovating process, and bore the Richmond C.S. stamp."[27]

Lorenz guns may well have gained a bad reputation from their association with older .71-caliber Austrian "Consol" or tube-lock muskets, which were conversions from flintlock. These guns, some of which were rifled, others not, were converted by a method devised by Giuseppe Consol of Milan and improved by General Vincent Augustin of the Austrian army. The Consol/Augustin system replaced the flintlock pan and frizzen with a two-piece priming chamber and installed a new hammer.

After muzzle loading the main charge in the usual manner, the Consol/Augustin was primed by bringing its hammer to half cock, lifting the top section of the priming chamber, which replaced the frizzen, inserting a small priming tube filled with percussion powder into a groove in the bottom section, which replaced the pan, then closing the chamber. The gun could then be brought to full cock and fired. The hammer hit a firing pin device in the chamber which, in turn, exploded the percussion tube and ignited the main charge. A number of these guns were converted to the standard percussion system before or after importation, but others, especially in the earliest days of the war, were placed directly in the hands of troops with their peculiar priming system intact.

Continental European guns were more commonly issued and remained in service longer in the western armies. Major General John C. Fremont purchased 25,000 tube-lock muskets in his desperate search for weapons in 1861 and at least 3,000 .71-caliber Delvigne chambered

Austrian "Garibaldi" rifles were issued to Minnesota troops. The men of the Twenty-sixth Illinois embarked on their military careers in September, 1861 armed with "hickory clubs," and were then issued "old English Tower" muskets, which they later exchanged for "old Austrian fuse primer [guns] altered and rifled" in February of 1862. By the end of the year an inspector classified the tubelock Consol/Augustin weapons as "nearly all... unfit for use."[28]

The Thirty-third Illinois began its career with smoothbored Austrian tubelocks, and Company C of the Thirty-third reported 3,155 "Austrian primers" on hand. One soldier accurately described the "Austrian primers" as "a little copper-covered stick of percussion, with a small twisted wire at the end of it." The men of the Thirty-third carried their tubelocks until early 1862.[29]

Although the Ninetieth Illinois was armed with .54 Lorenz rifles during the fourth quarter of 1862 and the first quarter of 1863, the recollection of veteran George P. Woodruff that the Ninetieth's initial armament, "the Austrian rifled musket... a very inferior arm" subject to premature discharge with stocks and bayonets "easily broken," does not seem to jibe of what we know of the Lorenz. Either the Ninetieth got an extremely bad lot of Lorenz-type guns or were issued Consol/Augustin rifles on enlistment, which were later exchanged for Lorenz guns.[30]

The Lorenz was issued in large numbers to Rebel soldiers as well. In contrast to the Federal experience, the number of Lorenz rifle-muskets in Confederate service actually increased in the final year of the war. In April of 1863, the Army of Tennessee reported 663 Austrian small arms in service; by the following spring, thirty-two percent of that army's men shouldered Austrian guns. The Lorenz was among the weapons tested by the Army of Northern Virginia's sharpshooters in the spring of 1864, and was found to be fully equal in accuracy to the Springfield and Enfield up to 500 yards.[31]

Perhaps surprisingly, considering that Delvigne and Minie had pioneered significant advances in firearms and projectiles and that the *Chasseurs de Vincennes* had developed new tactical theories around them, French rifle-muskets did not see as much use as British and Austrian models in the American Civil War. One reason for this might have been lack of availability. Despite the new developments, diehard tactical conservatives in the French army had fought a delaying action against the new weapons and tactics every step of the way. The British, finally divested of the Duke of Wellington, adopted the Minie system wholeheartedly and never looked back. By the late 1850s, the smoothbore musket was largely a thing of the past in British service. The French, on the other hand, issued rifled arms only to Guard regiments and Chasseur and Zouave light infantry outfits through the early 1860s.

French weapons, as well as Belgian copies of them, were purchased in some quantity in the wholesale weapons bazaar of 1861 and 1862. The French saw the American war as an opportunity to unload surplus Crimean war arms as well as earlier, less desirable guns. Although some weapons purchased by the Union in France and Belgium were late-model .58-caliber Minie rifles, Gallic guns used by the Union included older .69-caliber rifled muskets and even some obsolete smoothbores. A Belgian copy of a backlock-action .58-caliber French rifle examined by this writer appeared to be a quite well made and balanced arm.

Examples of an excellent German copy of the Springfield Model 1861 exist, but there is no indication that any significant number of these rifle-muskets found their way to America. Most imported German arms

Skirmisher Dave Dworak of the 69th New York with a .58 Belgian-made Minie rifle. This view shows back-action lock and a sight bearing a strong resemblance to that of an Enfield. *(Joseph Bilby)*

were surplus weapons. At the time of the Civil War, Germany was a decade away from unification, and arms purchasers dealt with individual states. Although some good quality rifled arms were obtained in the German states, the bulk of Federal purchases appear to have been smoothbore muskets which, though sturdy weapons, were merely stopgap purchases.

The famed gun-making center of Liege in Belgium was a source for all types of weapons, including copies of French, British and Austrian guns. Although quality varied, Belgian weapons, like German arms, filled a vital gap in the Federal arms inventory in the first two years of the war. Mostly by capture, Rebel units often found themselves similarly armed.

Rebel ordnance officer J. W. Mallet recalled that in "the early part of the war" Southern infantrymen were armed with "Springfield and Enfield muskets, Mississippi and Maynard rifles, Hall's and Sharp's carbines, and arms of English, German, Austrian and Belgian manufacture, of many different calibers." Mallet remembered that he had "at one time samples of more than twenty patterns of infantry weapons alone." Confederates, for the most part, however, avoided purchasing Continental arms other than the Austrian Lorenz, and concentrated on getting as many Enfields through the Federal naval blockade as possible. Due to the blockade's porosity, this proved to be quite a large number.[32]

Perhaps the last Federal issuance of Continental weapons in quantity occurred during the summer and autumn of 1862, when large numbers of "militia" regiments were formed, many from draftees, for nine months service. New Jersey fielded eleven such units. Some of them, according to state Quartermaster General Perrine, were issued "old Springfield smoothbore muskets, which from appearance had seen long and hard usage" by the Federal government, but two regiments, the Twenty-fifth and Twenty-eighth New Jersey Infantry, "were furnished with French rifled muskets, altered from flint to percussion." The quartermaster general described the guns as "of various manufactures, and in caliber ranging from 68 to 71, and differing in appearance and length as much as a rifle does from a musket, many of them bearing dates in the last century."[33]

When Perrine complained about the condition of these weapons to the War Department, "a person by the name of Forman, representing himself as an inspector of small arms for the Ordnance Bureau, called upon me after nine o'clock on the night of September 29th, [1862] to examine the arms, and after a superficial examination of some twenty muskets, by the light of a single lantern, he informed me that on his return he should report them to [Assistant Secretary of War] Mr. Watson as fit for service." By the end of their nine months' service in the summer of 1863, most of the Jerseyans had exchanged their smoothbores and old French arms for Springfield or Enfield rifle-muskets.[34] Although most Continental guns were no longer in active Federal service east of the Mississippi by late 1864, they remained in the hands of some frontier Yankees to the end of the war. Garibaldi and tube-lock Austrian weapons were still in the supply inventories of Forts Ripley and Snelling, Minnesota, in 1864, and the men of the Thirtieth Wisconsin carried .576-caliber German Dresden rifle-muskets into the Dakotas to fight the Sioux in 1863 and 1864.

Were most of the European guns refuse? Complaints about foreign, as well as obsolete American, weapons abound in both official and unofficial Civil War correspondence and memoirs, but it might be well to take at least some of them with a grain of salt. Some soldiers exaggerated or fabricated the defects of their guns, which, after all, had often been first-line firearms at one time or another in the best armies of the world. The assertion of a private in the Forty-fifth Massachusetts that his Austrian rifle-musket "would hardly carry a ball clear of its muzzle and [would] send it anywhere but in the desired direction" or of another Yankee that his company's Prussian muskets "burst at the first firing, and were more dangerous at their butts than at their muzzles" are patently absurd.[35]

It is, however, easy to blow the muzzle of a musket back like a peeled banana if the gun is fired with an obstruction like dirt clogging the muzzle. Some soldiers apparently abused issue weapons they didn't care for, whether foreign or obsolete American, in the hope that they would be replaced with more desirable Springfields or Enfields. Other Yankees were simply poorly trained and/or incompetent. Of the 4,291 .69-caliber rifled muskets issued by the state of New Jersey to its Fourth, Fifth, Sixth, Seventh and Eighth regiments, 2,490 were "condemned and turned into the Washington Arsenal as unserviceable" and returned to Trenton before the units ever saw combat. Perhaps deliberately, "and by the known recklessness and carelessness of the soldier, in a service of about six months [and no combat] they were very much injured and many of them rendered worthless."[36]

Other veterans no doubt "misremembered" the quality of their arms to weave a good story. George H. Otis of the Second Wisconsin recalled that after pulling the trigger on his musket he "was on my back, kicking for all that was out." While amusing, Otis' story is immediately revealed as a fabrication by anyone who has ever fired a musket, rifled or smoothbore. Guns gained weight over the years as well. Carlos Colby recalled that the "Belgian rifles, flintlocks, remodeled for percussion caps" issued to the Ninety-seventh Illinois weighed an unlikely "fourteen pounds, three pounds above the regulation standard."[37] Many soldiers knew nothing about guns before their enlistment, learned little during it, and forgot whatever they learned in the civilian life that followed, rendering their selective anecdotal memories more than a little suspect. In fact, although most were obsolete or, at best, obsolescent, the majority of foreign firearms issued in the first two years of the war were good enough to fill the temporary substitute role for which they were intended. This writer has fired a Prussian smoothbore musket of the era, and while a bit "clunky" and heavy in comparison to the U.S. Model 1842, it is a perfectly serviceable weapon—over 130 years after its issue to some Civil War soldier.

By 1864, with incompetent and fraudulent arms contractors weeded out, the latent arms-making capability of the North came into its own, and Model 1861 Springfield clones, with interchangeable parts, rolled out of factories across the northeast and were quickly placed in the hands of Yankee infantrymen. Although Harpers Ferry machinery continued to produce a respectable number of quality small arms in Richmond and elsewhere, the Confederate arms industry never really materialized. Despite this, Johnny Reb did not suffer for adequate infantry arms in the last two years of the war, and the Southern small-arms picture continued to improve. By 1864, most Rebel infantrymen (in the eastern theater at least) were armed with good quality imported Enfields and captured Springfields, along with a sprinkling of reliable Richmond rifle-muskets. While distinctions among the better quality rifle-muskets, including imported arms, are of interest to collectors, the guns are virtually indistinguishable from a tactical standpoint.

Much has been made of the rifle-musket's accuracy and the fact that it changed the nature of warfare on the tactical level. Officers had originally argued for the adoption of rifle-muskets precisely because they were believed capable of making "close shooting" at a distance of 500 yards, and effective on large formations at 1,000 yards. The British Minie Rifle's record in the Crimea sustained the validity of these conclusions. A closer analysis, however, suggests that the rifle-musket seldom achieved the potential expected of it in United States or Confederate service. This outcome was influenced by the realities of combat and terrain, ignorance of junior officers and poor or nonexistant marksmanship training. Even worse, most recruits, especially in Federal ranks, were totally unfamiliar with firearms. The historian of the Fourteenth New Hampshire freely admitted that many men in his regiment "cringed at every shot. Quite a number of them had never fired a gun in their lives; and several of them, when commanded to fire, would shut their eyes, turn their heads in the opposite direction, and blaze away."[38]

Fear of one's own musket made a bad thing worse. The inherent accuracy a gun displays under controlled conditions does not predict combat accuracy. Soldiers in action, especially untrained ones, tend to fire high and often wildly. This tendency was graphically demonstrated at the May 12, 1864 fight at Spotsylvania's "Bloody Angle." One of the more astute observers of the Bloody Angle's aftermath was Lieutenant Colonel John Schoonover of the Eleventh New Jersey Infantry. Schoonover was a cool soldier in action and a noted rifleman who often took a turn on the skirmish line with a Springfield. His observations are worth quoting in their entirety:

"The evidence of the continued fire at this point during the day and part of the night was everywhere apparent. The trees near the works were stripped of their foliage, and looked as though an army of locusts had passed during the night. The brush between the lines was cut and torn into shreds, and the fallen bodies of men and horses lay there with the flesh shot and torn from the bones. The peculiar whirring sound of a flying ramrod was frequently heard during the day. I noticed two of these that had fastened themselves in the oak trees nearby.

"While the great number of the enemy's dead and the terrible effects of our fire upon the logs composing the breastworks attested the general accuracy of our fire, the absence of the foliage from the top of the tallest trees made it evident that during a battle there is much random firing. There is a large percentage of men in actual battle who load carefully, aim deliberately and shoot to kill. On the other hand, it is *not an uncommon thing* for a soldier amidst the excitement of battle, to load his gun, shut his eyes and fire in the air *straight over his head*."[39]

Earlier in the war Confederate sharpshooter Berry Benson made a similar observation. After entering a woodlot where his regiment had fought on the Rebel right at Fredericksburg, Benson observed "the trees spotted and scarred with the marks of bullets, most of them just overhead, which shows that the average aim is too high. In one tree we found a ramrod which had been shot into it and wonderfully bent and twisted it was."[40]

Both observations lend credence to conclusions arrived at by John Gibbon's prewar *Artillerist's Manual*. While conceding the potential of rifled arms to stop most any advance, Gibbon, who would become a Federal general, concluded that even "the very best disciplined men will, in time of battle, fire with precipitancy and at too great a distance; from which results a great loss of ammunition and of effect upon the enemy."[41]

Wild firing is exacerbated when black powder smoke obscures the target. Anyone who has fired a rifle-musket at the N-SSA's Fort Shenandoah range on a humid, still day realizes how smoke hangs in the air with 400 or so shooters on the line. To properly envision the haze of battle, multiply that effect by 2,500 and add a heavy dose of three pound artillery powder charges. Connecticut Captain John W. DeForest recalled that, on one occasion, his men, unable to see their opponents, volleyed into the "hostile line of smoke which confronted them." Soldiers blazing away at each other along Antietam's "Bloody Lane" caught only brief glimpses of their opponents.[42]

Heavy brush or forest as well as gunsmoke often obscured enemy positions during the Civil War. These problems, coupled with the tendency noted by Gibbon of soldiers to fire uncontrollably once they began to shoot, led officers to control their men's fire until the enemy was very close, often well within 100 yards. This practice effectively negated the rifle-musket's range advantage over the smoothbore. Much of the fire delivered by rifle-muskets during the war was within the effective range of the old-fashioned smoothbore musket's murderous buck-and-ball load, which, in the hands of the men of the Irish Brigade, was responsible for much of the carnage in Antietam's "Bloody Lane."

Military historian Paddy Griffith analyzed a number of Civil War firefights and found that the distance between opposing forces ranged from an average of 104 yards in 1862 to 141 yards in 1864-1865, with an average for the whole war of 127 yards. These distances were about the same, Griffith notes, as musketry ranges during the Napoleonic wars, when the smoothbore reigned supreme and caused horrendous casualties. Extension of engaged ranges in the last year of the war is more likely due to the reluctance of veterans to advance into the more deadly closer range rather than deliberate use of the rifle-musket at longer range. In fact, the Yankee infantrymen of the Fifth New Jersey Infantry considered firing at the enemy at 200 yards "skirmishing and dueling at long range"[43]

According to Griffith, "decisive" Civil War musketry fights occurred at very close range—an average of thirty-three yards! It should be noted that Griffith had to assume that the distances reported by those involved were accurate. In some cases at least, they were probably shorter. Human recollection often fails. The actual distance of a deer shot at a hunter's estimated "one hundred yards" is often quite less.

On at least one occasion a Federal division commander who had the opportunity to use the rifle-musket's superior range and accuracy to good tactical effect demonstrated total ignorance of the gun's capabilities. At the battle of Fair Oaks/Seven Pines, the 104th Pennsylvania Infantry engaged a Rebel attacking force at a range of well over one hundred yards. The Pennsylvanians, equipped with Austrian Lorenz rifle-muskets, were shooting their smoothbore armed opponents to ribbons when General Silas Casey ordered the 104th and several other regiments to charge the Rebels. As the Yankees came within fifty yards of the enemy, they were subjected to a murderous barrage of buck and ball, which drove them from the field.

If Silas Casey, "author" of the Union army's standard tactics manual, had no real comprehension of the capabilities of the rifle-musket, then it is understandable that company and field-grade officers were even less enlightened. Then again, there is little evidence that most officers on either side displayed any kind of tactical innovation during the war. American Civil War commanders, North and South, generally ordered their men to hold their fire until the enemy was within the old "whites of their eyes" range. Tactics were largely limited to attempting to overlap an enemy's flank.

Unlike the British and French service, basic marksmanship training was virtually non-existent in Civil War armies during the first two years of the war. Although Cadmus Wilcox, later a Confederate general, addressed the effectiveness of long-range rifle fire on heavy columns, as exemplified by the British in the Crimea, in his French-influenced pre-war *Rifles and Rifle Practice*, the manuals used by American amateur soldiers to train their commands during the Civil War, by Winfield Scott, William J. Hardee and Casey, paid no attention to shooting other than to describe the method of loading a muzzle loader "by the numbers." All three manuals were largely plagiarized from French originals, with

Scott's decidedly oriented to an army armed with smoothbore muskets. Hardee's effort replaced Scott's for evolutions up to and including brigade level in the 1850s, but differed largely only in opening up skirmish formations and increasing the speed at which troops performed evolutions. Although he made some minor deployment changes, Casey's work was essentially a "politically correct" Union version of Hardee, who had become a Confederate general.

While paying lip service to a need to deal with "the revolution which has been wrought within a few years past in the weapons both of artillery and infantry," Casey simply advised commanders to speed up troop movements and increase unit intervals in response. Aside from drill in the separate motions used to load a muzzle-loading rifle or musket, the General's sole marksmanship tip, taken word for word from Hardee, was that the soldier should "... incline the head upon the butt, so that the right eye may perceive quickly the notch of the hausse, [rear sight] the front sight, and the object aimed at."[44]

To be fair, in advocating speed in the offense as a partial remedy to improved arms, Hardee and Casey revealed their familiarity with recent tactical developments in Europe, although failing to detail them in any case studies. The Austro-French war of 1859 in northern Italy provided the first instance where troops in both armies were armed with rifle-muskets. The French won such battles as Solferino by rapid advances and the steel-tipped bravado of a bayonet charge by elite troops in fine physical condition who were taught to shoot and think—revolutionary concepts for the day. That these examples were not totally ignored is evidenced in the victorious Union attacks at Second Fredericksburg and Rappahannock Station in 1863 and Colonel Emory Upton's successful, if brief, penetration of the Rebel lines at Spotsylvania on May 10, 1864.[45]

Casey's most useful suggestion was abstracted from the doctrine of the French Chasseurs who had proved so effective in combat in Italy. He recommended that two companies of every regiment, "composed of picked men, possessing the highest physical qualifications, marksmen as well" be detailed as permanent skirmishers. Inexplicably, this portion of Casey's book was "suspended" by Secretary of War Edwin M. Stanton when the manual was published.[46]

There is some indication that, despite Stanton's suspension, many Federal regiments largely armed with smoothbore muskets were provided with enough rifled arms to arm two companies for flank protection and skirmish duties. In September of 1862, the men of the newly raised

Company E, Fourth U.S. Colored Infantry. These African American Union soldiers are armed with a mixture of Springfield and 1861 Special Model rifle-
muskets. *(USAMHI)*

Eleventh New Jersey were issued "a new Austrian rifle for our flank
companies and the Springfield smoothbore, buck-and-ball musket for
the eight center companies." The Eleventh's Colonel Robert McAllister,
an experienced combat veteran, expressed himself "satisfied with this
arrangement." At around the same time the Twelfth Rhode Island and
Twelfth New Hampshire issued the same combination of Austrian
rifle-muskets and domestic smoothbores.[47]

Equipping one or more companies in an otherwise smoothbore-
armed infantry regiment with rifles was hardly an original idea in the
American military, and had been common practice since the early years
of the century. In early 1862, General Robert E. Lee, concerned about the
lack of rifled arms in the Confederate army, advocated that they be
distributed "to the flanking companies at least" of experienced regiments. Lee believed that "fine rifles [imported Enfields] will be more
efficient in the hands of tried troops."[48]

Sometimes rifle-armed regiments in a brigade otherwise equipped
with smoothbores were detailed for flank and skirmish duty. In the case
of the famed Irish Brigade, in which four out of five regiments carried
smoothbores longer than most Union outfits, the Enfield-armed Twenty-

eighth Massachusetts was detailed to permanent flank-guard duties on the march as late as the spring of 1864. Likewise, the Fifth New Jersey was issued Austrian rifle-muskets in January, 1862, while the other three regiments of the Second New Jersey Brigade remained armed with smoothbore muskets.

The selection of either companies or regiments for flank and skirmish duty was largely by happenstance, however, and there is no indication that, as in the case of the French Chasseurs, or as recommended by Casey, they were composed of "picked men" who were especially physically fit and trained in the elements of marksmanship.

With little else to go by, Union and Confederate regimental officers, largely military amateurs, buried their noses in Hardee's or Casey's work and their men often entered battle blissfully ignorant of the weapons they carried. The soldiers of the Eighth U.S. Colored Infantry had never even loaded their rifles with live ammunition before they went into action for the first time at Olustee, Florida in 1864. The situation of the recruits of the Thirteenth New Jersey, who fought at Antietam with only the most rudimentary training, was similar. One man from the Thirteenth apparently replaced the tompion, a plug intended to keep rain water out of the barrel on the march, in his Enfield's muzzle after loading it. When he fired his gun for the first time, the brass-tipped muzzle stopper hit another Jerseyman in the back, mortally wounding him. A veteran of the Thirty-fifth Massachusetts recalled that "men learned their weapons in battle or by stealth." Civil War reenactor and historian Ben Maryniak has aptly noted that "officers obviously lacked enthusiasm for this phase [target practice] of instruction in the art of war."[49]

Lack of instruction or practice did not limit the enthusiasm of officers and men to acquire rifle-muskets, however. Captain Henry Ryerson was delighted when his company of the Second New Jersey Infantry was detailed to the First New Jersey Brigade's "new battalion of sharpshooters." Ryerson's men swapped their smoothbore muskets for "the Minnie musket, rifled so that now we may with some propriety be called 'the Sussex Rifles.'" Ryerson left no indication that he planned to exercise his men in even familiarization firing of their new arms.[50]

Many soldiers apparently felt any lack of skill on their part would be compensated for by the inherent accuracy and power of the rifle-musket. A Rebel in the Forty-fourth Georgia noted that his comrades "all seemed proud of their guns [Enfields] and seemed to think that they could knock a Yankee over a half mile or more." Some of the Yankees

Private George Stevens, Company H, 9th New Hampshire Infantry, armed with one of the U.S. Model 1841 rifles the regiment received on its enlistment in August 1862. The regiment served with the well-traveled IX Corps, fighting at South Mountain, Antietam, Fredericksburg, Vicksburg and in the Virginia campaign of 1864. At Spotsylvania, the 9th lost almost half its strength in killed, wounded and missing. By 1864, this model had been replaced by the Model 1863 Springfield rifle-musket. *(USAMHI)*

were at least as optimistic. One marginally literate New Jersey soldier believed his gun would hit "secesh [at] 800 yards" and "kill stone ded through a stone six fot thick. And I can load it in the Twinck of an eie." An over-optimistic New Hampshireman, after reporting that his unit hit a target "the size of old Jeff" with 360 rounds at the unlikely range of 600 yards, noted that his Springfield "...will range 1500 yards with considerable certainty."[51]

Some soldiers were, or at least thought they were, more knowledgeable about the firearms they were issued. Although strictly forbidden by regulations to do so, these gunwise enlisted men occasionally "tuned" their weapons. When Sergeant James Sullivan of the Sixth Wisconsin drew a new Springfield after returning from convalescent leave, he "selected one with a curly stock and I mounted it with some silver ornaments and fixed the screw in the stock against the dog [sear] so it worked almost as easy as a squirrel gun, and I felt very proud of it." Sullivan accounted himself an excellent shot, bragging that he could "hit a canteen at a hundred yards." Other soldiers conducted their private target practice in a more grisly manner. Rebel guerilla Cole Younger reportedly lined up Federal prisoners one behind the other and shot them in order to test the penetration power of his newly acquired Enfield.[52]

In some cases, pre-war marksmanship training received by Yankee soldiers in foreign armies was put to good use. Although General Meagher of the Irish Brigade was firmly wedded to the concept of a blast of buck and ball and a rush with the bayonet, some of his men were not quite convinced. Many Irish soldiers in Meagher's ranks were combat veterans of the British army's wars in the Crimea and India and had been exposed to the Hythe system. When their brigade came under a heavy enemy skirmish fire while advancing at Antietam, some Irishmen "surreptitiously exchanged their muskets" for rifle-muskets and success-fully sniped at opposing Rebel skirmishers.[53]

The Irish skirmishers' success was not due to any instruction they received on this side of the Atlantic. Until at least mid-war, most army target practice was largely limited to occasional informal shooting matches. At one such, held among Union troops on duty at Newport News, Virginia in November of 1863, "a shooting match took place with rifles, at two-hundred-yards distance, and with revolvers at thirty yards." Interestingly, although men from the Ninth New Jersey, a regiment known for its marksmen, participated, the winner of both matches was "the chief bugler of Belger's Rhode Island Battery." It is safe to assume that the bugler acquired his skill with the rifle and handgun in civilian life.[54]

Some regiments, entirely on the responsibility of their commanders, engaged in limited target practice as early as 1861. This often occurred during guard mount changes. Lieutenant Benjamin D. Coley of the Sixth New Jersey's Company K "took the old Guard out and they fired at a target," with their smoothbore muskets. More formal, albeit limited shooting was also encouraged in the Sixth, and Coley "went out with the company at target practice and they fired four rounds," on October 9, 1861. When the company couldn't get out to the range, Coley and his fellow company officers took muskets out themselves "and had a shot at the target." The lieutenant was proud that he "made the best shot."

This 1861 Pennsylvania militiaman, a member of the Philadelphia Gray Reserves, is armed with a .54-caliber Model 1817 common rifle converted from flintlock to percussion. *(Michael J. McAfee)*

It should be noted that none of this practice included instruction of any sort other than loading and pulling a trigger.[55]

Although some official marksmanship practice took place in the Army of the Potomac prior to the campaign of 1863, it apparently accomplished little. On April 19, 1864, the Army of the Potomac's Provost Marshal General issued a circular order to "familiarize the men in the use of their arms," the order authorized "an additional expenditure of 10 rounds of small-arms ammunition per man...," and stressed that "every man should be made to load and fire his musket under the personal supervision of a company officer." The instructions were based on the belated discovery that "... there are men in this Army who have been in numerous actions without ever firing their guns and it is known that muskets taken on the battle field have been found filled to the muzzle with cartridges."[56]

What target practice took place that spring in the Army of the Potomac was limited and at known distances. On March 31, 1864 the 121st New York "had target shooting at 200 yds. and ten rounds per man." The New Yorkers returned to the range in mid-April and "shot five rounds 300 yards." On April 22, 1864, Colonel Penrose of the Fifteenth New Jersey authorized three days of target practice, with "a string of four shots...each practicing day at 300 yards." By the following spring, soldiers in the far west were engaging in target practice at three, four and five hundred yards. Private William Hilleary of the First Oregon Infantry recorded that the men of his Company F got "only two shots in

A soldier of the 53rd New York Volunteer Infantry (Tenth Legion) with his Enfield two-band rifle and fixed-sword bayonet.
(Michael J. McAfee)

target, [three by six feet] distance 5 hundred yards" with their Colt rifle-muskets.[57]

Available evidence suggests that even when senior officers became dimly aware of its value, target practice throughout the Union army was haphazard and lacked preliminary basic marksmanship instruction. Sophisticated concepts like range and trajectory estimation were beyond the comprehension of most officers on both sides outside of a few special sharpshooter outfits. Even officers who were aware of the need for important skills like range estimation had little faith that the average soldier could comprehend it. Colonel Willard of the 125th New York fretted at the possibility of a "soldier's mind ...perpetually occupied in guessing at distances." Willard recognized the potential value of the rifle-musket in the hands of men trained to use it—"thoroughly instructed 'light troops or skirmishers.'" He believed, however, quite correctly, that: "In this character of soldiers, our army is certainly deficient...."[58]

The deficiency was not innate. Although the War Department published *A System of Target Practice*, "prepared principally from the French," which included chapters on aiming, trigger control and range estimation, in 1862, there is little evidence the manual was put to use. As in the case of the April, 1864 order from the Army of the Potomac headquarters, target shooting was viewed mainly as familiarization firing.[59]

Colonel Benjamin F. Scribner of the 38th Illinois displayed unusual initiative for a senior officer when he reacted to his men's complaints of Confederate shooting superiority and the inferiority of their own ammunition and gun sights by establishing a range training-program prior to the Atlanta campaign. "Targets the size of a man were placed in position and rifle-pits were dug in front of them to protect the person who filled the bullet holes and reported the shots. The distances from the target of one, two, three, five hundred, and a thousand yards were carefully measured, and after several days of practice and application of careful tests, the conclusion was reached that both the powder and sights were right...."[60]

By way of contrast, British soldiers had to qualify on an *annual* basis by firing a ninety-round course of fire. Fifty rounds were fired in company formation in the standing and kneeling formation and included volley, file and individual firing as well as "ten rounds per man advancing and retiring between 400 & 200 yards." The remaining forty rounds

The 7th New York Militia was a stylish and well- equipped regiment, as evidenced by this 1861 photo. This militiaman, in the regiment's fatigue uniform, is armed with a U.S. Model 1855 rifle-musket, the same weapon carried by regular army soldiers at the outbreak of the war. *(Michael J. McAfee)*

of the course were expended in individual firing at ranges up to 900 yards.[61]

A notable exception to the general rule of indifferent marksmanship training in American Civil War armies was the case of General Patrick Cleburne's command in the Army of Tennessee. Cleburne, an Irish-born British army veteran, was well aware of the Hythe musketry school and its course of instruction. The general used men armed with rifle-muskets effectively as early as the April, 1862 battle of Shiloh, when he called for volunteer sharpshooters to pick off Yankee gunners supporting Brigadier General Benjamin Prentiss' position in the "Hornet's Nest." Following that fight, Cleburne personally visited each regiment in his brigade to select sharpshooters, who were formally organized into a company under his direct command. The Arkansas Irishman employed his sharp-shooters to good effect at Perryville and Murfreesboro.

By early 1863, Cleburne had acquired a copy of the British *Regulations for Conducting Musketry Instruction in the Army*, published by the instructors at Hythe. The Irish American general quickly mastered the manual and instituted a similar program in his division. Imitating the British cadre system, Major Calhoun Benham, Cleburne's chief of staff, instructed officers from each regiment in the division in the art and science of musketry. They in turn returned to their outfits and spread the knowledge, which included basic ballistics and range estimation, "with human flesh and blood as markers."[62]

On June 24, at Liberty Gap, Tennessee, one of Cleburne's brigades held off three Union brigades with withering long-range small-arms fire. One Federal officer reported that "within one half or three fourths of a mile of the enemy, the effect of their sharpshooters was terrible." Although Cleburne's sharpshooters, armed with deadly long-range British Whitworth rifles, played their part, much of the "terrible" effect was wreaked by Cleburne's ordinary infantrymen, properly trained in the use of the rifle-musket. Most soldiers, even in Confederate ranks, did not approach the shooting ability of Cleburne's men. In an effort to remedy this, Major Benham produced a small-arms manual based upon Cleburne's British training methods in the fall of 1863, and General Braxton Bragg ordered the publication distributed throughout the Army of Tennessee.[63]

Although they may not have been formally trained, soldiers west of the Mississippi were not reluctant to use their rifle-muskets at long range. In early 1862, Private Alfred B. Peticolas and other men of the Fourth Texas Mounted Volunteers "having *minie* rifles" traded shots with Yankees at ranges of between 300 and 600 yards at Valverde, New Mexico. Men and horses fell to long-range fire on both sides in this fight between Federal regular army soldiers and "Texas boys [who] are accustomed to the use of arms and never shoot away their ammunition for nothing."[64]

On rare occasions an infantry line outfit distinguished itself by its shooting ability. The men of the Ninth New Jersey Infantry, which was organized as a "rifle regiment," were recruited as sharpshooters but served as infantry. While the Ninth waited at Trenton to depart for the war: "A range was established for target practice, and scores were made that would put many sharpshooters of the present day [1889] to blush."

Men of the 30th Pennsylvania Volunteers (1st Pennsylvania Reserves) in camp with a stack of Springfield rifle-muskets. The weapons are stacked by intertwining the bayonets. The 1st Reserves served from 1861 to 1864, and lost 6 officers and 102 enlisted men killed and mortaly wounded. *(USAMHI)*

While encamped at Washington over the winter of 1861-1862 the Jerseymen continued their practice, and the regimental historian recalled that: "So thoroughly proficient did a respectable percentage of the men become with the new [Springfield] rifle..." that "the crack shots of the Berdan regiment, encamped near by, declined to compete with them."[65]

After leaving Washington for North Carolina in early 1862, however, the Jerseyans never formally practiced shooting during the remainder of their service. and were largely used as regular infantry, although often deployed as skirmishers. Replacements assigned to the regiment were not required to pass a shooting test, and the unit was never assigned long-range rifles with telescopic sights. The Ninth New Jersey retained its reputation as a regiment of good shots, however, and gave an excellent account of itself wherever it went.

At the battle of Roanoke Island the Ninth slogged through underbrush and waist-deep water to a position about one-hundred yards from a Confederate earthwork. Lieutenant Colonel Charles A. Heckman rotated his regiment by "divisions" (two companies formed a division within a regiment) and delivered a withering fire at the Rebel positions. Heckman detailed several of his best shots to silence a battery, which they did, killing the lieutenant commanding. While the Jerseymen actually hit few Confederates, the steady, accurate fire of their Springfields kept the enemy behind cover, and made a significant contribution to the Union victory. The Ninth repeated its performance at New Bern, where the Jersey boys, according to Brigadier General Jesse Reno, "opened a well directed fire upon a two gun battery only some 200 yards in front of them, and so accurate was their fire that the enemy could only occasionally fire their guns."[66]

The intelligent use of riflery by the Ninth New Jersey provides, however, the proverbial exception which proves the rule. Although soldiers armed with rifle-muskets may have been technically capable of picking-off cannoneers or breaking up an infantry formation at relatively long range, there is little evidence that such a scenario occurred with any degree of regularity. Except when they drew the attention of sharpshooter units, even unprotected field artillery positions generally became untenable only after they were subjected to very close-range fire, which would have been about as deadly (if not more so) if delivered with buck and ball.

Instead of the oft-repeated story of how it revolutionized warfare, the true tale of the rifle-musket in the Civil War is largely one of missed tactical opportunities. With notable exceptions, poor training and ignorant leadership led to a failure by commanders and soldiers to realize the weapon's deadly potential. Had they done so, perhaps the war would have ended sooner—or been even longer and bloodier.

Collecting and Shooting Rifle-Muskets Today

Although originally designed as a weapon of war, the rifle-musket's attributes of easy loading and good accuracy serve well in the hunting fields and on the target range today. These qualities, along with the ready availability of Lyman bullet molds, made the rifle-musket the first Civil

War arm to be returned to the firing line in the first of what has proved to be a very long line of Civil War "skirmishes." The first skirmish, a live fire-team competition, was held in Maryland in 1950 and led to the founding of the N-SSA. Interestingly, so lost had the lore of the rifle-musket become in the eighty-five years since it was last used in combat that some of the very first "skirmishers" loaded their rifle-muskets with round-ball projectiles!

Round balls were soon discarded, however, as shooters quickly turned to the projectile their guns were designed for—the minie ball. The secret of the rifle-musket's effective performance, in war or peace, lies in the conical hollow-based lubricated bullet which expands on firing to engage the rifling and scours the barrel of fouling deposited by previous shots as it travels up the bore.

The rifle-musket's relatively thin barrel walls, as well as the somewhat fragile bullet-base "skirt," limits usable powder charges to around sixty grains of FFG black powder—the army's original load. Most N-SSA shooters, who often fire up to forty shots in a match without cleaning, use a smaller charge of forty to fifty grains of the finer granulation FFFG, which produces less fouling and recoil. N-SSA skirmishers, firing off-hand against time, can consistently break clay birds mounted on a cardboard backer board fifty yards away and hit gallon jugs at a hundred yards. As many as three rounds a minute can be fired using preloaded plastic or cardboard tube cartridges. The tubes (unloaded) are available from sutlers and mailorder firms supplying Civil War shooters.

The Springfield or Enfield rifle-musket, which can be loaded with a

Euroarms Reproduction of the Springfield Model 1861 rifle-musket. The Model 1861, manufactured at Springfield Armory and by a number of private contractors, was the basic Union infantry arm of the Civil War. Large numbers did not begin to reach the field until the latter part of 1862 and early 1863, however. *(Euroarms)*

Euroarms Reproduction of the Enfield P53 rifle-musket. The most popular rifle in Confederate service and second only to the Springfield in numbers issued by the Union, the Enfield was supplied to both sides by private contractors in Birmingham and London. *(Euroarms)*

variety of massive 315- to 560-grain minie balls, has remarkable penetrating power. This writer once witnessed a 560-grain "Pritchett-style" minie cast from a Parker Hale mold and backed by forty-seven grains of FFFG penetrate a piece of sheet metal and two-two-by-ten boards and bury itself deep in a dirt backstop at 200 yards. The same load and bullet passed completely through a Whitetail deer at thirty yards. Tests conducted by the army in the 1850s revealed that the .58 minie ball could penetrate four inches of soft pine at a distance of 1,000 yards!

While original guns in good shape (see a good gunsmith for an evaluation.) are safe to shoot, and some are still seen on the skirmish line, most of today's musket shooters use reproduction firearms. New rifle-muskets are imported by a number of dealers, including Dixie Gun Works, Euroarms, Navy Arms and S&S Firearms. Custom American made guns are available as well. Excellent quality reproduction locks, barrels and other parts, as well as ninety percent inletted stocks, can be purchased by those who want to build their own guns. Many custom guns are composites of original and reproduction parts.

There are two basic rifle-musket styles available as reproductions, the British Enfield and the American Springfield. The Colt is sort of a hybrid of the two, but is closer to the Springfield. The Parker Hale Enfield, a copy of the original British rifle-musket, was formerly made in England, but is no longer in production. The Dixie Gun Works 1861 Springfield is produced in Japan. Other importers, including Euroarms, offer various Enfield, Springfield and Richmond rifle-musket copies made in Italy. For those in search of the unique, S&S Firearms imports a limited quantity of high-quality Italian-made Model 1855 Springfields. Colt Black Powder Firearms has offered a limited edition authentically

A New Jersey militia Zouave, possibly from the Communipaw Zouaves of Jersey City, poses with his converted and rifled smoothbore musket in 1861. *(Michael J. McAfee)*

marked "reissue" of the Colt Special Model 1861, an amalgam of Enfield and Springfield characteristics.

Springfields are only made with forty-inch barrels, but Enfields are available in thirty-nine-inch rifle-musket, thirty-three-inch rifle and twenty-four-inch carbine or musketoon configurations. Copies of original Richmond-made guns include the Euroarms rifle-musket and the S&S Richmond carbine, the latter sporting a twenty-five-inch barrel.

Ed Seiss of the N-SSA's 69th New York takes aim with a .54-caliber Austrian Jaeger rifle. Although the most common imported Austrian arm was the Lorenz rifle-musket, a limited number of Jaeger sharpshooter rifles were imported by the Union.

As manufactured, the Jaeger had no ramrod channel under the barrel. For reasons now unknown, Austrian soldiers issued the Jaeger carried its ramrod attached to their belts. Jaegers imported by the U.S. government had a ramrod channel bored in the stock.

The Jaeger has an unusual and advanced rear sight, which provides the shooter with a quick and effective elevation adjustment. It slides up or down in a slot and can be locked by a thumbscrew. This particular gun has had its barrel relined by R.A. Hoyt. *(Joseph Bilby)*

Other importers offer replicas of muzzle-loading Confederate carbines made by contractors like Cook and Brother and J. P. Murray. All are loaded and fired in the same manner, and, for the purposes of this discussion, will be considered as rifle-muskets.

Although not as popular with N-SSA shooters as it once was, a copy of the original Remington Model 1863 thirty-three-inch barrel "Zouave" rifle is still imported. There is no evidence that any American Zouaves, colorfully-dressed soldiers whose uniforms imitated those of French North African troops, were ever issued these guns. Few, if any, Remington 1863 rifles were issued to anyone during the Civil War, which accounts for the excellent condition of many surviving specimens. "Minty" original Zouaves were available in the 1960s and quickly became popular with N-SSA shooters. The short, heavy barrel of the Remington gun was faster to reload than a "three band" rifle-musket and dissipated heat better in a rapid-fire skirmish. While good shooting guns, reproduction Zouaves are generally forbidden at authentic reenactments.

Where the association of this gun with Zouaves, who were, incidentally, mostly Frenchmen rather than North Africans, originated is uncertain, although the term "Zouave rifle" was used to describe U.S. Model 1841 rifles with sword bayonets in storage at the New Jersey state arsenal at Trenton in December 1861. An 1861 photograph of a New Jersey militia Zouave shows him with a smoothbore musket, however. There is no evidence that these guns were reserved for Zouaves, and the descriptive term does not appear again in arsenal records. A reproduction gun with the same balance and other characteristics of the "Zouave" is the Model 1841 "Mississippi" rifle, imported by both Navy Arms and Euroarms. The Model 1841, in its original .54-caliber and rebored to .58, was widely issued during the Civil War.

Provided they are certified safe by a gunsmith, original guns in any condition but "factory new" may be fired without damaging their collectible value, provided they are carefully cleaned after shooting. Author prepares to place percussion cap on the nipple of an original U.S. Model 1841 Mississippi rifle which was once issued to the New Jersey militia.
(Fred Everson)

Skirmisher Dave Dworak of the 69th New York prepares to fire a .58 Belgian-made Minie rifle. This back-action lock weapon is typical of arms imported by the Union in the 1861-1862 period. Although foreign firearms were often characterized as junk, this weapon is very well made and balanced.

The Belgian gun's sight bears a strong resemblance to that of an Enfield. It should be noted that the manufacture of many Enfield parts was subcontracted by British gun makers to Belgian contractors. Belgian makers also produced complete Enfield rifles. *(Bill Goble)*

Another Civil War "non-gun" which has periodically given rise to controversy within the N-SSA, and elsewhere, is the "artillery model" rifle-musket. The "artillery model" is essentially a cut down Model 1861 or 1863 rifle-musket with a thirty-three-inch barrel and two rather than the usual three-barrel bands. Unlike the Model 1841 and 1855 or Remington Model 1863 rifles, these guns had the thinner barrel walls and other physical attributes of the rifle-musket.

Rifle-musket research pioneer Claud Fuller classified these bobbed rifle-muskets as government products, apparently based on the fact that Federal armories did, on occasion, shorten smoothbore muskets for use by fortress or heavy artillery troops in the years before the Civil War. There is, however, to date, no historical provenance for any Federal government alteration of rifle-muskets in this manner for use by ar-

N-SSA member Bill Adams of the 34th Virginia Cavalry Battalion holds a re-production of the Richmond Armory Mounted Infantry Rifle. These guns, made for use by mounted troops, are short, two-barrel-band versions of the Richmond rifle-musket, but are fitted with the Richmond muzzle-loading carbine front-sight and have no provision for affixing a bayonet. This reproduction was made from a Euroarms Richmond rifle-musket. *(Joseph Bilby)*

tillerymen. Although U.S. ordnance Captain Crispin commented that short imported Austrian Jaeger rifles "might do for artillery," heavy artillery units were issued the same small arms as infantrymen. Light artillerymen often carried artillery or cavalry sabres and revolvers, but most Civil War field artillerymen were unarmed. The primary use for artillery handguns appears to have been to shoot wounded or out of control horses rather than last ditch defense.[67]

Some Confederate state arsenals shortened damaged rifle-muskets for home-guard or militia use, but these guns were not intended for frontline troops. Recent research by the N-SSA's Bill Adams and Paul Davies, however, conclusively proves that the Richmond Armory produced a purpose-built short rifle-musket. Surviving Richmond Armory records indicate production of "Rifles, New, Short," along with rifles, rifle-muskets and carbines, beginning in at least September of 1864. Adams believes production actually began in the spring of 1863 and totaled at least 2,000 guns.

An inspection report on Confederate cavalry in East Tennessee in April of 1864 indicates that the Fourth Kentucky was armed with Enfield, Springfield and short Richmond rifles. Bill Adams, who has examined a number of surviving specimens and shot one as well, has identified several variant types of Richmond short rifle, including one produced out of cut down captured Springfield rifle-musket parts. All of these guns have rifle-musket dimensioned barrels, Richmond carbine-type front sights and have no provision for mounting a bayonet. Adams suggests that this abbreviated rifle-musket be called the "C. S. Mounted Infantry Rifle," a term which should supplant the old and admittedly inaccurate "artillery rifle."

Most of the short-barreled rifle-muskets still in existence, however, were professionally altered by commercial arms dealers in the years following the Civil War. They were, no doubt, used as drill weapons by the paramilitary cadet units spawned by the host of fraternal organizations which sprouted across America in the years between 1865 and World War I. Muskets cut down for hunting use usually had their stocks further shortened in "sporter" style.

In the 1950s, the founders of the N-SSA had to decide whether or not to allow these shortened military guns in competition. Using Fuller, the only available guideline, the artillery-model rifle-musket was authorized for N-SSA use and inspection parameters were established for it. In later years, when Fuller's error was discovered, hundreds of these guns were already in use, so the category of "artillery-style" guns was "grandfathered" into the N-SSA's group of allowable firearms.

Since the style rather than the existing guns was grandfathered, importers, manufacturers and individual skirmishers can still submit new "artillery-model" guns for inspection and use today. Some are custom guns and others are simply cut-down standard reproductions. Colt Blackpowder Firearms introduced an "artillery model" version of its rifle-musket in 1996. Those who prefer a more handy Springfield-style gun can purchase all the parts including a custom barrel to make their own Richmond carbine, 1855 rifle or artillery/mounted infantry gun. The latter are handy and accurate rifle-muskets, but, like the "Zouave," are banned from authentic reenactments. In light of the Richmond

N-SSA Inspector General Bill Goble holds his custom-made reproduction Fayetteville rifle with an R.A. Hoyt barrel. Original Fayetteville Armory guns were made in Fayetteville, NC, on equipment captured from the Harper's Ferry arsenal. Overall dimensions of Fayetteville rifles are similar to the U.S. Model 1841 and 1855 series of arms, but the Fayetteville was usually made without a patch box and has a unique curled hammer. *(Joseph Bilby)*

armory discoveries, however, the Richmond variant should be considered correct for Rebel cavalry reenactors.

Although minor dimensional differences from the original on some reproductions still irritate the purist, the average quality and authenticity of imported reproductions has improved greatly over the years. In general, the more expensive reproductions offer original-style progressive-depth rifling, which gets a deeper "bite" on a minie ball, and deeply hardened lock parts, which are more easily polished in "tuning" a trigger pull. Less expensive muskets, albeit with heavy trigger pulls and without progressive rifling, have, however, been known to shoot very well right out of the box, and can, with care and some parts rehardening, be tuned for a good trigger pull as well. For reenactment purposes, of course, trigger pull and rifling are irrelevant.

Custom replacement barrels are available for many reproduction and original rifle-muskets, and shot-out original barrels can be relined by custom barrelmaker R.A. Hoyt for use in custom guns. Because of their construction, most reproduction barrels are unsuitable for relining, given current technology. Needless to say, in this litigious age, neither manufacturers, importers nor this writer can recommend any alteration of their products.

Those who prefer a more handy Springfield-style gun can purchase all the parts including a custom barrel from twenty to thirty-three inches in length to make their own Richmond carbine, 1855 rifle or shortened artillery/mounted infantry model. A modern rifle-musket shooter who has some gunmaking skills and a yen for a truly big-bore gun can, with available custom parts, also recreate the thirty-three-inch barrel Plymouth Navy Rifle in .69-caliber. With an original lock and a few other parts in hand, reproduction stocks and barrels are available to make a .69-caliber Model 1842 rifled musket. A .685 semi-wadcutter bullet makes the .69-caliber rifle or rifled musket into the ultimate stake buster for skirmish competition. Custom musket maker Gerhardt Vikar of New Baltimore, Michigan, who specializes in short barreled military guns, has produced several modern-made Plymouths.

A musket can be "accurized" by glass-bedding the barrel in its channel in the stock, smoothing the action and reducing the trigger pull to around three pounds. With these minor modifications, best left to a professional gunsmith or talented amateur, reproduction factory or custom guns are quite capable of holding a two-inch or better offhand group at fifty yards, which falls well within the acceptance criteria for original guns.

Although nominally .58-caliber, barrels from different importers and makers have marginally different bore sizes, ranging from .575 to .581. Bore size on some original contract Springfields runs as high as .585. The closer the ball is to a musket's bore (not groove) diameter (.001 to .003 under) the more accurate the gun will be. Bullets which are too undersized will not "take" the rifling and will shoot wild, "keyholing" on the target. Correct size is a matter of compromise between easy loading and accuracy. A tight-loading bullet may shoot accurately, but the fouling produced by a few shots may make it too difficult to load. One exception to the rule appears to be the modified Parker Hale Pritchitt bullet. A

Like their forebears of 1861, many members of the N-SSA Wheat's Special Battalion, Louisiana Tigers carry Model 1841 Mississippi rifles and Bowie knives. Tom Berwick of the Tigers, pictured here, also manufactures a kit for making original-style revolver paper cartridges. *(Tom Berwick)*

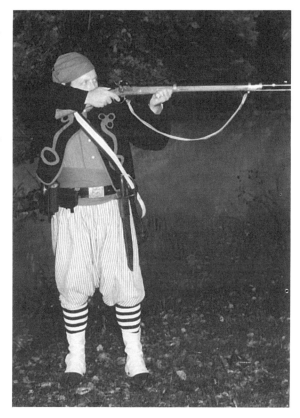

heavy, long slug with a shallow base, the Parker Hale, unlike the original Pritchitt, has American-style grease grooves and is fired unpatched. Although considerably undersize, it gives excellent accuracy in .575 diameter barrels.

As a general rule, British-made Parker Hale reproductions shoot .575 to .576 minie balls, while Dixie Gun Works Springfields work best with .580 to .581 bullets and Euroarms arms guns .577. These rules are approximate, however, and apparently depend on the state of wear on the manufacturer's rifling machine at any given time. A dealer or sutler like The Regimental Quartermaster or S&S Firearms can measure a gun's bore with a gauge and advise the buyer on what size bullet to use. Otherwise, unless the gun's maker recommends a specific size minie ball, the first thing a new rifle-musket owner should do is slug his gun's bore and measure the slug. To slug a rifle-musket barrel, remove it from the stock, place it in a vise and then remove the breech plug and drive a slightly oversized lead slug through the bore with a rod of brass or wood which will not mar the barrel's interior. After driving the slug through the bore, measure it for dimensions. It will provide a mirror image of the bore.

Bullet molds and sizing dies are made in increments ranging from .575 to .581. Because of varying wear rates of the "cherries" used to cut bullet molds, as well as varying temperatures of the molten lead poured into them, molds do not always throw bullets of the exact diameter they are supposed to. Pushing a minie ball through a sizing die enables the home caster to create a more consistent product. Rapine Manufacturing makes a simple manual-sizing die and S&S Firearms sells various diameter dies to fit the Lyman lubricator-sizer tool.

Although virtually all Civil War era minie balls were swaged by machines designed for that purpose, modern shooters must cast the big slugs. When casting minie balls, it is best to use an electric pot with a thermostat set at about 750 degrees or a bit higher. Some pots have handles to drop lead into the mold, while others require the use of a ladle. Since minies use a lot of lead, the bigger the pot the better. High heat assures that enough lead finds its way into all the nooks and crannies of the mold cavity. This, in turn, will assure a perfectly formed

Interest in the American Civil War and shooting Civil War guns has acquired an international following. Perth, Australia, dentist Dick Stein poses with his Parker Hale Enfield in the outback as a Louisiana Tiger.
(Dick Stein)

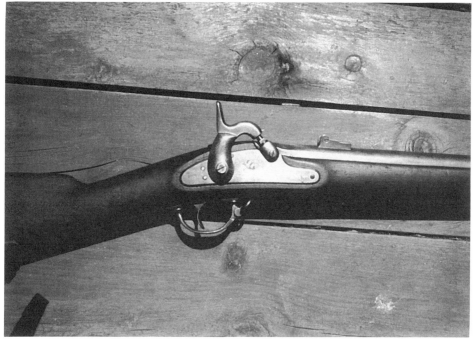

Original Model 1861 musket manufactured in 1864 in Trenton, NJ. The gun is marked "NJ" indicating purchase for New Jersey Rifle Corps or militia use. After 1861, New Jersey volunteer units were supplied with firearms by the Federal government. Many New Jersey Trenton-made muskets were still in storage at the state arsenal at the turn of the century. *(Michael Fanizzo)*

bullet rather than a misshapen hunk of lead. It will also cut down on any internal voids which will affect the ballistics of the slug.

Even with very hot lead, the first twenty or so bullets out of a mold are often wrinkled, a sign that the mold is still relatively cool. A frosted appearance on the bullet means the lead is too hot. Although these minie balls may not be aesthetically pleasing, they are safe to fire, provided they are completely formed. Many casters, however, return them to the pot. Minie balls with partially formed bases or "skirts" should always be returned to the pot, as they have a tendency to shed their skirts in the gun barrel on firing, leading to misfires and other safety hazards. Because of this possibility, one should *never* use the same rifle-musket for shooting live ammunition and reenacting.

When a mold is finally running perfect bullets, they should be dropped on a rolled up blanket to avoid damaging the delicate bases. Always use a piece of hardwood to hit the sprue cutter, which removes the sprue or tail left on the bullet nose by the molten lead. If a bullet sticks in the mold, a rap with the piece of wood where the scissorlike handles of the mold join will generally loosen it. *Never* hit the mold blocks themselves, as this might damage them. "Smoking" the inside of mold blocks with a candle before casting is sometimes used to ease release, and commercial mold releases are also available.

Minie balls should be lubricated to reduce fouling and prevent barrel leading. Although the Civil War era lubricant of beeswax and tallow is still effective, be aware that animal fats often contain salt, which may lead to bore rusting. Any of the lubricants used for "maxi" style hunting bullets, including the popular Wonder Lube[tm], and SPG[tm], a lubricant designed for use with black powder cartridge rifles, are also satisfactory for today's rifle-musket shooter. Pure Crisco[tm] vegetable shortening is an inexpensive and excellent lubricant for range shooting, but a bit messy in the cartridge box, especially in hot weather. Expert rifle-musket

Breech section of a New Jersey-marked Hewes & Phillips 1816/1822 .69-caliber musket conversion. The conversion, performed by the Newark, NJ, company in 1861, involved rifling the barrel, fitting a new breech (note line at the H of H&P where new breech was fitted) and installing a rear sight. *(Neal Friedenthal)*

Shooting 1860s firearms is a popular a popular pastime around the world, as evidenced by these lads of the Perth, Australia, Muzzle-Loading Club. The Diggers, as might be expected, favor the Enfield. *(Dick Stein)*

shooters, who believe lubricant is an important factor in accuracy, often experiment with various home brews. N-SSA skirmishers require a lubricant which will remain stiff during the course of a midsummer skirmish, and many use a 50-50 mixture of beeswax or candlewax and vegetable shortening. Melt this lubricant very slowly over low heat, so that it will mix well and not burn. Some skirmishers fill the hollow minie-ball bases with lubricant as well as filling the big bullets' lubrication grooves.

Chronograph tests made by Phil Seiss of S&S Firearms reveal that a forty-seven grain charge of GOI FFFG black powder loaded behind a 460-grain Lyman #575213OS "old style" minie ball lubricated with vegetable shortening and beeswax and fired in a Springfield rifle-musket registered an average velocity of 965 feet per second. This velocity is roughly equal to the ballistic pendulum velocity recorded in the mid-nineteenth century with the standard army load of sixty grains of "musket powder." Extensive testing by J. S. "Spence" Wolf has disclosed that the old "musket powder" is ballistically equivalent to today's GOI brand FFG black powder.

Using pure vegetable shortening lube, the 460-grain minie, again driven by forty-seven grains of GOI FFFG, registered 940 feet per second, indicating that the addition of wax, besides stiffening the lubricant for effective field use, contributes to a slightly higher velocity. The same load of FFFG behind a heavier 520-grain minie slug lubricated with a Crisco/beeswax mix chronographed at an average of 860 feet per second. It may not be all that fast, but it arrives like a freight train!

The same shooting and safety instructions apply to firing the rifle-musket as the smoothbore musket. The rifle-musket, a world-wide army stalwart of the 1860s, and its offspring, including rifles and carbines, fits the modern muzzle-loading shooter well as a plinking, target shooting and hunting arm. With minimal "accurizing" and proper-sized, well lubricated bullets, the rugged, reliable, easy-loading and accurate rifle-musket makes an excellent all around muzzle loader. With all that and historical ambiance too, you can't go wrong with a rifle-musket!

Colt Blackpowder Firearms' reproduction of the Special Model 1861 rifle musket. A hybrid of Enfield and Springfield characteristics, the Special Model was produced by Colt and other makers. This reproduction features progressive depth rifling, as did the original guns. (Colt Black Powder Firearms)

CHAPTER III

Sharpshooters

Sharpshooters have served in the American army since Virginia and Pennsylvania riflemen joined the American siege of Boston in 1775. Perhaps the most famous of these was Timothy Murphy, who shinnied up a tree at Saratoga, took a careful bead with his flintlock long rifle, and shot General Simon Fraser out of the saddle between 200 and 300 yards away, breaking British morale and turning the tide of battle decisively in favor of his American comrades.

Morgan's men were at their best while skirmishing and taking potshots at enemy officers at what were, for the time, long ranges. Since their rifles were not fitted for bayonets, however, riflemen could not stand the rush of a line of battle bristling with cold steel. General Washington later reduced the number of riflemen in his army, converting many into light infantrymen, who fought with smoothbore muskets and bayonets. In his second enlistment in the Continental army, Timothy Murphy himself shouldered a smoothbore in the Pennsylvania Line.

Ever after the role of the sharpshooter was muddled. In a largely smoothbore-armed army, the rifleman's job was to skirmish with the enemy, taking a toll on his line of battle until it was engaged by his own line of battle. Line regiments often had a company or two armed with rifles and assigned to skirmishing duties. Sniping officers and artillery crews at extreme long range was, if thought of, largely an afterthought. With rifles firing ballistically inferior round balls, it was also impossible.

In Civil War armies, where every man was, in theory, supposed to be armed with a rifled weapon firing a conical projectile capable of

Chauncy Maltby of the 2nd U.S. Sharpshooters with his Colt revolving rife. Although the sharpshooters turned their Colts in for Sharps rifles in the spring of 1862, the Colts were effective combat weapons. They were sent west, where they proved quite popular. *(Michael J. McAfee)*

long-range accuracy, the rifleman's prior special status as skirmisher became blurred. Every rifle-musket-armed soldier was potentially a skirmisher. What, then, would the role of the especially good shot become in the strife between the states? It took new men and new thinking to frame that role in its proper context. Enter Hiram Berdan.

When the word "sharpshooter" is mentioned in the context of the Civil War, the units that most often come to mind are Colonel Berdan's First and Second United States Sharpshooters (U.S.S.S.). These two regiments of green uniformed Federals gained an awesome reputation in the Northern press during the war and have maintained it ever since.

On July 2, 1863, at Gettysburg, Hiram Berdan's combat patrol of 100 sharpshooters and 214 officers and men of the Third Maine Infantry sparked the first serious fight of the day. Berdan later claimed that his

Colonel Hiram Berdan (1823-1893). A brilliant inventor, a fine shot and a relentless self-promoter, Berdan created the United States Sharpshooters in 1861. Unfortunately, Berdan's military qualities in the field were somewhat lacking. Nonetheless, he deserves a good deal of credit for fathering two of the finest regiments in the Union army. *(USAMHI)*

leadership and his sharpshooters' fast-firing Sharps breech-loading rifles had uncovered Lieutenant General James Longstreet's flanking move, severely damaged the Rebels and, by alerting the Union high command to the danger, saved the Army of the Potomac from defeat. At the risk of "sure death," recalled Berdan many years later, he had ordered his sharpshooters: "Follow me, advance firing" against the skirmishers of the Tenth Alabama infantry deployed in Pitzer's Woods that July morning.[1]

True? Well, maybe not. Hiram Berdan, born in New York and raised in Michigan, was a talented engineer, practical scientist and inventor responsible for such diverse devices as a gold crushing machine and a mechanical bakery. In addition, he was one of the premier American rifle shots of the 1850s. Berdan's inventive genius, applied to firearms, would secure his place in history. The Berdan centerfire primer for metallic cartridges, for example, is still in use worldwide. One thing Hiram Berdan was not, however, was a soldier. He was a self-promoting windbag.

Berdan's July 2 reconnaissance did not, as he maintained, reveal Longstreet's move. After pushing the skirmishers of the Tenth out of the woods, his task force encountered the remainder of the Tenth as well as the Eleventh Alabama Infantry. Both regiments were part of Brigadier General Cadmus Wilcox's brigade of Lieutenant General Ambrose P. Hill's Corps. Longstreet's flanking column was not in sight. In a brief firefight with the two Rebel regiments, the sharpshooters and Maine men expended most of their ammunition (ninety-five rounds each for the sharpshooters), then withdrew as the Tenth Alabama began to charge.

Despite the later claims of sharpshooters captured in the fight that they saw mounds of dead Rebels, losses were about equally divided, with sixty-six Yankees and fifty-six Confederates reported killed, wounded and missing. Most interesting to students of sharpshooter lore is the fact that the Eleventh Alabama, deployed behind a rail fence in a

Captain William Pulmer of the 1st Company, Massachusetts Sharpshooters, also known as Andrews' sharpshooters, with a typical Yankee long-range sharpshooter's rifle, which was actually a civilian target rifle. Pulmer commanded the company at Gettysburg, where the Massachusetts men performed good service by sniping at Rebels in the Bliss barn. While useful in fixed positions, rifles like the one pictured here were not very effective weapons in the field; the Confederate Whitworth was a much better choice for a sharpshooter in a fluid battle situation.
(Michael J. McAfee)

open field, lost only one officer and seventeen men wounded, despite drawing a blizzard of Sharps bullets at a range of about 300 yards. Later that day Wilcox's regiments joined Longstreet's attack, which fell just short of total success that evening.

Major General Daniel Sickles used Berdan's encounter with Wilcox as a rationale for advancing his III Army Corps to the Emmitsburg Road line, which many students of Gettysburg believe one of the greatest blunders of the Civil War. Berdan himself, far from leading the charge at Pitzer's woods, was most likely, historian Wiley Sword notes, "behind one of the larger trees once the fighting began."[2]

Despite Berdan's personal failings, including his strong reluctance to personally confront the enemy, which led to an unsuccessful attempt to convict him of cowardice and was a factor in his resignation from the army at the end of 1863, much of the reputation his men gained was genuine. And if it were not for Berdan, they may never have had the opportunity to gain it. At the outbreak of the Civil War, a number of people, including Caspar Trepp, a veteran Swiss officer then living in America, called for the formation of a special Union army sharpshooter corps. Berdan had the political influence, promotional ability and pure *chutzpah* to bring such a unit to life—and gain himself a commission as a colonel.

In the summer and fall of 1861, sharpshooter companies were raised in a number of states, including Minnesota, Michigan, New Hampshire, New York, Pennsylvania, Vermont and Wisconsin. Most, but not all, of these companies were consolidated into the First and Second U.S.S.S., the First commanded by Colonel Berdan and the Second by Colonel Henry A. Post. The First mustered ten companies and the Second eight. Two Massachusetts companies designated for the Second, "Andrews' sharpshooters," were, instead, attached to Massachusetts line outfits.[3]

In order to join the sharpshooters, a volunteer was expected to pass a qualifying marksmanship test. A Minnesota newspaper advertised for sharpshooter recruits who were "able bodied men used to the rifle." Prospective sharpshooters were expected to shoot "a string of 50 inches in 10 consecutive shots at 200 yards, with globe [aperture] or telescopic sights from a rest." None of the bullets were to be more than five inches from the center of the bull. A candidate shooting offhand was required to achieve a fifty-inch string at a distance of 100 yards.

A "string" score was made by measuring the length of a string which extended from the center of the bull to each of the bullet holes. The

A proud but unidentified Yank poses with a Sharps rifle.
(Michael J. McAfee)

criteria, roughly a ten inch group by today's standards, was not unusually demanding of a practiced rifleman. Needless to say, many future sharpshooters fired groups considerably under the minimum requirement. One, Charles H. Townsend of Wisconsin, "fired five shots at 200 yards with a total measurement of three and three-quarters inches." About fifty percent of sharpshooter aspirants were able to pass the shooting test.[4]

Sharpshooter recruits were promised $60 for the use of their own target rifles, should they desire to bring them to war. Recruiting officers promised those who reported unarmed, however, that they would be issued Sharps breech-loading rifles. This pledge led to problems for Hiram Berdan, as he had originally requested Springfield Model 1861 rifle-muskets for his men. Needless to say, Ordnance Chief James W. Ripley, who had a dim view of breech loaders for infantry use and didn't want to divert the Sharps factory from making much needed carbines, readily concurred with the new colonel's request. When Berdan changed his weapons preference to agree with that of his men, however, General Ripley "stonewalled" him.

Most of the men of the First and Second U.S.S.S. arrived in camp at Washington unarmed, and they remained so while Berdan, Ripley and assorted politicians wrangled over their eventual armament. One recruit, fifty-two-year-old Truman Head, also known as "California Joe," purchased his own Sharps Model 1859 rifle. When Joe brought his new Sharps to camp for inspection, sharpshooter enthusiasm for the gun increased. Eventually, the government agreed to buy 2,000 Sharps.

The sharpshooters spent the winter of 1861-1862 training for the coming fight. Their exercises appear to have been based on French chasseur tactical concepts, with extensive open-order-skirmish-drill and bugle commands. Drill was not the only example of European military thinking manifested in the sharpshooter regiments; their green uniforms, calfskin knapsacks with the hair left on and leather leggings set them apart from run-of-the-mill Union volunteers.

Interestingly, target practice was not on the sharpshooter training schedule. The men who brought their own rifles into service engaged in informal shooting matches, however, usually at a range of 220 yards. They were good. On one occasion Vermonter Ai Brown shot a string of four and a quarter inches. Colonel Berdan could shoot with the best of his men, and once turned in a five-and-nine-sixteenths inch offhand string.

Although the winds of war began to stir strongly in the spring of 1862, Berdan's sharpshooters remained virtually without weapons until March of that year, when they received Colt's revolving rifles, which they accepted reluctantly until the promised Sharps guns could be provided. The First Regiment, which accompanied General McClellan's army to the Virginia Peninsula, was issued its long-awaited Sharps rifles in May, 1862 and the men of the Second received theirs a month later. As predicted, the run of rifles had brought carbine production at the Sharps factory to a standstill for several months.

The Berdan Sharps model, of which 2,000 were produced, was the basic Model 1859 rifle fitted with a double-set trigger and a "fly" in the lock. One trigger would "set" the other, which then required very little finger pressure to drop the gun's hammer. The Berdan guns were designed to take a socket-style bayonet which slipped over the gun's

A Union soldier with his Sharps rifle slung over his shoulder in the field. Sharps rifles were issued to a number of units, but with the exception of the two regiments of Berdan's Sharpshooters and the Veteran Volunteers raised late in the war, usually in limited numbers. They were probably the best overall infantry weapons in use during the Civil War. *(USAMHI)*

muzzle, rather than the large sword bayonet which most Model 1859 rifles were designed to use.

Together, the two sharpshooter regiments never mustered 2,000 men, and, after active campaigning began, there were never more, and most of the time considerably less, than 1,000 sharpshooters on duty with both outfits at any one time. Excess Sharps rifles were stored in Washington.

Much to Colonel Berdan's dismay, a number of the guns in storage were issued to the "Bucktails," of the 13th Pennsylvania Reserves. A Michigan colonel also dipped into Berdan's Sharps trove. The sharpshooter colonel spent considerable time and effort, which coincidentally kept him away from the battlefield, trying to get his guns back. Despite these unauthorized issues, there were more than enough rifles in Washington to fill Berdan's requirements.

In March, 1863, both sharpshooter regiments turned in their weapons and were completely rearmed with new and reconditioned Sharps from the supply remaining in storage. There were still enough left over for periodic issue to recruits, men returning from sick leave and as replacements for worn out or combat damaged arms. Sharps rifles were also replaced or repaired within the units. Outfits like Berdan's, which were not armed with the standard rifle-musket, were authorized a regimental armorer, and first echelon repair, which included replacement of springs and hammers, was conducted at sharpshooter regimental level.

During the siege of Yorktown, Berdan's men discovered that the Rebels had some sharpshooters of their own. In April 1862, Private John S.M. Ide lost his life in a duel with a Confederate sniper. The green coated Yankees gave as good, if not better, than they got, however. Private George M. Case of the First's Company E singlehandedly kept a Rebel cannon crew away from their piece with his thirty-two-pound 'scoped target rifle.

The First's fast-firing Sharps were put to good use during the Seven days Battles, silencing a battery at Garnett's Farm and contributing materially to the defense of Malvern Hill. The regiment lost twenty men killed and mortally wounded in the Peninsula campaign.

While the First was bloodied on the Penninsula, Colonel Post's Second Regiment, assigned to Major General Irvin McDowell's Washington-covering force, skirmished with enemy pickets in northern Virginia. The first real fight for the Second was Antietam, where, assigned to an infantry brigade, the outfit lost twenty-one men killed.

Although the First U.S.S.S. distinguished itself at Chancellorsville, where it captured the Twenty-third Georgia regiment, in most battles the sharpshooter regiments were broken up into company- or battalion-sized units and deployed as skirmishers across a broad front. Although this was difficult and dangerous work, Berdan's men had been trained for it and they excelled. Sharpshooters often ended up fighting with other regiments, and some men from the Second fought side by side with the Twentieth Maine at Little Round Top.

As the war progressed, the sharpshooters seldom engaged in extreme long-range shooting, and the telescopic-sighted heavy target rifles several companies brought to the Peninsula and used at Yorktown were largely discarded. Some of these guns, apparently one per company, were retained and carried in the regimental supply wagons, however. Weighing as much as thirty pounds, the target rifles were brought forward and issued to "the most trusted and best" whenever the situation warranted. "When the unit moved," the sharpshooter a target rifle was assigned to "had to take the rifle to the case at the wagon train and put the rifle in it, for transportation." Although not as accurate at extreme range as the telescope-sighted heavy rifles, the Sharps was not a bad long-range rifle in its own right. Unfortunately, it was only sighted to 800 yards. On one occasion sharpshooters whittled wooden extensions for their rear sights and successfully drove Rebel signalmen off a tower some 1,500 yards away.[5]

In skirmishing, however, ranges were often short, and the rapidity of fire from the sharpshooters' Sharps rifles meant more than their accuracy. A corporal in the 1st U.S.S.S. remembered that he and his comrades fought pretty much on their own hook at Gaines Mill in 1862, and recalled that the enemy was engaged at about fifty yards. In a pinch, the sharpshooters could fire around ten rounds a minute from their breech loaders.

Although the First U.S.S.S. began its career in the V Corps and the Second in the I Corps, both were later reunited in General Birney's division of the III Corps. When the III Corps was dissolved in 1864, the sharpshooter outfits were transferred to the II Corps, where they retained their regimental organizations until the end of their three year enlistments. Despite the fact that the Union army was besieging Petersburg, a campaign where sniping was a daily occurence, the high command showed no interest in continuing the existence of these unique regiments beyond their original terms of service. Reenlisted veterans and recruits who had joined the sharpshooters since 1861 were transferred to line regiments from their respective states.

Why were such valuable units allowed to fade into history? Then, as now, commanders are often suspicious of, or openly hostile towards, elite organizations. Early on, Berdan's sharpshooters established a reputation for individuality and disregard of many military canons. On one occasion an inspecting officer discovered, to his horror, that most of them had thrown away their bayonets as useless appendages.

Berdan's regiments were not the only Union army "sharpshooters." The men of Birge's Western Sharpshooters, the Sixty-sixth Illinois Infantry, were originally armed with "the Demmick [sic] American deer and target rifle, but with meagre accoutrements" purchased from Horace E. Dimick, a Saint Louis sporting-arms maker. Although Dimick serial numbered and sold these half stock muzzle-loading sporting rifles to the government, he did not make all of them, purchasing a number for resale from other civilian gun makers. Most appear to have been fitted with rear sights purchased from the Sharps company. Calibers varied from gun to gun, (one surviving rifle is .48-caliber), and each man was supplied with his own bullet mold, serial numbered to his rifle, with which to cast an elongated minie-style "Swiss Chasseur" bullet. The Chasseur bullet differed from the minie in having a short post extend rearward from its base cavity.[6]

Most of the men in the Sixty-sixth later purchased their own Henry repeating rifles. The Henry was a splendid short-range skirmishing weapon, but hardly a proper sharpshooting tool. Similarly, companies of Ohio sharpshooters recruited in 1862 were eventually issued Spencer rifles, fine for the picket line but useless for long-range sniping.[7]

In the east, the two companies of "Andrews sharpshooters" raised originally for Berdan's regiments were attached to the Fifteenth and Twentieth Massachusetts Infantry regiments. Although Berdan apparently offered the Bay State marksmen some Sharps rifles from his original allocation, the Andrews sharpshooters chose to retain their heavy target rifles.

The Andrews company serving with the Fifteenth was "badly cut up at Antietam in a close engagement where rapid loading and quick shooting with them was out of the question, their guns being little better in that affair than clubs...." Asa Fletcher, a middle-aged recruit, joined the Fifteenth's company as it prepared to go into battle at Antietam. Although "an expert gunner, and a 'crack rifle shot'" Fletcher was hastily issued a .54-caliber Model 1841 rifle and nineteen rounds of ammunition. Fletcher managed to shoot five Rebels before his rifle fouled, but his war ended abruptly when he was severely wounded while trying to hammer a ball down its muzzle.[8]

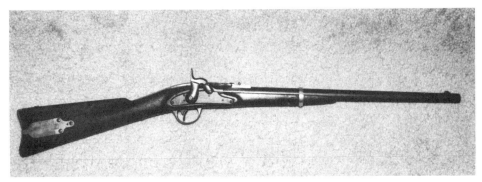

The Merrill carbine. The Merrill was a well-made and accurate gun which was issued in both carbine and rifle form. Massachusetts Sharpshooters were issued Merrill rifles. The Merrill's chief problem was the fragility of its delicate paper ammunition. *(Tony Beck)*

A breech-loading Sharps would have increased Fletcher's chances of survival considerably. Following the debacle at Antietam, the Massachusetts companies accepted Berdan's Sharps offer. They were also issued some Merrill breech-loading rifles, which, although quite accurate, used a delicate paper cartridge. The Andrews companies kept some of their target rifles for special service, and apparently the company assigned to the Twentieth used them on Rebels occupying the Bliss barn at Gettysburg. The Andrews monument on Cemetery Ridge features a heavy target rifle with telescopic sight.

A company of Minnesotans, which originally served with the Second U.S.S.S., was transferred to the First Minnesota Infantry in the summer of 1862 and never returned. The Minnesotans took their Sharps rifles with them to the First, giving the regiment its own sharpshooter company.

Although recruited in 1862 and 1863, the First Michigan Sharpshooters, many of whom were Native Americans, spent most of their service guarding prisoners and engaged in other rear area duties. When the regiment finally got to the front in the spring of 1864 it was attached to General Burnside's IX Army Corps and fought in the Overland campaign against Richmond, where it suffered heavy losses at Spotsylvania and Petersburg.

The First, armed with rifle-muskets, seems to have been used largely as a regular infantry outfit. At least some Wolverine sharpshooters were detailed to true sharpshooting duties, however. While on a sniping detail, Sergeant Wyman White of the Second U.S.S.S. joined forces with "a Michigan soldier" from the IX Corps who "was a full-blooded Indian." While crossing a cornfield, White, a splendid shot and a thorough soldier, learned a new trick from his partner, who instructed him to "Make self corn. Do as I do." The Michigan man cut corn stalks and stuck them "into his clothes and equipment." Thus camouflaged to break the outline of their bodies, the two Yanks "got a fine chance on the rebels."[9]

Ad hoc sharpshooter detachments were often formed within units. In the Fifteenth New Jersey, for example, Colonel William Penrose organized a shooting match at 300 yards distance in April, 1864 in order "to know which are the best shots in each company." The winners were then assigned to a detachment which would be detailed to "special duties." The Fifteenth's regimental sharpshooter squad was armed with standard-issue Springfield rifle-muskets. These Jerseymen may have been the best shots in the Fifteenth, but this did not guarantee they were

Berdan's Sharpshooters
were not the only Yankees
armed with Sharps rifles.
This member of Company A,
151st New York Infantry
(Bower's Independent Rifles),
carries a Sharps. Sharps-
armed soldiers in a regiment
would often be members of
the flank companies, used
for skirmishing and flank protection.
(Michael J. McAfee)

any better than the general run of infantrymen. They certainly had no special training. Later on that year the Fifteenth's brigade created a sharpshooter detachment which was armed with Spencer rifles, good for skirmishing, but not very good at all for sniping beyond 200 yards.[10]

Strangely, although the First Michigan Sharpshooters and the sharpshooter detachments of regiments like the Fifteenth New Jersey had to make do for the most part with rifle-muskets, other line regiments were armed, in whole or in part, with Sharps rifles. The state of Connecticut purchased a number of Sharps rifles, some of them originally intended for the Egyptian government, in 1861, and the First and Second Connecticut Infantry were partially armed with these weapons at Bull Run.

Two companies of the Fifth New York Zouaves carried Sharps rifles in the Peninsula Campaign, and used them to good effect at Gaines' Mill on June 27, 1862.

In late 1863, twenty Union units, including the First and Second U.S.S.S., carried Sharps rifles on their ordnance reports. These ranged from a high of 176 in the Forty-Second Pennsylvania in the fourth quarter of the year to a low of thirteen in the Second Indiana Infantry. By June 30, 1864, there were thirteen Yankee infantry outfits still carrying Sharps rifles. They were most numerous in the ranks of the Eighth Connecticut (603) and least common in the Third New Hampshire (14). Those units with a handful of Sharps-armed men undoubtedly used them for sharp-shooting chores.[11]

The men of Major General Winfield Scott Hancock's Veteran Volunteer Corps, formed in early 1865, were amply supplied with Model 1863 Sharps rifles, along with some repeating Henrys. Except for a skirmish with Rebel guerrillas, however, Hancock's veterans, who served largely on garrison duty in the Shenandoah Valley, got little chance to use their breech loaders in battle before the end of the war. With the dissolution of Berdan's regiments, 466 Sharps Model 1859 rifles remained in service scattered throughout the Army of the Potomac.[12]

Much less is known about Confederate sharpshooters than their Union counterparts. Limited, for the most part, to muzzle-loading weapons, sharpshooting Rebels easily matched their Yankee opponents in courage and shooting skill. While they might have been at a disadvantage on the skirmish line against Federals armed with breech loaders and repeaters, Confederate sharpshooters were quite effective, and, as the war progressed, some of them perfected the art of long-range sniping.

Confederate sharpshooters increased in numbers, sophisticated weaponry and tactical effectiveness during the course of the war. This was in marked contrast with the Federal policy of allowing Berdan's sharpshooters, who made their reputations in the first two years of the conflict, to decline in numbers and eventually cease to exist as distinctive organizations.

Initially, however, the Rebels had to play catch-up. In the spring of 1862, the Confederate army "reorganized" its regiments, which had initially enlisted for one year's service, essentially conscripting their men for the remainder of the war. As might be expected, there was more than a little grumbling and some mini-mutinies occurred as a result of this action. To stifle some of this opposition, Southern soldiers were given the authority to elect new officers and, in some cases, form new outfits.

One new unit was the "Palmetto Sharpshooters," formed by men from the Second, Fourth, Fifth, Sixth, and Ninth South Carolina Infantry. Marksmanship requirements for joining the regiment, if any, are unknown. It appears the Palmetto Sharpshooters believed they would, like

Berdan's men, serve as skirmishers and flank guards and, when the occasion demanded, snipers. Like the First Michigan Sharpshooters, however, the Palmetto Sharpshooters spent most of their war fighting as line infantry.

Although the Confederate Congress authorized the raising of sharpshooter battalions for each brigade in the army in April of 1862, most Rebel sharpshooter outfits were unofficial detachments of men detailed from line regiments and virtually never appear as distinct units on any Confederate army's table of organization. Unlike the Union standard of a ten-inch group at 200 yards from a rest, Confederate sharpshooter qualification criteria were never officially specified; ad hoc competitions were established to find the best shots in any given unit, who were then detailed as sharpshooters. Unlike the case of the Fifteenth New Jersey, however, competition for sharpshooter positions was broader based; usually at brigade or even division level.

Until the war's final year, Confederate sharpshooter units were often disbanded at the close of a campaign. Sharpshooter battalions were formed in at least some brigades of Lee's army in the spring of 1863. Applicants accepted from the line regiments of General Samuel McGowan's South Carolina Brigade that year were expected to be young men who were active and very good shots. McGowan's 120 sharpshooters were divided into three companies. The battalion was assigned to skirmish and picket duty, and could be deployed at the brigade commander's discretion in a general engagement.

Berdan's regiments largely gained their reputation with rapid and accurate skirmish fire at short to medium ranges up to 500 yards. The Federal practice of arming sharpshooters selected from line units late in the war with Spencer rifles, which were essentially short range weapons, indicates a doctrinal belief that the primary role of the sharpshooter was that of an elite skirmisher.

In general, Confederate concepts of the tactical role of sharpshooters in the Army of Northern Virginia were similar to those held by Union officers. In early 1864 Brigadier General Cadmus Wilcox suggested to General Robert E. Lee that a sharpshooter battalion be formed in each brigade of the Army of Northern Virginia, formalizing the battalions raised, then disbanded, the previous year. Lee approved Wilcox's proposal. The battalions, which were to assume all skirmishing, scouting and picket duties when the army was in contact with the enemy, were composed of three or four sixty-man companies each. Assignment to the sharpshooter battalions was predicated upon good marksmanship, courage in battle and "fidelity to the Southern cause." Following the French concept, they were intended to be shock troops, adopting tactical roles similar to World War I German Storm Troopers.[13]

The training regimen established for Lee's sharpshooters was probably the most thorough of any implemented during the Civil War. "This scheme was presented in the form of a *brochure*, translated from the French by General C. M. Wilcox...." All veteran soldiers when they joined, sharpshooters conducted intense drill in small unit tactics abstracted by Wilcox from the French Zouave and Chasseur a Pied manuals, which stressed the four man group of *"comrades de battaille."* To French light infantrymen and their Confederate counterparts, "comrades in battle" meant much more than a convenient drill formation. The equivalent of a modern fire team or squad, the "comrades" ate, slept,

Soldiers of the 71st New York Infantry. The man on the left holds an Enfield rifle. Shorter than the Enfield or Springfield rifle-musket and fitted for a sword bayonet, the Enfield rifle was favored for mounted infantry use by Confederate Generals Forrest and Morgan. It may also have been the weapon of choice for rank and file sharpshooters in the Army of Northern Virginia's sharpshooter battalions. *(USAMHI)*

marched and fought together, and each had the total trust of the others. Shooting was as important as discipline, drill, and morale. Sharpshooter Berry Benson recalled that, in addition to target practice: "We practiced judging distances also, for it is essential to a soldier to know how far his enemy is from him, in order to adjust his sights properly."[14]

As might be expected, sharpshooter small-arms selection was given considerable thought. To simplify logistics, and with the limitations of the Confederate arms industry in mind, only muzzle loaders were considered. Rifle-muskets, including Springfield, Enfield, Austrian and French weapons, were carefully fired from a tripod rest (in the British manner) at ranges up to 1,000 yards. While all of these guns proved equally accurate at 500 yards, the Enfield was clearly superior beyond that range. As a result of these tests, the sharpshooter battalions took the field in the spring of 1864 armed exclusively with new Enfields and cartridge boxes filled with fresh British-made ammunition. It appears that the "rifle" version of the Enfield, with its thirty-three-inch barrel, was the weapon of choice.

As with Berdan's men, in addition to their skirmishing duties, Confederate sharpshooters were tapped for sniper duty, although the term "sniper" was not formally used. Selected marksmen in each sharpshooter battalion were issued British-manufactured Whitworth sniper rifles fitted with telescopic sights. The .45-caliber Whitworth weighed about the same as a rifle-musket and was easily portable in the field, which gave it a great advantage as a weapon of tactical opportunity over the cumbersome target rifles used by Yankee snipers. Whitworth armed Rebels were always ready to capitalize on such opportunities; a Confederate carrying a Whitworth killed VI Corps commander Major General John Sedgwick at Spotsylvania.

Confederate arsenals also converted a number of civilian target and "country" rifles into sniper guns by reboring them to .54 or .58 military calibers, and equipping some with imported telescopic sights. Imported British Kerr rifles were also issued to some Confederate sharpshooters, most notably those in the Kentucky "Orphan Brigade." The Whitworth, however, became the primary, and best, Rebel sniping tool.[15]

Irish born Confederate General Patrick Cleburne was notable for training his line infantrymen how to shoot properly—a skill which most commanders ignored—at ranges up to 900 yards. Cleburne quickly perceived the advantages of the Whitworth; his sharpshooter units evolved into true sniper detachments which delivered fire at extreme

Major General Patrick Ronayne Cleburne. Born in County Cork, Ireland, in 1828, Cleburne served as an enlisted man in the British army before emigrating to America. He began his Confederate military career as colonel of the 1st Arkansas Infantry and rose to the rank of major general. Perhaps the only general officer in either army to fully realize the true potential of the rifle-musket and sharpshooter rifle, Cleburne was killed in action at Franklin, TN, on November 30, 1864.
(Irish Brigade via Charlie Laverty)

ranges on enemy artillery batteries and officers, affecting combat situations far out of proportion to their numbers.

Although the Whitworth, invented by British engineer Joseph Whitworth, was not a common gun in the Confederacy, recent research indicates there were a lot more of them—perhaps several hundred—in service than previously believed. More than a hundred cartridge boxes specially modified for use with Whitworth ammunition were shipped from the Atlanta arsenal during the war.[16]

The .45-caliber Whitworth was rifled with a hexagonal bore with a pitch of one turn in twenty inches and fired a long, 530-grain .451 bullet backed by eighty-five grains of powder. It was remarkably accurate at ranges up to 1,500 yards. Some Whitworth bullets were factory swaged in a hexagonal configuration to mechanically fit the rifle's bore. Others, however, were cylindrical, and a mold for these was packed with each Whitworth rifle. Accuracy appears to have been roughly equal with either slug, and both types have been recovered by relic hunters at Rebel campsites, target ranges and on battlefields, although the cylindrical are far more common.

The Whitworth was an expensive weapon. According to one Rebel, each rifle, including accessories, tools and 1,000 cartridges, cost the Confederacy $1,000. This cost may well reflect devalued Southern currency, as the British government paid £10 each, or around $50 U.S., for Whitworth rifles in 1858. Interestingly, the British paid £20, 7s, 3d. to have a Davidson telescopic sight fitted to a Whitworth. Whatever the cost, Southern sharpshooters no doubt thought the money well spent. One of them, Isaac N. Shannon, who served in the Army of Tennessee, did not "believe a harder-shooting, harder-kicking longer-range gun was ever made than the Whitworth."[17]

Although some Whitworths imported by the Confederacy were apparently fitted with "globe" or aperture sights, most came equipped with both open sights graduated up to 1,200 yards and Davidson sights. The Davidson telescope nestled in quick detachable, externally adjustable mounts on the gun's left side. The sight's elevation could be corrected by adjusting a swivel on the rear mount. Windage corrections were made by moving an extension on the front mount, which projected through the Whitworth's stock from left to right behind the rear barrel band. The Davidson sight was meant to be used with the shooter lying on his back, supporting his head with his left arm and resting the rifle muzzle on his leg or foot. Awkward as this may seem, it was a popular position for extreme long target shooting at the time.

The Whitworth's accuracy, light weight (less than ten pounds with 'scope sight mounted) and consequent portability, made it the war's best sniper rifle. With all its technical expertise, the Union could produce nothing comparable. Strangely, considering the large number of Enfields purchased by the Federal government, the Yankees do not appear to have ever considered using the Whitworth as a military weapon. One authority notes that "fifty Whitworth rifles, complete with bayonets and fifteen thousand cartridges" perhaps booty from a captured blockade runner, were offered for sale, apparently to the general public, in New York in 1862.[18]

At least one firearms expert thought the Yankees should have considered the Whitworth. H. W. S. Cleveland, one of the most-noted American riflemen of his day, commented in *The Scientific American* in 1864 that most Northern civilian target shooting was done with "a dead rest, a rifle too heavy for any man to carry and provided with a patent muzzle and telescopic sight, neither of which are admissable except on rare occasions in field service." He added that it was "impossible on our principle of construction of both rifle and projectile to attain a very long-range without making the gun too heavy for field service."[19]

Cleveland, who had attended rifle matches in Canada, was well aware of the British system of offhand marksmanship training and the superiority of the Whitworth as a practical military sniper rifle. He complained that "our gunsmiths have not yet adopted the principle which Whitworth and many others have proved beyond all question, that to secure precision at a very long range without giving such weight to the gun as to admit the use of an enormous charge of powder, it is necessary to use a bullet of great length in proportion to its diameter."[20]

With the appearance of the Whitworth, long-range sniping, especially in the Army of Tennessee, where General Cleburne's influence was most strongly felt, became a Confederate specialty. At one point during his brilliant fight at Liberty Gap, Tennessee, in 1863, Cleburne, an officer not given to exaggeration, reported: "I had no ammunition to spare and did not reply to the continual fire of the enemy except with five Whitworth rifles, which appeared to do good service. Mounted men were struck at distances ranging from 700 to 1300 yards."[21]

Kentucky sharpshooters in the Orphan Brigade were instructed "never to approach within four hundred yards of the Yankees but to use their superior weapons to bring down Federal artillerymen and officers." The Kentuckians used their British-made Kerr rifles, perhaps with longer range Whitworth ammunition, to good effect during the Atlanta Campaign, spending thirty-three straight days in the line without a break. Rebel long-range sharpshooters did not go about their business with impunity, however. Yankee sharpshooters dueled with the Rebels with some success and, more importantly, artillery batteries often concentrated their fire on a single sharpshooter, with considerable effect.[22]

Although Whitworths gained fame in both the Army of Northern Virginia and the Army of Tennessee, they were also used with great effectiveness by the Confederate defenders of Charleston. As many as eighteen Whitworths were issued to sharpshooters attached to Battery Wagner on Morris Island. Although much of the fighting at Wagner was at close quarters, negating the long-range capacity of the Whitworths, the pinpoint accuracy the guns were capable of at closer range made it hazardous for any besieging Federal to expose even a small part of his anatomy. Union Major Thomas B. Brooks noted: "The least exposure above the crest of the parapet will draw the fires of his telescopic Whitworths, which cannot be dodged."[23]

The Yankees made desperate attempts to counter the "constant and accurate" fire of the Morris Island Rebels. Although it might have been a good idea to request that a company of Berdan's men be sent to Morris Island on detached duty, an ad hoc sharpshooter unit armed with Springfield rifle-muskets was created instead. Major Brooks deemed them "inefficient." and detailed why: "First, they are not good shots; second, their arms are not in good condition; third, they are not in sufficient numbers, even if they were efficient; fourth, they are not properly officered."[24]

Following the fall of Battery Wagner in September, 1863, the Whitworth sharpshooters removed to Fort Sumter, where they, like the Germans at Monte Cassino in World War II, burrowed into the the rubble and repelled all attempts to take the ruins. The Yankees did not recapture Sumter until Charleston was evacuated as Sherman's army surged northward in 1865.

Rebels with Whitworths continued to harass the Federal besiegers of Charleston until they abandoned the city. On September 19, 1864, Major General John G. Foster requested "telescopic rifles" from then Ordnance Chief Brigadier General George D. Ramsay. Foster felt "there is no place where from ten to fifty of these rifles could be used to better advantage than in the front works of Morris Island. I would respectfully suggest that from ten to fifty of these rifles be sent here." Interestingly, the general did not request trained riflemen, evidently in the mistaken belief that the mere possession of such guns would silence the dead-shot Southerners.[25]

With all their skills, there is no evidence that Civil War sharpshooters, North or South, ever dramatically changed the course of a major battle. One exception to this maxim often claimed is the first day's fight at Gettysburg, which might have had a different outcome had not General Reynolds been killed in its initial stages. Over the years, there have been a number of assertions that Reynolds was shot by a Rebel sharpshooter armed with either an Enfield or a Whitworth, and several claimants to the honor of dispatching the general have either stepped forward themselves or been nominated by historians.

The most recent scholarship on the circumstances surrounding Reynolds' death, however, effectively contradicts the lone sharpshooter theory. In his definitive *Gettysburg July 1*, Dr. David Martin concludes that Reynolds "was probably felled by directed fire from [Brigadier General James J.] Archer's line, either by troops aiming directly at the

General's party, or by shots fired by Archer's infantry at and over the line of the 2nd Wisconsin."[26]

Although a sharpshooter may not have ended the life of General Reynolds, a number of commanders, high and low, including Sedgwick, fell to the long-range guns of snipers on both sides. Civil War sharpshooters were more than fine shots, however. As Colonel Berdan himself was to prove, it took more than shooting ability to be a sharpshooter. Superb marksmanship coupled with courage, discipline and fieldcraft, however, made the Union and Confederate sharpshooters some of the finest American soldiers ever to don a uniform.

Collecting and Shooting Sharpshooter Weapons Today

It is possible to partially replicate both the Union and Confederate Civil War sharpshooter experience today. Sharps rifle reproductions are available from a number of dealers. Navy Arms advertises a special Berdan Sharps rifle with the double-set triggers of the originals and Dixie Gunworks offers set triggers which may be installed on its Pedersoli-made Model 1859 rifle. The only design feature absent from modern-made Sharps guns is the pellet-primer magazine, which, although present, is inert on the reproductions. The pellet-priming concept was based on the seeming improbability that the primer magazine would successfully propel a priming pellet towards the gun's nipple as the hammer began to fall. Ideally, the hammer would catch the primer in mid air and slam it down on the nipple, firing the gun. The system was intended to raise the Sharps' rate of fire by eliminating the need for the shooter to place a percussion cap on the nipple for each shot. Most accounts stress the unreliability of the pellet primer, although sharpshooter Wyman White praised its efficiency and used it often.

Loading and firing a Sharps rifle does not differ materially from a Sharps carbine. Sharps carbines are fairly common on N-SSA firing lines during individual and team carbine matches. Sharps rifles are permitted for N-SSA breech-loading rifle competition and have proved more accurate on the 100 yard phase of that match than Henry and Spencer rifles.

The Sharps, which fired a combustible cartridge ignited by a percussion cap, was the most popular breechloading single-shot rifle and carbine issued during the Civil War. Civil War-issue ammunition for the Sharps was made from glazed linen with a .54-caliber bullet, although the gun was nominally .52-caliber. Many original Sharps rifles and carbines can be safely fired (after a thorough inspection by a qualified gunsmith) but a number have severe gas leakage problems due to corroded breech seals. Correcting this problem may, however, affect the collectible value of the gun.

Back in the '60s (1960s, that is) I did some shooting with a friend's original Sharps rifle which had a replaced gas seal and I don't recall any problems. Empirical historian Tony Beck uses combustible paper cartridges loaded with forty-five to sixty grains of FFG black powder in an original Sharps carbine. (Loading and firing data are applicable to both carbines and rifles.) Beck, who has fired two-inch fifty-yard groups with original Sharps carbines, recommends the lighter load for target shooting.

The majority of today's Sharps shooters use reproduction guns. Some non-N-SSA shooters breech seat a bullet with a dowel and then fill up the chamber with loose powder. Although a Sharps can be loaded and fired in this manner, recoil will be heavy. Loose powder loading also increases the danger of powder grain migration between the gun's frame and forestock, which may result in the forestock blowing out or off, with injury to the shooter's psyche, if not his/her person. This possibility is not as remote as some may think. Small-arms parts specialist Phil Seiss of S&S Firearms received a replacement request for an exploded Sharps forestock from a shooter in England, and Tony Beck's carbine stock shows signs of repair from an old blow out.

A unique way to load the Sharps is with skirmisher James Burgess Jr.'s "Fast and Accurate Sharps Cartridge" described in the May/June 1980 issue of *The Skirmish Line*. Burgess created cartridges using three-and-a-half inch long yellow .45-caliber vinyl tubes from the Winchester Sutler loaded with forty-five grains of GOEX FFFG black powder and Lyman #557489 "Ringtail" bullets with their driving bands sized down to .545 to easily enter the Shiloh Sharps chamber.

To make the Burgess Round, drop the powder charge into the cartridge tube and then insert the "ringtail" portion of the bullet into the tube, leaving the rest of the slug exposed. Then dip the bullet end of the cartridge into a 50/50 mixture of melted alox-beeswax and petroleum jelly—or whatever lubricant you prefer—and remove excess lube.

To load the cartridge in your Sharps, insert the cartridge tube, which also serves as a bullet starter, into the front of the chamber and twist it to release the bullet. Then withdraw the tube, depositing the powder charge behind the slug. Burgess reported fast loading and good accuracy with his unique ammunition.

Some years back my N-SSA unit fielded a sorrowful ad hoc carbine team at a regional skirmish. Pressed into service, I borrowed a Shiloh Sharps with cartridges ostensibly loaded according to the Burgess method. Although they were a wee bit unwieldy, the rounds seemed to load reasonably well, but I shot terribly. I later learned that the bullet driving bands were not sized as per Burgess' instructions so the bullets weren't seated far enough forward in the chamber.

A clogged nipple channel and the resultant hangfires and flinches, as well as unfamiliarity with the gun, didn't help matters. The tortuous channel linking the Sharps nipple and chamber, should, by the way, be thoroughly cleaned after every shooting session.

Original and reproduction Sharps rifle and carbines, like all guns, are often singular in their ammunition preferences. Bil Nolze of the N-SSA's 69th New York shot a Sile Sharps carbine for years using the Burgess cartridge without sizing the ringtail bullet's driving band, and experienced excellent accuracy.

Probably the most common way to shoot a Sharps is with nitrated paper cartridges, which can be made using kits available from Dixie Gun Works, the Regimental Quartermaster and other dealers. Making paper cartridges is labor intensive work, but they work well and are authentic. Some Sharps enthusiasts make paper cartridges from scratch. Among these stalwarts is veteran Sharps shooter Joe McAvoy, who fired 15,000 rounds through his Shiloh Sharps carbine in fifteen years and has won his share of medals with the gun.

Joe crafts his cartridges from 100% cotton-fiber paper, which he soaks in a potassium nitrate solution for fifteen minutes before drying. McAvoy forms his cartridges on a dowel, sealing the seams and base with sodium silicate or "water glass," purchased in a paint supply store. He loads the formed paper tubes with thirty-seven grains of FFG powder, followed by Cream of Wheat filler and then a bullet. Although Joe has tried several slugs in his carbine, he has settled on the 430-grain Shiloh "Buffalo Bullet" sized to .542. He prelubes his Buffalo Bullets with vegetable shortening and beeswax melted together and then dips the bullet end of the loaded cartridge in hot lubricant.

McAvoy's rounds are approximately one and seven eighths inches long, and, like original Civil War linen ammunition, just fill the gun's chamber. Joe's success with his chamber-filling cartridges reflects the results of government weapons trials conducted in March of 1860, where longer paper cartridges with their ends sheared off by the breech block in loading proved inferior in accuracy to chamber-length linen rounds. As a result of that test, the shorter linen cartridges were standard Federal issue for Sharps guns during the Civil War.

Confederate paper rounds were sheared by the breechblock, which might have resulted in powder grains working their way between frame and forestock, and may have been the source of the explosions recorded with Richmond-manufactured copies of Sharps carbines. Joe McAvoy's motto: "You can't go far wrong by trying to recreate the way they did it in the old days" is well worth considering.

It's a harder proposition to shoot a Whitworth today than a Sharps. Original guns are rare, and for the most part, too valuable to their owners to shoot. Years ago, Parker Hale produced a Whitworth reproduction, made in Britain, which closely resembled the company's "Volunteer" rifle. It is no longer in production. In 1994, impending production of an Italian-made "Whitworth" was announced, although at the date of this writing it has not yet appeared. Whether or not the gun will have original Whitworth-style rifling is unknown.

Compared with the Sharps, few people have garnered experience shooting a Whitworth. One who did was Cleves H. Howell Jr. Howell, who wrote on the Whitworth in the January 1952 *American Rifleman*, owned "a nearly new, cased military model [Whitworth] practically complete with all accessories, including an original mold." He used the mold to cast some cylindrical bullets (Whitworth factory bullets were swaged) and loaded them in front of various charges of FFFG, FFG and FG black powder. His most accurate load proved to be eighty-five grains of FFG, which produced a three-inch group at 100 yards with open sights.

After a friend crafted a custom mold for hexagonal bullets, Howell, who made no claims to being an expert shot, intensified his tests. He fired 300 rounds, most from the prone position, at 100 yards, with five shot groups averaging "from 2 inches to 2 ½ inches."

At 200 yards groups averaged around four inches, with occasional three-inch spreads. Howell reported that "on two occasions, a Whitworth gave slightly smaller groups at 200 yards than a M1903 Springfield [.30-06] when fired by the same rifleman." Groups at 500 yards averaged around fifteen inches. At that distance the bullet drifted twenty inches to the right, as predicted by the "drift scale" packed with the rifle. Howell found the sights so perfectly calibrated that if "the original load is used, the bullets will strike within a few inches of the point intended, regardless of range."

There is no reason to believe that a modern-made Whitworth, sharing the same bore dimensions and quick-rifling twist of the originals, will not perform similarly to Howell's original gun.

In fact, they do. The Parker Hale reproduction, made in limited numbers between 1978 and 1989 to the specifications of the original Whitworth, has an enviable reputation for accuracy. Tom Conroy of Honeoye Falls, New York, "the lucky owner of two Parker Hale Whitworths," reports some excellent shooting with his rifles. Conroy has fired "1½- and 2-inch groups from a machine rest at 200 yards using 570- grain pure lead hexagonal bullets (cast in a mold by Englishman Peter Dyson) over 80 grains of GOEX FFG powder" contained in a combustible paper cartridge. A dry-lubed felt wad cut to the configuration of the hexagonal bullet rests between powder charge and slug. Tom soaks his bullets (to keep friction to an absolute minimum) in Dura Lube[tm], lubes the bore after loading powder and before loading the lubricated bullet and "religiously" cleans, dries and lightly lubricates his Whitworth's barrel between shots.[27]

Civil War sharpshooter weapons shoot just as well as modern guns similarly sighted, and, with some care and attention to trajectory, will shoot exceptionally well at long range. Modern-made reproductions of the Sharps and the Whitworth are among the most expensive replicas on the market. But, like the men who carried them in the 1860s, their owners think them well worth the money.

CHAPTER IV

Breech-Loading Carbines

In March of 1865, the largest, most heavily-armed column of cavalrymen ever assembled on the North American continent set out on a campaign to pierce the hollow shell of what was left of the Southern Confederacy. Major General James Wilson led his three divisions of Yankee horse soldiers, bristling with seven-shot Spencer repeating carbines, Model 1860 light cavalry sabres and a variety of revolvers, deep into Alabama, scattering his outnumbered and undergunned opposition like chaff before the winds of victory.

Wilson's raid is often cited as a demonstration of the industrial and military might of the Union, which assured Confederate defeat. The Spencer repeater has long been touted as a symbol of that superiority. There was much more to Wilson's success than Spencers, however. The Federal troopers who trotted towards Selma in that high spring of 1865 were experienced, well-trained and superbly-led, attributes at least as important as their carbines, which, for many of them, were recent acquisitions. The confident Yankee cavalrymen of 1865 were as unlike their bumbling, poorly-armed selves of 1861 as they were soldiers from another era—another world.

When war fever swept the nation following the attack on Fort Sumter, United States government stores held 4,076 muzzle-loading and breech-loading carbines. Since the strength of a cavalry regiment was 1,000 or more men at muster-in, it was readily apparent that the available supply of weapons would be rapidly depleted if volunteer horse soldiers rushed to the colors.

A natty horse soldier from the 15th Pennsylvania Cavalry poses with his saber and his Sharps carbine slung over his shoulder. A mounted cavalryman inserted the muzzle of his slung carbine into a small leather carbine socket attached to his saddle. The gun was fully exposed to the elements and could get banged around quite a bit while riding in wooded terrain. These stresses often told on the less durable patent arms.
(Michael J. McAfee)

There was a general consensus, shared by the conservative Union Chief of Ordnance, General Ripley, that single-shot breech-loading carbines, which could be reloaded more readily on horseback, were preferable to muzzle loaders for cavalry service. Acquiring significant numbers of these guns quickly presented problems, however. "Patent" breech-loading guns using semi-fixed ammunition—a paper, linen, rubber or metal cartridge ignited by an external percussion cap—were invented and manufactured by private individuals, most of whom were in no position to mass produce their products.

Many Federal officers who believed the coming conflict would be an infantry war felt that the five regiments of regular army cavalry would suffice and that large numbers of breech-loaders wouldn't be needed. This belief, along with the fact that horse soldiers required a longer training period than infantrymen, and cavalry regiments were expensive to maintain, led to a reluctance to recruit volunteer mounted units.

Following Bull Run, however, where a small regular army mounted force proved totally inadequate, this policy was reversed. Volunteer cavalry regiments sprung to arms across the North. For the most part, the arms they sprung to were not caplock breech-loading carbines. Most new cavalry units received sabers, handguns or infantry weapons, which were in greater supply than the complicated carbines. The Fourth Iowa Cavalry got a mix of revolvers and imported Austrian infantry rifle-muskets and the First Kentucky Cavalry was issued "old infantry muskets" apparently .69-caliber smoothbores.[1]

The troopers of the Seventh Kansas Cavalry were armed with a hodge-podge of weapons, including Model 1855 pistol carbines and imported Prussian muskets. As late as March of 1862, the Third Wisconsin Cavalry was issued awful little .71-caliber Austrian carbines with fourteen-and-a-half-inch barrels. All of these regiments were better off than the First Maine Cavalry, however, which remained totally unarmed

Colonel Charles Jennison of the 7th Kansas Cavalry. A renowned border warrior and Jayhawker before the Civil War, Jennison raised the 7th Kansas, a hard-fighting outfit which became as well known for its pillaging as its combat skills. This is probably a pre-war picture of Jennison, who is shown with a slant-breech Model 1853 Sharps of the type associated with John Brown. *(USAMHI)*

from its October 1861 enlistment until March of 1862. The Maine men performed guard duty with axe handles!

The few carbines available were carefully rationed within units. The First Vermont Cavalry issued carbines to a dozen men in each company. When the First Maine finally received seventy-two carbines, the guns were distributed throughout the regiment. Seeking to concentrate firepower for greater effect, the Second Michigan Cavalry massed its carbines in a "dragoon" battalion, which was balanced by a gunless "saber" battalion.

Most of the limited number of new breech-loading carbines issued were Sharps arms, since Sharps was the only carbine manufacturer capable of mass production at the outbreak of hostilities. Various models of Sharps breech loaders were in service in the U.S. regular army and the British military. They were also popular with gunwise civilians on the frontier. The Sharps served successfully around the world, including in the exotic ranks of Frederick Townsend Ward's "Ever Victorious Army," as it moved against the Chinese Taiping rebels.

Almost 6,000 New Model 1859 carbines were delivered to the Federal government by the end of 1861, with more than 17,000 more forwarded by December 31, 1862. The Model 1859 was eventually replaced by the New Model 1863, the same gun sans patchbox. Almost 100,000 Sharps guns eventually saw service during the Civil War, most of them cavalry carbines. Aside from the repeating Spencer, the Sharps was the most desirable carbine issued during the war. The Sharps was the most common carbine used by Federal cavalry at Gettysburg, with 4,724 in action. The closest competitor was the Burnside, with 1,387 guns represented at that climactic battle. A Sharps in the hands of Lieutenant Marcellus Jones of Company E, Eighth Illinois Cavalry, fired the opening shot at Gettysburg.[2]

As late as March of 1865, with the end of the conflict around the corner, the Second Illinois Cavalry petitioned to "obtain Sharps in the place of Burnside carbines." At war's end, almost 100 Union cavalry units were armed, in whole or in part, with Sharps carbines.[3]

Although some men from the Eighth New York Cavalry were issued the coveted Sharps, most carried obsolete Mexican War-era Hall breech loaders when their regiment rode up the Shenandoah Valley in the spring of 1862. As the New Yorkers retreated before General Stonewall Jackson's Rebels, they took the opportunity to discard most of their Halls, which were apparently picked up by Rebel horsemen, who had few breech

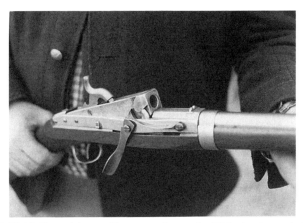

U.S. Model 1843 Hall carbine with open breech. This last model of the Hall carbine uses a side lever to open the breech for loading. The Hall's paper catridge was torn open and powder and ball loaded into the chamber. The breech was closed and a cap placed on the gun's nipple before firing. Although sturdy, the Hall's design allowed a noticeable amount of gas to escape when firing, which was disconcerting to the shooter.

The Model 1843 Hall saw wide use in the Civil War on both sides. Some Union cavalry units in the West were still carrying Halls in the spring of 1865. Although most 1843 Halls were .52-caliber smoothbores, this particular gun was one of 5,000 purchased from the government as surplus, coverted to .58-caliber and rifled and then sold to General Fremont at a considerable, some thought unconscionable, profit. The ensuing scandal became known as the Hall Carbine Affair. (*Joseph Bilby*)

loaders of any kind. Halls were not unfamiliar to the Virginians, as their state had issued some of the obsolete guns to mounted units in the summer of 1861. Surviving records indicate that the First and Second North Carolina Cavalry were issued over 600 Halls early in the war. In February of 1864 an inspecting officer reported that seven of the seventy-three long arms carried by members of the Second Florida Cavalry's Company I were Halls. Some Halls were still in Federal service at the end of the war, even though all of the Yankee cavalry officers queried on the gun's reliability reported it as "worthless." One commented that the Hall "does not carry well, gets out of order easily, they burst and blow the powder out and burn the men."[4]

The Confederates would always have less access to breech loaders than their Northern opponents and Southern production facilities would never become capable of producing large numbers of the more modern guns. Richmond-made copies of the Sharps were most common, and about 5,000 were eventually made. A few Southern-designed breech loaders were made in small numbers. The most notable of these was the Morse, of which Texas governor Sam Houston (a Unionist) wanted to acquire "seven or ten thousand" for a proposed invasion of Mexico in 1860. About a thousand Morse carbines were manufactured in South Carolina during the war. In a startling reverse of technology, one Confederate armsmaker actually converted Hall breech loaders to muzzle loaders! Despite this technology lag, however, in the first months of the war most Confederate cavalrymen, east and west, were at least as well armed as Federal horse soldiers.[5]

It could be argued that the Confederate cavalry, besides being blessed with good leadership and organization, excellent horseflesh and trained riders, was initially *better* armed for the task at hand than Union mounted regiments. A detachment of twenty-eight men from the Fifth Ohio Cavalry, armed with Joslyn .44 revolvers, some sabers and four Sharps carbines, were driven from a positon by Rebel horsemen armed with double-barreled shotguns. The officer commanding the detachment blamed the Joslyn sixguns, which he referred to as a "spurious weapon, made out of cast iron, and one half of the time will neither cock or revolve." More Sharps carbines would no doubt have altered the incident's outcome.[6]

In some cases, there was no need to speculate. One company of the First Mississippi Cavalry was superbly equipped with excellent Maynard breech-loading carbines, sabers and Colt revolvers. Maynards were also issued to Florida and Georgia troops. In all, Mississippi, Florida and Georgia bought 1,600 Maynard carbines, made in Chicopee Falls, Massachusetts, in the six months prior to the April, 1861 outbreak of hostilities. Still more Maynards in both .50 and .35-calibers were purchased by individuals and militia companies throughout the South. Some of the Georgia-purchased Maynards were issued to the Confederate Navy.

The Maynard, perhaps the most inherently accurate of the Civil War caplock breechloading carbines, used a reloadable brass cartridge which was fired by a musket cap on an external nipple. Although Maynards were issued to the U.S. cavalry on an experimental basis in the 1850s, and a few saw action in the hands of regulars in the early part of the war, it was very late in the Civil War before they got into the hands of Yankee volunteers.

Although Confederate horsemen in the eastern theater were fairly well equipped with sabers and revolvers, the double-barreled shotguns used in lieu of carbines by many Southern troopers proved extremely effective in close range shock action encounters. The Rebel ascendancy would not last, however. By November of 1862, while General Nathan Bedford Forrest's brigade was still armed with shotguns, squirrel rifles and smoothbore flintlock muskets, most Federal units east of the Mississippi were rearming with rifled breechloading carbines. In August of 1863, the Confederate Army of Tennessee's cavalry force still carried an eclectic collection of shotguns, smoothbore musketoons, Sharps, Hall, Maynard and Smith carbines. The Southern cavalry small-arms picture gradually improved, however. By May of 1864, Forrest's command was somewhat better armed, with most of his men carrying .58-caliber Enfield style rifles made in Asheville, North Carolina, .54-caliber "Mississippi" rifles and captured Sharps carbines.[7]

The Peninsula campaign established that carbines could greatly enhance the effectiveness of cavalrymen and, as 1862 closed, Burnside, Sharps and Smith carbines began to roll out of Northern factories and were quickly put into the hands of troops. Some Yankee cavalrymen operating west of the Mississippi, however, carried muzzle loaders throughout their service. At the end of 1862, most of the men of the Seventh Iowa Cavalry were armed with muzzle-loading French rifle-muskets, while a number of soldiers in the First Colorado Cavalry carried U.S. Model 1841 "Mississippi" rifles rebored to .58-caliber.

Although they remained technologically handicapped, Confederate cavalrymen also improved their armament as the war progressed, largely replacing their smoothbore muskets, sporting rifles and shotguns with muzzle-loading Enfield carbines, rifles and rifle-muskets as well as Richmond carbines and mounted infantry rifles. Although slower to load, these guns were easier to supply with ammunition and outranged the Yankee breech loaders.

Breech-loading carbines, firing lighter bullets with smaller powder charges than rifle-muskets, were not long-range weapons. The Sharps was probably the best long-range carbine. A prewar test of the Sharps Model 1859, perhaps the best and most accurate of the single-shots, involved five cavalrymen firing at a ten-foot-square target as individual skirmishers and by volley at various ranges. As might be expected,

This soldier carries a Sharps carbine and a Model 1860 Colt .44-caliber revolver. The Sharps and the Colt were the most popular weapons of their class during the Civil War. *(Donald V. Bates Collection)*

individual fire was more accurate than volleys. In individual fire, the shooters scored nineteen hits out of twenty-five shots at 100 yards, fourteen out of twenty-five at 300 yards and a mere three out of twenty-five at 500 yards. When paper cartridges which were sheared off by the gun's breechblock and spilled powder in the action were replaced by linen cartridges, Sharps accuracy improved dramatically. All shots fired at 100 and 300 yards hit the target and there was only one miss at 500 yards.

Richmond-manufactured Sharps copies and captured Yankee carbines supplemented the Confederate muzzle loaders. The "Richmond Sharps," however, gained a reputation as a poorly-made weapon prone to malfunction, breakage and even explosion in the field. Georgia soldiers were luckier than most Rebels, as the state purchased 1,600 authentic Sharps carbines from the factory in Hartford, Connecticut, prior to the outbreak of hostilities. Aside from poor quality control, some of the Rebel-manufactured Sharps' problem was, no doubt, due to the use of paper ammunition. Federal soldiers using linen cartridges, which fit in the chamber without spilling powder, did not experience similar problems.

Of necessity, then, the Confederate cavalry long-arms picture remained somewhat simpler than that of the Union throughout the conflict. The very industrial strength and diversity of the North, however, created nightmares for Federal cavalry and ordnance officers. Hordes of eager inventors and their publicists overran Washington and the Ordnance Department at the outbreak of war. Although hindsighted critics have pilloried General Ripley for being too conservative in his approach to new arms, and there is some justification for this, the general provided a real service in disposing of many of these cranks. The need for cavalry arms, especially carbines, was so great, however, that contracts were let for a number of forgettable firearms.

Yankees who had complained in 1862 that they had no carbines, were complaining in 1863 about the carbines they had. One dubious design, the Cosmopolitan or Union carbine, apparently purchased due to political considerations, was described by the troopers of the Eighth Ohio Cavalry as "a worthless arm." The Starr, an inferior knockoff of the Sharps design, was considered "a technically poor weapon" by an officer of the Twenty-fourth New York Cavalry. Colorado cavalrymen engaged in a firefight with an Indian war party in August of 1864 found that only two of their eleven Starrs would fire! Sixty-one of eighty-eight officers polled on the reliability of the Starr classified it as "poor" or "worthless."[8]

The Union purchased two types of Joslyn carbines: the Model 1862, some of which used semi-fixed paper ammunition and a percussion cap and the Model 1864, which, like most 1862s, was chambered for the .56-56 Spencer self-contained rim-fire cartridge. Although army tests of the Joslyn found it "as little liable to get out of order as any breech-loading carbine," Captain F.C. Newhall, an inspector assessing the Army of the Potomac's cavalry in the spring of 1864, characterized the Joslyn carbines of the Nineteenth New York Cavalry as "unreliable and worthless." Eight out of nine field officers asked to comment on the Joslyn believed it a "poor or worthless" arm. Many rim-fire Joslyns were apparently improperly chambered, and their breechblocks had a disconcerting propensity to blow open on firing![9]

Fortunately for the Union cavalry, the Gibbs carbine factory located in New York City was burned down by anti-draft rioters in July of 1863 after only 1,052 carbines had been shipped to the army. An ordnance inspector noted that the Gibbs was "liable to catch all dirt, and the smallest stick or pebble getting into it renders it unserviceable." Five of seven Union officers evaluating the field service of the Gibbs considered it "worthless."[10]

Most of the 20,000 Ballard carbines and rifles that went to war ended up in the hands of Kentucky troops. On the surface, the Ballard, which went on to have a distinguished career as a civilian target and hunting arm after the war, appears to be a simple, foolproof gun. Chambered for a nominally .44-caliber rim-fire cartridge (some have been converted to fire the centerfire .45 Colt cartridge for N-SSA competition), the gun has a lever-actuated breech and a manual extractor. Not everyone was satisfied with the Ballard, however. Captain Joshua W. Jacobs of the Fourth Kentucky Mounted Infantry, whose Company A was armed with Spencer repeaters, trashed the Ballards carried by six companies of the Fourth, noting "the utter worthlessness of the Ballard rifle.... A great many became entirely useless during the action; some bursted from firing; others became useless by the springs [extractor] which threw out the old cartridge."[11]

Although 18,000 Gallager carbines were purchased by the Federal government, one officer whose regiment was issued these guns felt they

A heavily-armed Union horse-man displays his Remington revolver, Smith carbine and saber. By the end of the war most Federal cavalrymen were equipped with sabers, revolvers and carbines. *(Donald V. Bates Collection)*

were useless and and requested double-barreled shotguns to replace them. The Gallager, which developed extraction problems as it heated up in action, was well detested by many of the troops to whom it was issued. Lieutenant Eugene F. Ware of the Seventh Iowa Cavalry, whose Gallager-armed regiment was rearmed with new Gallagers prior to being sent west to fight Indians in 1864, classifed the gun as "an exceedingly inefficient weapon."[12]

Even the Smith, a simple break-open-breech design, generally regarded as one of the best-designed Civil War carbines, had its detractors. Although highly regarded by today's N-SSA shooters, the Smith was probably the least popular of the "big three" (with the Sharps and Burnside) single-shot breech-loading carbines used by the Union. Over 30,000 Smiths were purchased by the Federal government, and captured Smiths were carried into action by Southern cavalrymen as well. Nevertheless, horse soldiers who participated in Colonel Benjamin Grierson's famous 1863 raid felt their Smiths were not trustworthy firearms. After a fight at Snicker's Gap on November 3, 1862, Lieutenant Colonel Horace B. Sargent of the 1st Massachusetts Cavalry requested permission to turn in his Smiths, which often failed to go off until several caps were snapped on their nipples, for Sharps carbines. His request was granted. General Wilson had a low opinion of Smiths and the officers of the First Connecticut Cavalry believed Smiths in the hands of their men were "entirely unreliable."[13]

To be fair, some of the Smith's problems may have been due to extraction difficulties caused by widespread use of the paper and foil "Poultney's Patent" cartridge in the gun, rather than the more durable rubber round it was designed to fire. Other problems inherent in the Smith's design caused the joint between barrel and frame to wear and subsequently wobble after a period of heavy use in the field. Overall, the Smith seems to have given satisfactory, if not stellar, performance. When queried as to the Smith's serviceability in the field, seventeen officers rated it as the best weapon in the service, forty-six as "good," eleven as "fair" and four as "poor." Eight pronounced the Smith "worthless."[14]

There were few complaints lodged against the Sharps, indisputably the favorite caplock breech loader in the service. Sharps linen or paper cartridges were occasionally damaged by the jostling they received in horsemen's cartridge boxes, however. Bad weather could also affect

A well-equipped Yankee horse soldier with saber, Remington revolver and Burnside carbine. Durable and accurate, the Burnside was one of the best percussion breech loaders. *(Donald V. Bates Collection)*

Sharps ammunition. Rain rendered the Seventh Kansas Cavalry's Sharps cartridges unserviceable in a fight on August 19, 1864.

A Major Patton of the 3rd Indiana Cavalry registered the following minor complaint against the Sharps: "The small springs in the locks are more easily broken or damaged than any other part of the gun. An armorer could easily repair most guns condemned as unfit for service if extra articles of this kind were provided."[15]

Burnside tapered-wrapped foil or drawn copper or brass cartridges were more sturdy than either Sharps or Smith rounds, and the .54-caliber gun that fired them was durable, reasonably accurate and popular with most of the troopers who carried it. A soldier in the Twelfth Illinois Cavalry rhapsodized about his newly issued "celebrated Burnside patent" carbine. When the Sucker horse soldiers of the Twelfth tried out their new arms they found they could "load and fire them 10 times per minute with care and take a very deliberate aim; in some target practice...a ball was shot 400 yards through a sheet iron car which is about 1/16 inch thick and almost through the other side."[16]

The Burnside, with its lever-controlled tilting breechblock, was the only Civil War single-shot breech loader, other than the Ballard, with an ejector or sorts, which bumped the empty case loose from the bottom of the chamber. This ejector was not foolproof, however, as evidenced by occasional complaints of sticking cartridge cases. Some soldiers wet metallic cartridges in their mouths before loading. This field expedient seems to have aided in extraction of fired cases.

First Model Burnsides saw limited service in the prewar regular army, and "Second Model" Burnsides were in the hands of troops by late 1861. Addition of a forestock resulted in the "Third Model" Burnside. Most of the more than 50,000 Burnsides issued from 1862 on were the very similar "Fourth Model" guns.

Dave Burns assumes a skirmishing position with a Fourth Model Burnside carbine. Cavalry skirmish lines were relatively thin, as every fourth man was detailed to hold horses. *(Tony Beck)*

When queried as to how they would rate their men's Burnside carbines in an Ordnance Department survey which included the categories "best, good, fair and poor," the overwhelming majority of officer respondents categorized the Burnside as a "good" weapon. One regarded the gun as a "very good weapon, second only to Spencers." Although Lieutenant G.T. Elgin of the First Texas (Union) Cavalry qualified his evaluation of the Burnside as an "excellent arm" by stating it was "not quite strong enough for rough service," the men of the First New Jersey Cavalry were quite fond of their Burnsides, which were eventually replaced by Spencers. The troopers of the Second Ohio Cavalry actually grumbled when they turned in their Burnsides for Spencers because of the latter arm's greater weight. The Buckeyes were doubly doubtful about the exchange when their new repeaters failed to fire because of defective ammunition.[17]

Cartridges for breech loaders were not only occasionally defective, but often in short supply. As carbines became available to Union cavalrymen in quantity, supplying correct ammunition became a problem for ordnance personnel. In June of 1863, soldiers of the Sixth and Seventh Illinois Cavalry, armed with Cosmopolitan and Smith carbines, could find no ammunition for their guns in the whole Department of the Gulf. At one point, the troopers of the First New Jersey Cavalry, with only ten rounds of Burnside ammunition per man, held a critical position largely by bluff.

On another occasion, the Second West Virginia's cavalrymen found themselves totally without ammunition. Yankee horsemen on Brigadier General William Averill's Virginia raid of 1863 were supplied with only thirty-five rounds of carbine ammunition per man. Ammunition supply did not necessarily improve as the war went on. As late as August of 1864, the men of the Eighth Ohio Cavalry, armed with the deplorable Cosmopolitan carbine, had only fifteen rounds each in their cartridge boxes.

Ammunition difficulties were often complicated by the fact that many Union cavalry regiments, even during the last year of the war, carried a variety of carbines, which, when out of order, were often not readily replaced. In the spring of 1864, the First Brigade of the Third Division of the Army of the Potomac's Cavalry Corps had "large deficiencies of carbines and pistols in all the regiments but one."[18]

In November of 1864, the men of Brigadier General August Kautz's cavalry division attached to the Army of the Potomac, which was armed with everything from state of the art Henrys to the woeful Starr, was described as having "a great deficiency in the arms and equipments of the men present for duty." A Union cavalry brigade serving in East Tennessee in late 1864 was armed with six different types of long arms—Sharps, Henry and Enfield rifles and Burnside, Smith and Union carbines.[19]

The situation was worse in the Trans-Mississippi. Perhaps the most extreme example of mixed firearms in a single Federal unit was the First Missouri State Militia Cavalry, an outfit which was constantly in action against Rebel guerrillas. In September, 1864, at the time of General Sterling Price's raid into Missouri, the men of the First carried sixteen different patterns of breech loaders, nine different types of muzzle loaders, and a few double-barreled shotguns. Some of the Missourians were armed with nothing but revolvers. Needless to say, the spare parts problems in such units were at least as bad as the ammunition difficulties.

It was, no doubt, uniformity of armament as well as firepower that General Wilson had in mind when he requested Model 1865 Spencers to arm his three divisions in the spring of 1865. When these were not forthcoming, he stripped Model 1860 Spencers from some of his units to arm those making the raid. Several of Wilson's regiments turned in Hall carbines, still in service in the spring of 1865!

Thus the picture often drawn of the Federal cavalry bristling with Spencer repeaters from Gettysburg through to the end of the war is not an accurate one. If the conflict had lasted another year, even another six months, probably every Federal on horseback would have had a Spencer slung over his shoulder, but such was not the case.

Despite the varying quality of their carbines, cavalry commanders in the field had more tactical flexibility than their infantry counterparts. In the years prior to the Civil War, there were, theoretically, different types of horse soldiers in the U.S. regular army. The First and Second Dragoons were armed with carbines, single-shot pistols or revolvers and sabers, and were expected to fight on foot as well as horseback. The First and Second Cavalry were more lightly armed, with revolvers and some carbines and expected to do most of their fighting on horseback. The Mounted Rifle Regiment was a mounted infantry outfit with rifles which outranged the dragoons' carbines. In fact, however, the equipment and tactical role distinctions between these units had become increasingly blurred by 1861—so much so that they were all classified as cavalry shortly after the war broke out.

Although some theorists believed that the cavalry should be armed solely with revolvers and sabers, most Union cavalry regiments became, in effect, dragoons, armed with carbines (in some cases rifles), revolvers and sabers. There was diversity of thought in the Rebel service as well, and Major General J.E.B. Stuart, a veteran of the U.S. Cavalry, retained a strong belief in such traditional cavalry tactics as the saber charge. Stuart seems to have had little interest in using his men as mounted infantry. Other Rebel horse outfits, although organized and denominated as cavalry, were true mounted infantry armed with rifle-muskets, who would dismount and fight on foot in infantry line of battle formation. Nathan Bedford Forrest's men were some of the best mounted infantry of the war.

Outside of commanders like Forrest, who was at his best when on his own, cavalry, even when organized in divisions or a corps, was largely employed for screening, scouting and raiding. Seldom did it exert a significant influence on the course of a battle. For all his reputation as a dashing leader, J.E.B. Stuart never delivered a crushing blow to the Army of the Potomac. One of his more signal accomplishments, the ride around McClellan's army on the Peninsula, would not have fazed a more effective Federal commander. Stuart was caught almost literally with his pants down at Brandy Station and his failure in the Gettysburg campaign is a matter of record.

Even with his limitations, however, Stuart was a generally good cavalry leader, made to look even better by the mediocre opponents he faced in the first two years of the war. Although the Federal horse gained parity with Stuart's men in 1863, it was not until General Sheridan's Shenandoah Valley campaign of 1864 that it was used in the role European military men envisoned for the mounted arm. Sheridan was the only leader in the war to use massed, Napoleonic-style charges to exploit a breaking enemy infantry force. At Winchester and Cedar Creek, these charges proved irresistible. As has been said about politics, however, all Civil War cavalry tactics proved local. What worked for Forrest or for Mosby's Partisan Rangers or the Missouri guerrillas operating behind Union lines was not necessarily appropriate for cavalry attached to an army.

A commander of a well-equipped cavalry unit could call on three weapons, saber, revolver and carbine. The first two were used for mounted fighting. Although breech-loading carbines were favored for cavalry because they were easier to reload on horseback, the carbine was generally used by dismounted men. In a typical small unit action, a commander would dismount a portion of his command to provide carbine fire support for the remaining mounted men, who would then try to charge the enemy (usually another cavalry outfit) or manuever them out of position.

The effectiveness of carbine fire may be fairly questioned. With its short-sight radius, ballistically inferior bullet and relatively low powder charge, the average Civil War carbine, with the notable exception of the Sharps, was a short-range arm. It is also doubtful that troops armed with carbines had the skill to exploit the capabilities they did have. As with the infantry rifle-musket, carbine target practice was seldom held by commanders, at least on the Federal side. Stephen Z. Starr, the definitive historian of the Union mounted arm, notes that: "Not more than a handful of cavalry regiments are definitely known to have had target practice, and it can be deduced from incidental comments that the great majority had none."[20]

Infantrymen routinely disparaged not only cavalrymen, but the accuracy of their weapons. Lieutenant Colonel Thomas Hyde recalled many years after the war that: "We had a belief in the infantry that these carbines would not hit anything, and I confirmed the belief so far as I was concerned by borrowing one from a wounded man and firing in the line for an hour. To be sure there was nothing but smoke to fire at as a general thing, and although in dead earnest then, I am happy in the conviction that I did not hurt anybody."[21]

A dismounted cavalry regiment immediately lost one fourth of its potential combat strength when it deployed to fight on foot. In defense or offense, dismounted horse soldiers were generally deployed in a skirmish formation, which was not designed to bring a great volume of fire on the enemy. The greatest service Brigadier General John Buford's horse soldiers performed on the first day at Gettysburg was to force the advancing Confederate infantry to consume a great deal of time in deploying. Once the Rebel foot soldiers began to move in earnest, however, there was little the cavalry could do but retreat. If breech-loading carbines played a role in Buford's stand, it was probably more due to the noise they made than their ability to mow down Rebel infantrymen.

As evidenced by Buford's stand at Gettysburg, dismounted cavalry could position itself in the defense to slow down an infantry attack. Offensive manuevers against infantry were quite another matter, however. One Federal horse soldier recalled that "one brigade armed with Enfield rifles and posted behind earthworks ought to be a match at any time for more than an entire division of dismounted cavalry." A New York cavalry sergeant informed Captain De Forest of the Twelfth Connecticut Infantry that: "At close quarters we can whip [Brigadier General Lunsford L.] Lomax's men; they have no sabres and generally no revolvers. But at long range we are rather afraid of them; they carry Enfields which shoot farther than our carbines."[22]

The muzzle-loading Enfield was indeed a superior weapon for infantry fighting, and a better gun than most of the "patent" carbines thrust into the hands of Union horsemen during the Civil War. The Union cavalry fought its war in large part with a hodgepodge of single-shot percussion-ignition breech-loading carbines of varying quality. Although the best of these, like the Sharps and Burnside, were generally fine arms, the worst were some of the poorest weapons ever issued to American soldiers.

Collecting and Shooting Breech-Loading Carbines Today

In November of 1992 I had the pleasure of attending the New Jersey Outdoor Writers' Association pheasant, chukar partridge and quail hunt and game dinner at the B&B Pheasantry in Pittstown, New Jersey. What, one might ask, does a bird-shooting safari and fine dining have to do with Civil War carbines? In this case it provided an introduction to a rather unique individual who provided an interesting story relating directly to the matter at hand. Good stories are where you find them.

When I met him, Hank Ricci, a retired outdoor writer who formerly penned articles for the Long Branch, New Jersey *Daily Record*, was still going strong and dropping birds with aplomb at the age of seventy-seven. Besides being a lifelong outdoorsman, Hank, who knew genuine Civil War veterans in his youth, was, for me, a living link to America's past.

Back in the 1930s and 1940s, when use of a muzzle-loading rifle in the hunting fields was considered an eccentricity, Hank Ricci went afield with an original ('twern't no repros then) flintlock Pennsylvania long rifle. When I met him he could still shoot a score of 49 or 50 on a National

Tom Willard (who is related to Colonel Willard of smoothbore musket fame) of the N-SSA Washington Artillery takes a bead with his reproduction Italian-made Sharps carbine. Tom uses paper cartridges made from hair-curler paper in his Sharps. His cartridges are constructed so that they enter the breech completely before it is closed, leaving no paper to shave off and no stray powder grains to ignite in the wrong place. *(Joseph Bilby)*

Muzzle-loading Rifle Association target at fifty yards with one of his original guns.

Just after World War II, Hank came across an old Vermont hunter who had downed a deer with a rather unusual firearm—a Sharps and Hankins Model 1862 carbine. Most of the production run of around 13,000 .52-caliber rim-fire Sharps and Hankins guns went to the Navy, although a few were issued to cavalrymen, most notably in the 2nd New York Veteran and the 9th, 10th and 11th New York Cavalry. Here, more than eighty years later, one was still dropping deer in the Green Mountains. The old timer refused to sell or trade his ancient Sharps and Hankins, which had required but a single shot to make meat every year. He was, however, a little apprehensive about his diminishing store of "cattiges" which he kept in an old shoebox, and asked Hank if he knew where he could get some more. Hank subsequently encountered another old Vermonter potting pike along the shore of Lake Champlain with a Sharps and Hankins.

Hard to come by then, shootable cartridges for any type of Civil War carbine shortly became impossible to obtain. I'm as sure as I can be that those old Sharps and Hankins carbines are no longer harvesting game in Vermont. (Shooting fish is no longer legal.) Sure, and a little sad. One of the major themes of this book, however, is that the tide has turned and, with a little ingenuity, I'm sure a creative black powder gunsmith could get almost anything shooting today. This was not true a mere thirty years ago.

Cartridge breech loaders externally primed with percussion caps have proved easier to get back into action than rim-fire guns like the Sharps and Hankins. The N-SSA has been the main vehicle for the renaissance in Civil War caplock breech-loading carbine shooting. Beginning with individual matches in the organization's early days, carbine shooting was elevated to the status of team competition in 1971. N-SSA demand led to the production of specialized carbine bullet molds and sizers by Rapine Bullet Mold Manufacturing Company as well as a variety of cartridge cases by different makers for the old guns.

Since my own carbine shooting experience is somewhat limited, I ransacked my files and interviewed a number of experienced carbine shooters before tackling the subject. Fortunately, there are people who have given a good deal of serious thought to shooting Civil War era breech loaders. Some of these dedicated shooter/researchers might be more properly termed "empirical historians," since their work sheds much needed light on the probable tactical performance of breech-loading single-shot carbines during the Civil War.

The most popular breech-loading carbine of the war was the Sharps carbine, which like the Sharps rifle made famous by Berdan's sharpshooters, fired a combustible cartridge ignited by a percussion cap. Shooting a Sharps rifle today is covered in the chapter on sharpshooters, and the same information can be applied to shooting Sharps carbines.

Perhaps the most popular original carbine in N-SSA ranks, especially for team competition, is the quick-loading break-action Smith. Although Civil War soldiers had problems with the nominally .50-caliber Smith in the field, it is considered the ideal caplock breech loader by many modern shooters. Restoring Smiths to shooting shape and building shooters out of "junkers" and mixtures of reproduction and original parts has become a cottage industry. R.A. Hoyt relines original and reproduction Smith barrels and Larry Jensco supplies fitted new barrels for the gun. Original and quality reproduction parts, including new stocks, are available from Dixie Gun works, S&S, Larry Gollohan and others.

The Smith's popularity has inspired two revivals since 1865. Mike Yeck, who turned out some excellent musket barrels (I'm still shooting one) and reproduction muskets in the 1970s, manufactured a limited number of reproduction Smiths, most of which are still seen on the firing line. Navy Arms now markets a good-looking Italian made reproduction Smith, but cartridges which fit original Smiths do not chamber in the Navy Arms gun, which requires a special cartridge.

Original Smith cartridges were rubber, but most used in the Civil War were apparently the Poultney round, made from a composite cardboard-type material. Reloadable Smith cartridges are currently available in plastic and brass. Plastic rounds are cheaper, but the brass ones last longer, providing you clean them thoroughly after a range session. Either type are immeasurably better than the original ammunition. Reduced capacity brass cases are popular with target shooters, and are available from dealers like Bill Osborne of Lodgewood Manufacturing. Bill also stocks a full range of original and excellent quality reproduction parts for a number of carbines and other Civil War guns.

As with most original black powder breech loaders, Smith bore diameters vary. Nineteenth century gun makers depended on the "push" of a black powder charge to boost undersized bullets into the rifling grooves. Oversize bullets were swaged down in the gun's barrel. For the best accuracy, shooters of original carbines like the Smith should slug the bores of their guns to better match bullet to barrel for the best accuracy. Rapine offers Smith molds in .520 and .525 diameters to match varying bore diameters. Some shooters size Smith bullets to assure they are consistently .001 to .002 above groove diameter for a closer fit, while others shoot them as cast. Recent research on the post-Civil War .45-70 cartridge, adopted in 1873, suggests that using over-groove diameter bullets to asure accuracy, a modern cast bullet concept, does not necessarily apply to black powder cartridges and firearms. If you feel like experimenting, try groove diameter bullets, or even slightly undersized slugs. Bullet alloy is not as critical with breech loaders as muzzle loaders, and many shooters use a harder alloy with good success. Lubricants for carbine bullets are generally the same as those used on minie balls for muzzle loaders. Carbine powder charges range from twenty-eight to forty grains of FFFG or FFG black powder, with and without filler material. The finer FFFG sometimes leaks out the ignition hole in the Smith cartridge's base, a problem solved by placing a small square of tissue paper in the base before filling it with powder.

The Maynard, although strange looking, is probably the most technologically progressive of the single-shot capping breech loaders, and the only one to survive into the self-contained cartridge era as a target and hunting arm. Harper's Ferry Arms offered a reproduction Maynard back in the early 1970s, and a new reproduction is rumored to be entering the market, but most Maynard shooters use original guns. Although the gun was highly praised in pre-war government tests, the Union did not purchase any Maynards until late in the Civil War. Most of those being shot today are   original .50-caliber guns from this lot. Earlier model .50 and .35-caliber Maynards, many of which saw Confederate service, are rather rare.

Should you acquire an original Maynard with a shot-out or rust-pitted bore, R.A. Hoyt will reline it. If your Maynard needs a barrel, fitted replacement tubes are available from Steve Jensco. Other Maynard parts are available from Larry C. Gollahon, S&S Firearms, Lodgewood and other dealers.

The Maynard was originally chambered for a rimmed copper cartridge with an ignition hole in the center of the base where the primer is found on a modern centerfire round. Bullet molds in .515 and .520 sizes and reloadable brass cases for both .50 and .36-caliber Maynards are available from most sutlers and dealers who specialize in black powder shooting supplies.

N-SSA skirmisher Joe McAvoy loads twenty-eight grains of FFFG behind a .518 sized bullet in his .50-caliber Maynard cases, filling up the space between the powder charge and bullet base with Cream of Wheat and a wax wad, the latter seated directly behind the bullet. Joe cuts wads for his Maynard, as well as his Henry, out of wax wad sheets available from J&J Ltd. Skirmisher Bud Scully, who uses unsized bullets cast from a .520 Smith carbine mold in his Maynard, reports that those who use reduced loads without filler material in standard Maynard cases risk hangfires. In the past few years, reduced capacity Maynard cartridge cases in both brass and plastic have come on the market and are favored by many shooters, including Scully. The plastic cases are flexible and accept bullets of varying diameters more readily than brass rounds.

Acceptable short-range accuracy is possible with a variety of loads in a Burnside carbine. All a shooter needs is a reproduction case and powder measure, and some bullets, in this instance ranging from round balls to minie balls. With some work, a Burnside shoots as well as a Sharps. *(Joseph Bilby)*

The Gallager is a relatively rare choice among today's carbine shooters, but some are still in service. Not very popular among the troops during its heyday, the Gallager was reproduced briefly in the 1970s by the German Erma firm. Erma Gallagers were beautifully-made guns, although one I am aware of had a groove diameter of .550. Unfortunately, available reproduction Gallager cartridge cases are designed for a .540, 300-grain two-step heel-style bullet. Even with black powder, .010 is a bit much to boost up a bullet!

Modern reloadable brass Gallager cases, which will fit original guns and the Erma copies, have a ridge inside them against which the "heel", which is of a smaller diameter than the rest of the bullet, rests. Powder charges for the Gallager fall into the same range as those cited for the Smith and Maynard.

N-SSA Skirmisher Steve Garratano's experience with an original Gallager may be considered typical of the problems faced by carbine shooters who dabble with the more esoteric arms. Steve's Rapine Gallager mold threw a .539 bullet, but his particular bore slugged out at .525 groove diameter. With no smaller diameter heeled bullet available, and unwilling to have a custom mold made before exploring other alternatives, Steve took a .525-diameter Smith bullet, increased the bullet's base bevel with an X-acto knife, and loaded it into the Gallager case using a small "C" clamp, which shaved a small concentric ring off the slug. He reports that the gun shoots quite well with this improvised ammunition.

Even fewer Burnsides than Gallagers are seen at a typical N-SSA skirmish. Many years ago, before I started skirmishing, I owned a Fourth Model Burnside in very good condition with a spotless bore. I bought a handful of reloadable brass cases and did a little haphazard firing with around forty grains of FFG loaded behind a .530-grain round ball as well as some .54-caliber minies I happend to have around. The results, as might be expected, were less than spectacular, and I swapped the

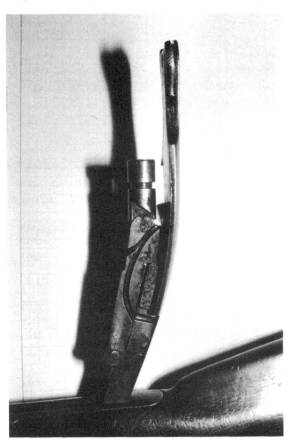

The Merrill breech opened. The plug served as a gas seal to keep escaping powder gases within the breech. The only paper cartridge breech loader which sealed gas better was the Sharps. *(Tony Beck)*

Burnside for a Winchester Model 1873. Today I regret that trade, as I have come to the conclusion that the Burnside has definite potential as a shooter. With new, inexpensive plastic cartridges available from Lodgewood Mfg. the Burnside is easier and cheaper to load than ever.

The work of Tony Beck, an "empirical historian" of the first order, has been influential in shaping my new conclusions. Beck's instructions on the Burnside are the last word at present on Burnside shooting. He recommends a "short, wide, 375 grain .56 bullet" cast from molds available from Dixie Gun Works, The Regimental Quartermaster, S&S or Rapine. Although the Burnside case holds fifty grains of powder, Tony prefers a twenty-one grain charge of FFFG black powder for fifty yard shooting and thirty-eight grains for 100 yards, the space between powder and bullet base filled with "cotton fluff." I am sure that any of the usual fillers would serve as well. Beck reported minimal recoil and accuracy equal to that obtained in his original Sharps carbine with the twenty-one grain load.

Beck has found the Burnside's tumbler and mainspring, which can be easily broken by dry firing, to be the gun's weak points. Since parts are hard to come by, don't dry fire your Burnside! The same advice applies for Gallagers and other odd carbines. Steve Garratano has sought a spare Gallager tumbler for years with no success.

Tony Beck has also experimented with a Merrill carbine, not a favorite in the 1860s and almost unheard of except as a collector piece these days. Although the Merrill rifle enjoyed some popularity among Massachusetts sharpshooters, the carbines were adjudged "poor" or "worthless" by fifty-nine of the ninety-one Union cavalry officers asked to comment on them.

Beck was still willing to give the Merrill a try. After inconclusive experiments with a Burnside bullet, he made a mold based on some battlefield dug Merrill slugs. The Merrill, according to Beck "shoots surprisingly well and leaks [gas] much less than an unmodified [original] Sharps." He reports that the biggest problems reported by Civil War era commentators on the Merrill "were the fragile paper ammunition and the propensity for the sight screws to break, causing the sights to fall off." Tony's tests verified both of these defects. Apparently due to chamber dimensions, paper for the Merrill cartridge has to be quite thin. Beck correctly notes that "neither of these [problems] is a big deal for skirmishing."

Subsequent study of and experimentation with the Merrill led Beck

A rare sight, two working Merrills. Tony Beck *(standing)* and Jim Kenner *(kneeling)* fire their Merrills at a site near Tucson, Arizona, in 1995. *(Dave Burns)*

to use hair curler paper for cartridges. Although fragile, rounds made with this paper (it also works in a Sharps) work well in the gun. An easier cartridge is made by using the plastic tubes designed for rifle-musket cartridges. Load "about 35 grains of FFFG powder" and then insert the bullet. When loading the gun, extract the bullet from the cartridge case, insert it into the breech and close the breech to seat it. Reopen the breech, drop the powder charge into it behind the bullet, close, cap and fire.[23]

Skirmisher Lee Terry of the 13th Virginia Infantry (N-SSA) aims a "captured" Burnside carbine at an N-SSA regional skirmish. *(Bill Goble)*

Carbine shooting with caplock breech loaders is more popular today than at any time since the 1860s. I believe that the future of carbine shooting will witness even more progress than we have witnessed in the past forty years, with a growth in the variety of good reproduction guns. The next time you're browsing around a gun show or a sutler's table, give these short-barreled cavalry arms more than a casual perusal. For a new shooting challenge as well as a good perspective on the arms of the Civil War horse soldier—try a carbine.

CHAPTER V

Sixguns—and Some Cold Steel

Despite his later triumphs, Samuel Colt's early efforts in the gun business were not successful. The Patent Firearms Company of Paterson, New Jersey, an entity established to manufacture and market the inventor's repeating rifles and revolvers, failed in 1840. Sam was out of the gun business, perhaps, he may have thought, forever.

In Texas meanwhile, his "revolving pistols" were sowing the seeds of a legend. The Texas Navy ordered 180 Paterson revolvers and a like number of revolving rifles in 1839. The U.S. Army and Navy also purchased a number of Paterson revolvers and carbines from Colt, and then the company which bought out his assets, between 1838 and 1845. Some of the Texas navy guns ended up in the hands of the Texas Rangers, who wrote the most notable combat chapter in the early history of the revolver. In 1844, an outnumbered company of Rangers shot up a band of Commanche Indians with their .36-caliber Paterson "five shooters," giving birth to the saga of the Colt.[1]

The outbreak of war with Mexico in 1846 led a suddenly revolver-hungry U.S. military to scour gun shops for remaining Colt handguns. Colonel Samuel Walker of the U.S. Mounted Rifles, a former Texas Ranger who had witnessed the power of the Paterson in the 1844 Commanche fight, traveled east to look up Sam Colt and offer some ideas for an improved version of the gun. The result was the massive, six-shot .44-caliber "Walker" Colt.

Despite a disturbing tendency to blow up in a shooter's hand, the "Walker" put Colt back into the gun business for good. For the next

Private E.L. Dye of the 7th Kansas Cavalry displays his 12mm pin-fire Lefaucheux revolver. The Lefaucheux was unique in that it fired a self-contained cartridge. A small tube containing priming compound jutted out at a right angle from the cartridge case and, when hit by the gun's hammer, fired the round. Most of these French guns ended up in the western Federal armies, although one company of the Maryland Purnell Legion cavalry carried Lefaucheux handguns at Gettysburg. *(USAMHI)*

twelve years, the terms "revolver" and "Colt" were synonymous. The born-again Colt firm churned out a number of handgun models, from .32-caliber pocket guns to big .44-caliber Dragoons. Perhaps the most popular Colt model among civilians was the Model 1851 .36-caliber Navy revolver. Following the 1857 expiration of Colt's patents, a number of new revolvers appeared on the market. Although the Colt 1860 Army, a streamlined gun which retained the effective .44-bore diameter of the Dragoon, became the predominant handgun of the Civil War, the Federal government also purchased large numbers of Remington, Starr and Whitney revolvers, as well as the guns of other makers, including the bizarre looking Savage, with its second "ring trigger" which cocked the arm, and the sidehammer Joslyn. Most of the Joslyns were turned in in 1862 "due to their utterly worthless field service."[2]

All major Union handguns, save one, were loaded with combustible cartridges or loose powder and ball, ignited by percussion caps fitted to nipples on the rear of each chamber. The exception was the imported French Lefaucheux, which fired a self-contained pinfire round. Privately purchased Smith and Wesson revolvers, which chambered small caliber self-contained rim-fire cartridges, also found their way to the front.

Confederate soldiers were initially armed with an assortment of privately-owned revolvers, as well as sixguns from state arsenals and confiscated Federal stores. These guns were later supplemented by arms purchased from the North prior to the actual outbreak of hostilities. Sam Colt was more than willing to fill orders from the Confederate States of America until he was ordered to desist by the Federal government. The Rebel revolver supply was later bolstered by captured weapons, a few imported handguns like the British Adams and Kerr and a small number of domestically-produced revolvers, most of them copies of older model Colts.

Some Confederate soldiers, at least indirectly, may have purchased their revolvers from Yankee cavalrymen. The Colonel of the Second Michigan Cavalry issued an order threatening that "any noncommissioned officer who shall lose, sell or otherwise lose his arms will have double its value deducted from his pay." In December of 1862, some Yankees from the Second Illinois Cavalry sold their Colt Navies to civilians for from $50 to $75 each as part of a scam in which the buyers

This Yankee displays a Colt Model 1851 Navy. *(Donald V. Bates* Collection)

Corporal Henry Harrison Hibbs, 104th Pennsylvania Infantry, displays a .44-caliber Colt Model 1860 Army in his belt in a photograph taken on Morris Island, SC. This is probably Hibbs' personal weapon, as infantry corporals wre not authorized to carry revolvers. Photographers occasionally used weapons as props, but that does not seem to be the case here, as photos of other members of the regiment were taken by the same photographer, but none of them display handguns.
(James M. Heayn)

were immediately arrested and the guns returned to their original owners, who kept the purchase money. What happened to any sixguns sold by members of the Second Michigan is less clear.[3]

Some volunteers who flocked to the Union colors in 1861 brought their own handguns with them. More than a few of these recruits were ignorant of the basics of gun safety, and often mixed gunpowder with alcohol. Two Jersey City militiamen on their way to the front in 1861 shot a fellow soldier while "skylarking" with their revolvers, and a Jersey City officer chased a private through his regiment's crowded camp, taking pot-shots at him with his sixgun.

In the Fifteenth New Jersey Infantry, an 1862 regimental order banned handgun possession by enlisted men after an accidentally discharged ball bounced into a major's tent and caromed off his boot. Although such prohibitions were widely disregarded, many infantrymen sold or discarded their personal pistols, along with much other excess gear, after their first forced march.

Some foot soldiers did, however, keep their handguns. Private Alfred Bellard of the Fifth New Jersey Infantry lost his when it was stolen, along with the rest of the contents of his knapsack, while he was tending wounded men following the battle of Williamsburg in May, 1862. Sergeant John Crater of the Fifteenth New Jersey, a champion forager, used his revolver to dispatch ducks, chickens, pigs, rabbits and other edible enemies of the Union. Violating regimental orders, Private George Henderson of the Fifteenth hung on to his sixgun until May 3, 1863, when, at the battle of Salem Church, it saved his life by stopping a minie ball.

Some infantry colorbearers, including those of the Fourteenth and Fifteenth New Jersey, were issued or requested handguns. During the Atlanta campaign, Confederate infantrymen received revolvers for use in a successful trench raid. Generally, however, infantry enlisted men on either side seldom carried revolvers after 1861.

Pennsylvania cavalryman, with a saber and Starr revolver. Invented by Ebenezer Starr, the Starr revolver, which came in double- and single-action versions and .26- and .44-calibers, was a better arm than the Starr carbine, yet not in the class of the Colt or Remington. One Kentucky officer stated that the contractor who sold Starrs to the government and the person who purchased them should have been "hanged as traitors." Over 40 Union cavalry regiments were at least partially armed with Starr revolvers. *(USAMHI)*

Corporal Kimball Pearsons of the 10th New York Cavalry. The 10th served in the Army of the Potomac and was present at Gettysburg. Like most of the Yankee cavalry units at that battle, the New Yorkers of the 10th carried Sharps carbines and Colt 1860 army revolvers, like the one Corporal Pearsons has stuck in his belt. The 10th also reported some Colt .35-caliber Navy revolvers on its ordnance reports. *(USAMHI)*

Private Bill "Nick" Nicholson of the Thirty-seventh Mississippi Infantry was an exception. Nicholson, a former Texas Ranger, was reluctant to give up his "old six-shooter," even though its weight was a burden on the march. Following frontier custom: "'Nick' every few weeks went out into the bushes and tried his pistol at a tree; then for a couple of hours he cleaned and reloaded it." It was two years before he ever found a use for it. After escaping Yankee pursuit at the battle of Peachtree Creek in July, 1864, Nick returned to his comrades with an empty gun and claimed that he "got five" of his pursuers with the revolver.[4]

Although sixguns were often supplied to light artillery batteries, their actual issue was usually limited to non-commissioned officers and drivers, who used them primarily to shoot wounded and out of control horses. Both infantry and artillery officers usually carried privately purchased handguns, but, since an officer's job was to direct his men and not get engaged directly in the vulgar brawl of combat, these were seldom fired except in dire circumstances. Officers of the 116th Pennsylvania Infantry used their handguns in close-quarter fighting at Gettysburg, and the occasion was such an exception that it was noted in the regiment's post-war unit history.

There was no formal revolver training or range qualification requirement for officers, and any shooting practice was purely voluntary. Captain De Forest of the Twelfth Connecticut Infantry amused himself while on shipboard bound for New Orleans thusly: "I load my revolver and shoot at gulls or floating tufts of seaweed...." Lieutenant Colonel Elisha Hunt Rhodes of the Second Rhode Island Infantry was more gunwise than the average officer. During the siege of Petersburg, Rhodes recorded that he and his fellow officers "practice fencing every day and a little pistol firing."[5]

Most of the revolvers purchased by the Federal government, as well as those captured or bought by the Confederacy during the course of the war, wound up in the hands of cavalrymen. The story of the handgun in the Civil War is, therefore, largely a cavalry story. There was general military agreement that the revolver was an ideal weapon for cavalry. One Texas cavalryman thought horses and sixguns "just run together like molasses." For most horse soldiers, revolver meant Colt. Arms

A Yankee soldier with a British Pattern 1858 Enfield rifle. The short Enfield, issued to the rifle brigade and sergeants in the British army, had variations, but this snub-nosed variety, also known as the Pattern 1856 No. 2, or [bayonet] Bar-on-Band, is rare. The revolver stuck in his belt appears to be an Allen and Wheelock Navy. Many infantry recruits discarded their personal handguns after the first hard march.*(Harry Roach)*

historian John D. McAulay notes that "eighty-four percent of all the [Union] revolvers on hand [at Gettysburg] were the Colt M1860 Army."[6]

As with other small arms, especially in the trans- Mississippi theater, Confederate soldiers were often required to provide their own weapons in the first year of the war. Former Texas Ranger Ben McCulloch required each recruit for his First Regiment, Texas Mounted Riflemen, to "provide his own horse, saddle, blankets, canteen, 'six shooting pistol' and, if possible, a shotgun or rifle."[7]

Even in Texas, sixguns were not always available, and many cavalrymen on both sides set off for war with old-fashioned single-shot "horse pistols." The soldiers of the Third Texas Cavalry left for the front armed with, in addition to an eclectic assortment of shotguns, "common rifles" and Sharps rifles, 1,547 "pistols." Although the terms "pistol" and "revolver" were often used interchangeably during the Civil War, most of these handguns were, no doubt, part of the "consignment of 1,550 brass mounted [single-shot] pistols" delivered to the regiment in July, 1861. South Carolina and Virginia also issued old .54-caliber smoothbore single-shot pistols, some converted to percussion and some in their original flintlock configurations, to cavalrymen in 1861.[8]

Despite the industrial superiority of the North, there weren't enough modern handguns to arm all the Yankee horse soldiers flocking to the colors either. The U.S. government dug several thousand horse pistols out of storage and bought more from private arms dealers. The state of Massachusetts purchased 200 of the big single-shot handguns in August, 1861. Colonel Charles W. Carr of the Third Illinois Cavalry, raised in August, 1861, reported at the end of February, 1862 that his men had "never been furnished with revolvers of any kind." By the end of that year, the 135 Colt revolvers the regiment reported in service were outnumbered by the regiment's 249 "U.S. pistol[s] m/1822-1840." As late as the second quarter of 1863, the men of the Third still carried 156 horse pistols.[9]

Some Federal theorists argued that handguns and sabres were the only weapons a cavalryman needed. The Yankees of the numerically inadequate cavalry force that General McClellan brought to the Virginia Peninsula in the spring of 1862 quickly discovered that the theorists were wrong. Union horsemen of the Fifth United States and Sixth Pennsylvania (Rush's Lancers) Cavalry found themselves at a serious disadvantage when confronted by Rebel cavalrymen armed with shotguns and muskets.

A Federal cavalryman with a Starr revolver and a saber. Some authorities thought "cold steel" and sixguns were all a horse soldier needed. *(Donald V. Bates Collection)*

By the end of the war, most Union cavalry outfits were armed with carbines, sabers and revolvers, and developed ad hoc small unit tactics integrating these weapons. Units sometimes attacked with the front ranks wielding sabers and the rear ranks, revolvers.

Confederate regular cavalrymen relied more on longarms, particularly Enfield rifle-muskets or the shorter Enfield rifle, as the war progressed. Despite common belief, neither side totally abandoned the saber, however. Even Jefferson Davis, who introduced the rifle-musket to the U.S. army during his tenure as Secretary of War, remained an advocate of the saber for cavalrymen. As late as August 14, 1864, in a conversation with his ordnance chief Josiah Gorgas, Davis "...spoke again of a long Sabre that Gen. [Wade] Hampton wanted made for his cavalry, and remembered that on a previous occasion, he spoke of the armament of cavalry and said that if they had sabres they should not have guns, but be made to depend on the sabre." The Confederate chief executive firmly believed "that if our cavalry were to depend on the sabre alone that they would then come to close quarters, & run off their antagonists who depend on their long-range guns."[10]

Saber drills, first dismounted and then mounted, were part of every Union and many Confederate unit training schedules, although a Prus-

Private Oliver Sweitzer, Company A, 132nd Pennsylvania Infantry. Sweitzer has a Bowie knife and a Colt Model 1855 side-hammer Root Model revolver stuck in his belt. The small-bore side-hammer Colts were not purchased by the government, and this handgun is either a photographer's prop or a personal weapon. The 132nd was a nine-months regiment which served from August 1862 through May 1863. It fought at Fredericksburg and Chancellorsville. *(USAMHI)*

sian observer "declared it 'apparent that the American does not understand how to use the saber properly.'" Properly or not, they were used. A perusal of Stephen Z. Starr's definitive three volume study, *The Union Cavalry in the Civil War*, reveals forty-six saber charges. The vast majority of these assaults were, however, on the squadron, battalion or regimental level.[11]

Due to organization, training and terrain, saber-armed cavalry was seldom given the opportunity to perform in the huge massed formations that had established its reputation as a shock arm in Europe. When opportunity arose, however, even during the last year of the war, the saber—or the threat of it—was put to good use. The mere possibility of a saber charge by Brigadier General William Gamble's brigade on the flank of an advancing Confederate infantry unit on the first day of Gettysburg caused the Rebel foot soldiers to halt and deploy. The subsequent delay in the Confederate advance allowed the remains of the badly battered I Corps to fall back to Cemetery Ridge and safety. It is hard to say what would have happened if Gamble's men had actually charged. Colonel Elon Farnsworth led two cavalry regiments to disaster and his own death in a charge against Rebel infantry on the battle's third day. When infantry was already in a disorganized retreat, however, as at the 1864 battles of Opequon and Cedar Creek, massed federal saber charges proved quite effective. Confederate Colonel John Hunt Morgan's "Kentucky Squadron of Cavalry" charged a disorganized Yankee skirmish line at Shiloh with good effect, although one participant recalled that "real execution" was only accomplished with "[shot]gun and pistol," while some of the men's attempts "trying to cut them down with the saber" resulted in "ridiculous failures."[12]

The saber charge was usually reserved for cavalry to cavalry combat, however. On June 27, 1863, a hell for leather charge by Brigadier General Robert H.G. Minty's brigade of Yankee horsemen thoroughly trounced Confederate Brigadier General Joseph Wheeler's Rebel cavalrymen near Shelbyville, Tennessee. "Of the 256 Rebels killed and 549 wounded, most [fell] beneath the stroke of the saber." Minty, an Irish veteran of the British army, was such a "cold steel" enthusiast that his brigade was nicknamed the "Sabre Brigade."[13]

The saber was successfully employed at Brandy Station, Toms Brook and the battle of Opequon. One of General J.E.B. Stuart's staff officers noted after Brandy Station that "most of the dead bore wounds from the saber, either by cut or thrust." At Opequon, on September 19, 1864, in the largest and most successful saber charge of the Civil War, twenty regiments of Federal horse soldiers advanced across a field "open and free from obstructions," against the Confederate left flank. According to one participant, the Federal "horses rapidly increased from the walk to the trot and from the trot to the gallop.... The scene as we rode into the rebel ranks baffles description." The Rebels, infantry and cavalry, breaking already from an overwhelming infantry assault on their front, took to their heels.[14]

Despite successes like Opequon, however, one prominent Confederate horse soldier openly scoffed at sabers. Countering the opinions of officers who argued that a saber was "always loaded," John Singleton Mosby believed edged weapons were "of no use against gunpowder." Mosby's partisans, who favored the .44 Colt Model 1860 Army above all other handguns, found rapid fire revolvers ideal for close-range surprise charges on supply wagons or Federal patrols. James J. Williamson, one of Mosby's men, remembered that: "With us the fighting was mostly at close quarters and the revolver was then used with deadly effect."[15]

Many Yanks agreed with Mosby. A Federal officer wrote that his

Captain George Grayson, a Native American officer who served in the Second Creek Regiment, CSA, which fought in the Indian Territory (Oklahoma), holds a Colt navy revolver, a favorite with border warriors. Grayson was temporarily blinded when one of this men fired a flintlock squirrel rifle next to his face.
(Smithsonian)

regiment "had never yet drawn the saber in a charge, and never would charge with anything but pistols." Union General James Wilson noted that "the saber is just as much out of date for cavalry in a country like ours as the short sword of the Roman soldier is for infantry. It is in the way and is of no value whatever in a fight." Wilson placed his greatest faith not in the revolver, however, but in the repeating Spencer carbine.[16]

Perhaps the most significant devotees of the sixgun during the Civil War were the irregular warriors of the border states. In contrast to Mosby, whose men were enlisted in a recognized unit and whose partisan operations had a clear military purpose and value, Kentucky, Missouri and Arkansas guerrillas, whether they professed loyalty to the Union or the Confederacy, were often little better than bandits—a trade many adopted as a postwar career. Like Mosby, however, the guerrillas found sixguns ideal for ambushes, where a blizzard of bullets rapidly delivered at close range negated the range advantages of rifle-muskets or breech-loading carbines.

Men who depended on the revolver as a primary weapon often carried a number of them. Many of Mosby's troopers holstered two

Popular myth has held that Rebel guerrillas switched cylinders on horse-back to reload their revolvers. As evidenced by this disassembled Euroarms copy of a Colt Model 1865 Navy, this is hardly a likely scenario.

handguns on their belts and another two on their saddles. Private Joseph Edwards of Mosby's Forty-third Battalion, Virginia Cavalry, declined to surrender his weapons at the end of the war and rode home with four .44-caliber Model 1860 Colt Armies, a Colt shoulder stock and a Sharps carbine. Rebel guerrillas in Missouri outdid the Virginia partisans and often carried as many as six sixguns. On one occasion, Cole Younger, who fought with William C. Quantrill's guerrilla command, was described as having "four dragoon pistols belted about him." As early as 1861, the infamous Quantrill was "armed with a Sharpe's [sic] carbine and four navy revolvers."[17]

In September of 1864, Federal troopers in Missouri "killed 6 of ["Bloody Bill"] Anderson's gang, taking from their bodies 30 revolvers." Bloody Bill himself met his end shortly afterward, and the Yankees removed "four revolvers, two watches, and about $500 in gold and greenbacks" from his body. When another bushwacker, Bill Stewart, was killed by cattleman W. H. Busford, who he was attempting to rob: "Four revolvers were taken off his person." Although it has been written that guerrillas carried spare loaded cylinders to speed revolver reloading, and this may have been the case on occasion, they preferred multiple handguns to boost firepower. Anyone who doubts this should dissasemble a percussion Colt and imagine himself doing so on the back of a bucking horse![18]

Since the usual Federal issue was one handgun per soldier, Union troops operating in guerilla-infested areas like Missouri and Arkansas, or on the Indian frontier, often increased their personal armament by private purchase. Those who did not occasionally paid the supreme penalty. Lieutenant Stephen Watson of the First Oregon Cavalry was killed in a fight with hostile Indians on May 18, 1864. According to an observer, Watson's men "discharged their pistols and...had no reserve fire" by the time they reached the Indian position.[19]

Given the chance, any sensible horseman in hostile territory carried more than one handgun. William M. Hilleary of the First Oregon Infantry, who cautiously rode up Willow Creek Canyon in October of 1865, admitted: "my thoughts would *sometimes* wander to the ambush that might be here, while at the same time two navy revolvers hung at my sides." Fortunately for Hilleary, the only thing he got to use his navies for was potting grouse.[20] Louis A. Garavaglia and Charles G. Worman report in their *Firearms in the American West: 1803-1865* that a sergeant in the Twelfth Kansas Cavalry purchased ten Remington .44-caliber Army revolvers, one Colt .44-caliber Army and two Remington .36-caliber Navies in a Leavenworth gun store in the summer of 1864. A lieutenant in the Second Colorado Cavalry, a unit operating against Missouri guerrillas, bought seven Remington Armies in the same store.

According to John N. Edwards, author of *Noted Guerrillas*, the Missouri irregulars had an intense relationship with their handguns. Edwards, who also innocently recorded several cases of guerilla transvestism, portrayed one bushwacker disassembling his sixgun who "touches each piece as a man might touch the thing that he loves."[21]

It should be noted here that Edwards, a source on the Missouri guerrillas for many later writers, including ex-guerrillas who plagiarized much of their "memoirs," along with the misspelling of Quantrill's name, from his work, should be taken with much more than the proverbial grain of salt. During the war, Edwards served as adjutant to the dashing Confederate cavalryman General Joseph O. "Jo" Shelby, and was singlehandedly responsible for the purple prose which characterized Shelby's official reports.[22]

Edwards, whose fondness for bourbon was legendary, spent his post-war years as a newspaper editor and apologist for Jesse James, Cole Younger and other former guerrillas turned bandit. *Noted Guerrillas* appeared in 1877, after the bullet-riddled Youngers were incarcerated following the failed Northfield, Minnesota bank robbery. It is largely dedicated to glorifying and exaggerating the role of the James and Younger brothers as paladins of the Confederacy.

Much of Edwards' work, especially concerning Federal casualties and guerilla shooting skills, does not stand up to a perusal of the *Official Records* or the technical capabilities of the cap and ball revolver. Carefully read, however, *Noted Guerrillas* provides much information on handgun use. Edwards interviewed numerous ex-guerrillas and, once the romantic hyperbole is pared away, there is a solid core of information in his book.

Without access to regular supply channels, guerrillas had to exercise a good deal of creativity to supply themselves with both handguns and ammunition. Most brought their personal revolvers to the war, and supplemented them with captures and surreptious purchases. According to Edwards, Quantrill, on one occasion, purchased "an unusually large number of revolver caps, one hundred and sixty-eight new navy revolvers—worth every one of them its weight in gold...." on the civilian economy.[23]

Although most Federal and Confederate regular soldiers were provided with combustible cartridges for their revolvers, the guerrillas were never able to capture or purchase enough of these convenient rounds. Instead, they cast their own bullets and rolled their own paper cartridges, which had to be torn open like musket rounds in the loading process.

Powder, lead and paper were in good supply in rural Missouri. Percussion caps were not readily available, however, and necessitated secret buying trips into larger towns and cities. As late as 1862, many guerrillas were not equipped with cartridge boxes and carried their spare cartridges in their pockets, which must have led to pockets full of loose powder and lead on more than one occasion.

According to Edwards, Quantrill spent time training his riders to fire their revolvers accurately while mounted. This in itself is not singular. The men of the Fourth Ohio Cavalry practiced sixgun marksmanship on horseback in 1861, although it seems doubtful they were ever as good as the guerrillas. Edwards' claim that: "A revolver in each hand, the bridle rein in the teeth, the horses at a full run, the individual rider firing right and left—this is the way the Guerrillas charged," may well be at least partially true, as some guerrillas were noted horsemen. Charley

"Ki" Harrison, one of Quantrill's men, allegedly "practiced that kind of revolver shooting which consisted of drawing and the act of firing." Harrison believed his time of two seconds was faster than almost anyone's. Modern western movies to the contrary, it probably was.[24]

It is extremely unlikely, however, that such quick handgun shooting was ever more than accidentally effective at the ranges of up to 200 yards claimed by the alcoholic ex-major. Edwards' assertions of guerilla shooting ability were given the lie during the James gang's botched Northfield, Minnesota robbery, where the supposed ex-guerilla wizards of the sixgun were slaughtered in the streets by ordinary armed citizens.

It is inarguable, however, that the average Southern cavalryman was a better handgun shot than his Federal opponent. Although rifle target shooting was a recognized sport in the north and gave rise to competent sharpshooter units, the average Yankee, whether a farm boy or urban dweller, was unfamiliar with handguns. A veteran of the First Maine Cavalry recalled: "With revolver in hand, the trooper was more likely to shoot off his horse's ears, or kill his next comrade, than hit an enemy, however near."[25]

There were a few deadly handgun artists in Yankee ranks, however, and one drew the attention of the Federal equivalent of John Edwards. George Ward Nichols, a former Union officer, came across one James Butler Hickock, Federal army scout and man about town, in Springfield, Missouri in the summer of 1865. According to Nichols' subsequent story in *Harper's*, "Wild Bill" Hickock had done in battalions of Rebels with his trusty Colt Navies. Although Hickock was, in fact, a remarkably good gunhand, the reality of his life and abilities, along with those of Jesse James, Cole Younger and other border warriors, gave place to myth. In the years to come, the work of Nichols and Edwards was absorbed into tales woven by bad novelists and even worse screenwriters.

Although revolvers were significant in certain theaters of the Civil War and proved ideal for certain tactical uses, they had no significant impact on the course of the war. The use of the sixgun by certain combatants, however, expanded a legend with origins, like many over the years, in Texas. It was with a good deal of truth that John Mosby claimed his partisans "did more than any other body of men to give the Colt pistol its great reputation." So did Jesse James, Cole Younger, James Butler Hickcock, and perhaps most significantly, John Edwards and George Ward Nichols—Civil War soldiers all.[26]

Collecting and Shooting Sixguns Today

No weapon is as personal as a pistol. And there is no handgun, with the possible exception of the Colt Single Action Army, which evokes memories of things past better than a cap and ball revolver. History literally leaps into the hand of the shooter who draws a bead with a percussion sixgun.

Although the collapse of the Confederacy effectively brought the brief military career of the rifle-musket to a close, the end of the Civil War did not toll a death knell for the percussion revolver. Although challenged by rim-fire cartridge conversions produced by arms factories and individual gunsmiths, the cap and ball revolver remained a state of the art fighting handgun until the close of the turbulent 1860s. The first competitive large-bore cartridge revolver to challenge the dominance of percussion Colts and Remingtons was the Smith and Wesson First Model American .44, which appeared in 1869. The famed Colt Single Action Army .45, which supplanted the popular 1860 in Colt's lineup, was not introduced until 1873.

The reputation of many famous and infamous characters of the post-war "Wild West," including Civil War veterans Jesse James and Wild Bill Hickock, were established with percussion revolvers. Although Jesse later switched to cartridge guns, Hickock carried cap and ball sixguns throughout his active career.

Even with the general availability of metallic cartridge handguns in the 1870s and 1880s, many percussion revolvers remained in use. They were perfectly satisfactory arms for those who did not require a rapidly reloadable weapon. J. P. Stelle and William H. Harrison, authors of *The Gunsmith's Manual*, published in 1883, concluded that "although inconvenient, compared to the cartridge pistol of more modern make, the old Colt's revolver is yet an excellent arm."[27]

It remained so. During the early years of the twentieth century, renowned sixgun savant Elmer Keith dispatched trapped bobcats with an ivory stocked .31-caliber cap and ball Colt.

The revival of muzzle-loading shooting, heralded by the birth of the National Muzzle-loading Rifle Association (NMLRA) in the 1930s, also sparked renewed interest in "the old Colt's Revolver" and other percussion sixguns. The growth of the N-SSA in the 1950s added another group of nostalgic shooters who enjoyed popping away with elderly cap and ball revolvers.

Euroarms reproduction of the .36-caliber Colt Model 1851 Navy. The .36-caliber Colt was very popular on the frontier prior to the Civil War and, although government purchases came nowhere near the quantities of 1860 Army Colts, continued to be popular with individual users during the conflict. *(Euroarms)*

In 1960, Jeff Cooper, the father of modern combat pistol shooting, recruited black-powder shooters to test the sixgun expertise attributed to Wild Bill Hickock and, by implication, the guerrilla riders of Missouri. All of these pistoleros relied on original guns, which were available in a finite and inevitably diminishing number. Navy Arms' introduction of an Italian-made copy of the 1851 Colt Navy in 1959, however, provided a real boost to cap and ball sixgunning. Navy soon expanded its line of reproductions and other firms followed suit.

Every percussion Colt and Remington model (as well as copies of Confederate handguns) has been reproduced with more or less accuracy by some company at one time or another since. Recent years have witnessed the reintroduction of the Rogers and Spencer, a gun contracted for by the Federal Ordnance Department but never issued, as well as the exotic Confederate LeMat, with its underslung smoothbore shot barrel.

Many, if not most, reproduction cap and ball sixguns were bought in a fit of nostalgic enthusiasm, shot a few times, then hung on a wall or stuck in a drawer. Some were put to work plinking at tin cans or rolling rabbits for the stew pot. Others were used in reenactments and living history presentations. A smaller number found their way to the formal target range.

The open-framed Colt Army and Navy were the most popular percussion revolvers during the Civil War. When he fled Richmond in 1865, President Jefferson Davis, who could have obtained any handgun he desired, carried a presentation Colt Navy he had received from Sam Colt in happier days. The Colt is still a favorite with many plinkers and reenactors. NMLRA, N-SSA and International target shooters, however, prefer Remington or Rogers and Spencer sixguns. The latter arms have solid topstraps with rear sight grooves, which provide a better and more consistant sight picture than that offered by the Colt's hammer notch rear sight.

Some Remington-style reproductions are fitted with modern adjustable rear sights, as is the Ruger "Old Army," a modern percussion design. While interesting, adjustable sighted handguns were not used in the Civil War and will not be considered here.

Whatever their sights look like, all cap and ball revolvers are loaded the same way. The usual procedure is: first, disassemble the gun and check to make sure it is unloaded; second, swab the revolver's barrel and each chamber of the cylinder with a dry cleaning patch to remove any residual oil; third, snap a percussion cap on each nipple to burn off any oil remaining in the nipple channels; fourth, load each chamber with a measured charge of FFFG black powder, usually fifteen to twenty grains for a .36-caliber or twenty to twenty-five grains for a .44, followed by a soft lead swaged or cast round ball rammed home with the gun's integral loading lever; fifth, slather grease over the mouth of each chamber; sixth, pointing the gun in a safe direction, slip caps over the nipples. The sixgun is now ready to cock and fire.

Civil War soldiers loaded their cap and ball revolvers with six rounds and let the hammer down on one of the safety pins located between chambers on Colts or the cylinder safety notches in the later Model Remingtons. Since we no longer depend on percussion handguns for

Euroarms reproduction of the Remington .44-caliber Army revolver. The Remington-style gun, with its solid frame and backstrap, is popular with modern target shooters. The .44-Colt 1860 Army, which balanced better for snap shooting, was more popular during the Civil War. *(Euroarms)*

combat, it is safer to let the hammer rest on an unloaded chamber when carrying a holstered gun, whether loaded with blanks at a reenactment or ball ammo in the hunting or plinking fields.

It is also safer and more convenient to carry premeasured powder charges to the field or range instead of loading directly from a powder flask. Inexpensive flexible plastic tubes which hold both powder charge and bullet are sold by dealers such as The Winchester Sutler. Although a revolver can be loaded with a powder flask and loose balls, cartridges of some sort are required for N-SSA competition.

Although some Civil War soldiers, mostly Southerners, may have occasionally loaded their revolvers with a powder flask and others from prepared cartridges made from paper which was discarded in the loading process, most Civil War sixgun cartridges purchased from commercial contractors were combustible. Nitrated paper, "skin," (animal membrane) and collodian were among the materials used to contain the bullet and powder charge in this ammunition, which was entirely consumed on firing. These somewhat fragile rounds were usually packed five or six to a two piece wooden box. Combustible cartridges were sometimes wrapped in individual stiff paper tubes for added protection. Before loading, the tube was opened by ripping off a piece of tape.

A handgun shooter using combustible ammunition simply inserted a cartridge in the front of each revolver chamber, rammed them home and capped the gun's nipples. It was the fastest method ever devised to load a percussion sixgun, and reloading speed could mean the difference between life and death in the turbulent 1860s. Today the chief virtue of original-style combustible rounds is convenience. To craft such cartridges, a paper sheet of the correct thickness and type must be soaked in a proper nitrate solution to insure complete combustion. When dry, individual cartridge papers are cut from the sheet, rolled, glued and loaded.

If you want to shoot combustible cartridges without the hassle of starting from scratch, the answer is one of the cartridge kits marketed by Tom Berwinkle of C.S. Arsenal Works. A seasoned black-powder shooter, skirmisher and reenactor, Tom examined original cartridges, researched arsenal and contractor records and experimented with different types of paper and nitrate solution compositions before marketing his cartridge kit, which is available in .36 and .44-calibers.

Cartridge making with the C.S. Arsenal Works kit is a relatively straightforward affair. First, lay the pattern provided on the nitrated paper, trace it and then cut out individual cartridge papers. If you're lazy and have cooperative children, you can detail tracing and cutting to them. Authentic reenactors should note that children often worked in Civil War cartridge factories!

Second, roll the cartridge paper around the wooden mandrel; third, apply glue to the overlapping seam and smooth down; fourth, apply glue to base, fold over and set aside to dry for fifteen minutes; fifth, drop a measured powder charge in the cartridge cylinder and then insert a ball. A bit of glue around the ball's midsection makes it adhere to the paper and helps to hold the round together. The whole process is easier than it sounds. Although the finished cartridges are, like originals, somewhat fragile, they are sturdy enough for normal handling.

Tom recommends tearing the base of the cartridge before loading to assure ignition and smearing grease over the bullets after loading. Berwinkle's manual provides plans for making wads out of common toilet paper to use in rolling blanks for reenactments. According to Berwinkle, combustible blank cartridges made with these wads go off with a satisfying, realistic, loud bang.

I field tested ball ammo combustible cartridges made from this kit in my Colt .44 First Model Dragoon, made during the Colt "reissue" program of the 1970s and 1980s, and in my old reliable Navy Arms Remington .44 reproduction, as well as my original Remington New Model .44. Ignition was flawless and accuracy was up to usual standards with the dozen rounds I fired from each gun. I was able, as promised, to reload more rapidly than with any other method I have tried. The C.S. Arsenal Works combustible cartridge kit makes revolver shooting a lot easier and is, coincidentally, the most authentic way to go afield with a cap and ball revolver.

Some shooters, including myself, prefer to load .44 cap and ball sixguns with the twenty-five to thirty grain service charge they were designed to use, in order to more closely replicate the historical experience of shooting a Civil War revolver. Many target shooters, however, download to fifteen to twenty grains of FFFG in their .44 handguns. When a ball is rammed down on such a light load, there is a noticeable gap between it and the end of the chamber. Since this situation is not considered conducive to accuracy, most shooters fill the space behind the ball with corn meal or cream of wheat.

Ideally, the revolver ball should shave a small ring of lead off on the cylinder face as it is seated, assuring a snug fit. Most authorities recommend .451-diameter round balls for reproduction .44 revolvers, .454 for orginal guns and, if chambers are oversized, .457. There are, however, exceptions to this rule. The chambers of original and reproduction revolvers often vary from the accepted dimensions. Custom pistolsmith Tom Ball reams the chambers of his tuned reproduction N-SSA approved target sixguns to take a .457 ball. A good rule of thumb is to use the largest ball which will shave lead and still load with a reasonable amount of effort. Shooters of .36-caliber guns will usually find that either a .375 or a .380 ball will fit their guns correctly.

Modern cap and ball revolver enthusiasts generally shoot round balls in their handguns. Although 146-grain round balls were occasionally loaded in .44-caliber cartridges during the Civil War, most such rounds carried 215-grain conical bullets. The heavier, pointed slug was preferred by the military because of its superior penetrating power.

Elmer Keith loaded his original guns with heavy charges of black powder and round balls, which he believed more accurate than conicals. Shooters who wish to try old-style conical bullets in their revolvers can cast them in original or reproduction brass molds. (Wear heavy gloves

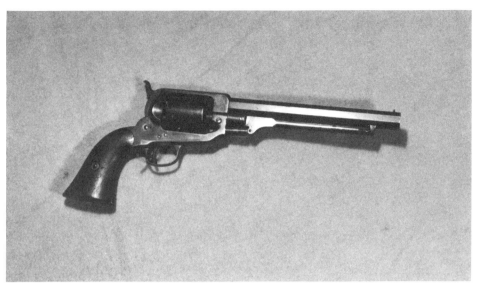

Whitney .36-caliber revolver with New Jersey markings. These revolvers, pur-chased by the State of New Jersey, were issued to officers of the New Jer-sey Rifle Corps and Militia. After the war, some were re-issued to prison guards. *(Neal Friedenthal)*

or wrap the handles—these molds get hot!) Other bullet styles are available from modern mold makers like Lee, Lyman or Rapine. I have found the Lee bullet, with its grooves filled with SPG lubricant, quite accurate when loaded ahead of twenty grains of FFFG in a Tom Ball accurized .44. Although most mold makers also offer round-ball molds, many shooters prefer the convenience of commercially swaged balls, which are available from Speer, Hornaday and other makers in the popular .375, .451, .454 and .457 sizes for .36- and .44-caliber revolvers. For best accuracy, cast balls should be loaded with the sprue, left over from the casting process, facing upward. Swaged bullets have no sprue and are, therefore, faster to load.

The late and lamented Alberts bullet company produced a slightly hollow-based round-nosed dry-lubricated swaged conical bullet for .44 revolvers. These slugs shot splendidly, but alas, the company is no longer in business. The Buffalo Bullet Company, however, markets a similar projectile in .375, .451 and .457 diameters. The Buffalo bullets are lubricated with what appears to be SPG or something similar and come with lubricated-over-powder wads. Although a bit pricey, they shoot quite well.

Lubrication of some sort is necessary to reduce powder fouling and keep a sixgun shooting. A revolver's cylinder pin should be coated with grease and some sort of lubricant used atop each loaded chamber or between powder charge and bullet. Pure vegetable shortening applied to the front of each loaded chamber is cheap, effective and popular, but it has its drawbacks, including a tendency to melt in hot weather.

Commercial lubricants sold by a number of companies also perform effectively and are more heat resistant. Elmer Keith used beeswax and tallow- (the original black powder lube) soaked felt wads between powder charge and ball in his percussion sixguns. The Ox-Yoke Originals Wonder Wad improves Keith's system. Wonder Wads are now available impregnated with the excellent Wonder Lube 1000. Wads are less messy than applied grease and are, I believe, more effective in sweeping fouling from a revolver's bore. The old-fashioned homemade wads, often cut from an old felt hat and greased with tallow and beeswax, occasionally stuck to a ball after it left the barrel, possibly causing a "flier" on a target.

Most shooters (and gun writers) believe that greasing chamber mouths also prevents chainfires, which occur when more than one chamber goes off at once. A chainfire is a decidedly unpleasant and potentially dangerous experience that I, in almost thirty years of cap and ball sixgun shooting with a number of original and reproduction revolvers, have fortunately never experienced. Why and when someone first advocated the use of grease on chamber mouths to prevent multiple discharges is unclear. No one, to my knowledge, advocated such a procedure during the heyday of the cap and ball sixgun. Although the army and navy experienced chainfires with the first lot of Colt Paterson revolving carbines bought by the government, and an otherwise "satisfied customer" ended up "missing a couple of digits on his left hand" from a multiple discharge of his Paterson revolving rifle, Sam Colt always maintained that one of his guns, *properly loaded*, would not chainfire.[28]

William B. Edwards tested old Sam's premise and reported on it in his classic *Civil War Guns*. Edwards' loaded a .56-caliber Colt revolving-rifle cylinder with powder charges and unlubricated snug-fitting minie balls. Without applying grease to the chamber mouths, he covered the rifle's cylinder face with loose powder which he touched off with "a long match." Although the powder "'whooshed' up," none of the chambers went off. Edward deduced that: "A Colt's [percussion] revolver, loaded with proper bullets rammed home, is as safe from accidental discharge as is an ordinary metallic cartridge .38 Police Positive Special."[29]

Edwards believed multiple discharges were caused by "corrosion pitting joining two chambers, or sympathetic detonation across two adjoining caps," or "excess cylinder slap with possibility of shock from the standing breech setting off a cap." He concluded that chainfires resulted from "mechanical defects which condemn the maintenance, not the design" of the Colt revolver.[30]

Elmer Keith learned how to use cap and ball revolvers from cowboys and Civil War veterans who had once depended on them for their lives. He recommended a greased wad between powder and ball to reduce bore fouling—*not* to prevent chainfires. Keith experienced several multiple discharges, but believed they were caused by loose caps, as the "recoil of one charge will jar the cap on another chamber; the flash may get into it and fire a second or third chamber at the same time." Keith also contended that caps that "were too small and did not seat fully, [would] fire the charge of other chambers from recoil which threw them back against the frame of the gun." He asserted that the danger of chainfire could be eliminated by the use of proper size caps.[31]

A friend of mine has experienced two multiple discharges, one in 1979 and another several years later. The first incident occurred with a Model 1851 .36-caliber Navy and the second with a .44-caliber Model 1860 Army. Both guns were reproductions. The Navy's chamber mouths were filled with vegetable shortening and the Army was loaded with Wonder Wads between ball and powder charge. When queried about the circumstances of each incident the shooter could only recall one common factor—the same lot of *loose fitting caps* was used at each range session.

Another shooter reported one chainfire in forty years of cap and ball sixgunning. One summer's day in 1963 he was clearing brush on his Virginia farm when he encountered a rattlesnake, drew his reproduction Remington .44 and fired. Six chambers went off at once, shredding the serpent and shocking the shooter. The Remington was loaded with buckshot which varied in diameter and had its chamber mouths smeared with vaseline. The shooter could not recall how well the caps fit.

West Point Museum curator Robert F. Fisch advises that he "had a three chamber volley" in "a somewhat scruffy [original] New Model Remington" during the 1950s while using .45 revolver bullets pulled from old metallic cartridges. The bullets were not a tight fit and Fisch used no wads or grease behind or in front of the slugs. He believes that, since the chambers of his revolvers were "slightly tapered from wear and erosion," inertia pulled the bullets forward where they became loose enough for flame to leak past them."[32]

Fisch also witnessed a series of multiple discharges experienced by another percussion revolver shooter at a local range. The shooter, largely ignorant of cap and ball revolvers, believed the chainfires were just a part of the cap and ball sixgun experience. When loading his revolver, he had smeared a light coating of grease, which apparently blew out on firing, over the chamber mouths. After investigation, it appeared that the revolver manufacturer had chamfered the mouth of each chamber but left burrs behind. This anomaly resulted in the loaded balls being swaged *under chamber diameter*. These loose-fitting balls moved forward under recoil and, with the light coating of grease blown out the chamber mouths, created a unique situation which fostered frontal chainfire ignition. Fisch reports that "after the burrs were removed this man never fired another volley."[33]

Outdoor writer and black powder expert Robert "Red" Meinecke reports one multiple discharge of a revolver in a long cap and ball sixgun career. Red was teaching a hunter safety course when he loaded up a reproduction Colt Model 1860 Army. Although he emphasized greasing the front of the chambers to prevent a chainfire, he was distracted during his presentation and forgot to do so.

When Meinecke touched off his sixgun at an empty can: "That old army bucked and thundered and spit lead and flame in fourteen different directions. The pop can sailed into the sky and landed about ten feet from where it was originally." On initial inspection, Red discovered that four rounds had gone off at once. A subsequent detailed inspection revealed a crack in the wall of one of the chambers. Although he can't exactly say what caused the explosion, Meinecke now loads his revolvers with felt wads under each ball and grease slathered over the chamber mouths.[34]

After some reflection, I have concluded that Keith was *mostly* correct, and that ill-fitting caps are the source of *most*, if not all, chainfires, providing proper-size balls are used. In order to avoid these incidents be sure to slightly crimp all loose caps before pressing them on revolver nipples. Although Remington #11 percussion caps fit my original revolvers and my "second generation" Colt First Model Dragoon well, I invariably have to pinch caps of any brand before they will fit snugly on the nipples of my reproduction guns. I often wonder why reproduction revolver makers and cap makers don't get together to standardize their products. Good fitting caps should eliminate most of the risk of a chainfire.

Neither Yanks nor Rebs applied grease to the chambers of their loaded sixguns. There are, however, few reports of Civil War multiple discharges. In his extensive research on frontier and Civil War firearms use, historian Charles G. Worman has not encountered any accounts of "incidents of multiple discharges from revolvers." I have only been apprised of one such incident, involving Corporal Eben Pulsifer, First Maine Cavalry, who was transferred to hospital duty after he was "wounded by a double discharge of his revolver, losing two fingers." In order to incur such an injury, Pulsifer must have steadied his six gun by placing one hand in front of the cylinder, a dubious practice at best, as it exposes the non-firing hand to powder blast and lead and cap fragments.[35]

Considering all of the sixgun rounds fired during the Civil War, it appears that the case of the unfortunate Corporal Pulsifer is the excep-

Provided all safety rules are followed and adults closely supervise, young shooters can get an early start with Civil War guns. The author's daughter, Kate "Scarlett" Bilby, at age eight with an original .44-caliber Remington revolver.

N-SSA shooters may officially shoulder muskets at the age of fifteen.
(Joseph Bilby)

tion, proving the rule that tight-fitting bullets and caps should provide ample protection against chainfire incidents. Although it seems unlikely that a spark could enter the front of a revolver chamber and slip past a tight bullet to reach the powder charge, such incidents, given other variables, are, however, possible. The prudent percussion sixgunner should use wads and/or grease his gun's chamber mouths as an extra precaution.

Excluding the misadventure of multiple ignition, well made percussion sixguns, whether original or reproduction, are as inherently accurate as similarly sighted modern handguns. For instinct or snap shooting, the Colt 1851 Navy and 1860 Army patterns, favorites of Yankee horse soldiers and Rebel partisans alike in the old days, reign supreme.

Despite the ramblings of John Edwards in *Famous Guerrillas*, most old-time handgun work got done at very short range, where the well-balanced Colts excel. Within the realistic accuracy parameters of com-

Replicas can shoot! This Euroarms copy of a .44-caliber model 1860 Colt Army fired five shots into one ragged hole, with a sixth shot just outside the group, at a distance of fifteen yards. The gun's forcing cone was reamed to a uniform concentricity by custom gunsmith Tom Ball. *(Joseph Bilby)*

bat-style shooting, they don't do badly at longer ranges either. I can scare the hell out of a tin can at fifty yards with my Colt Dragoon loaded with combustible cartridges crafted from the C.S. Arsenal Works kit. But, then again, the can doesn't shoot back.

The Colts cannot, however, compete with solid frame revolvers for formal target shooting. Some original and reproduction Remingtons are fitted with dovetailed front sights, which make the task of windage (left to right) adjustment much easier than with a Colt-style gun. If a Colt style gun has windage problems, some correction is possible by installing a wider front sight, which may be filed on one side or the other to move the bullet's point of impact. If compliance with N-SSA rules is not a necessity, a Colt barrel may be dovetailed for a movable front sight. This practice was common among nineteenth-century frontier gunsmiths.

Elevation is another problem often encountered with cap and ball revolvers. A perennial complaint voiced by modern shooters against original and reproduction guns in both Colt and Remington configurations is that they shoot too high. This feature was not much of a problem in the 1860s, as revolvers were sighted to hit somewhere on a man-sized target at the longest point-blank range possible. Installation of a higher front sight lowers a gun's point of impact. More recent Remington reproductions tend to have taller front sights, which makes them shoot closer to the line of sight at normal modern revolver ranges.

In an effort to reduce the variables of revolver shooting, some dedicated cap and ball target shooters use only one chamber of their guns in competition. Percussion sixgun chambers, like those of modern revolvers, vary slightly in dimensions. In order to discover your gun's most accurate chamber, number each one with nail polish, then set up an NMLRA six bull target at fifteen yards. Load and fire the chambers from a secure benchrest position in numerical order, one at each of the six targets. Clean the gun, reload, and repeat the process in the same order until each bull has five or six rounds in it. The bull with the best group will indicate the potentially most accurate chamber.

Many percussion revolvers need some tuning and interior parts polishing after purchase in order to enhance their performance. Although I have hazarded a bit of polishing in my time, I generally let professionals or talented friends work on my guns, especially revolvers, which are much more complex than muskets. Knowing what has to be done to tune a gun and then actually doing it are two different things. Work on triggers, which should break at around three and a half pounds of pressure, is best left to a skilled individual. For a complete "accuriz-ing" job, contact Tom Ball.

A tuned percussion sixgun, loaded up with proper powder charges, lubricated wads, soft lead balls or conical bullets and snug-fitting caps, is as effective today as it was 135 years ago, both on the range and in the field. If you're a Civil War enthusiast who doesn't own one, it may be time to fill your hand with some history.

CHAPTER VI

Repeaters

In late May of 1864, Lieutenant Colonel Thomas W. Hyde, a staff officer in the Army of the Potomac's VI Army Corps, found himself leading a catch-all command of a few hundred cavalrymen, most of them troopers of the First District of Columbia Cavalry. While on a foraging expedition, Hyde's force was fired on by a small enemy patrol.

As the boys of the First D.C. responded with a fusilade of fire, the Rebels scooted away. Hyde's attempts to stop the shooting were futile, and the Yanks didn't cease firing until they emptied their guns. The din startled Major General Horatio Wright, who, believing Hyde's men were seriously engaged, rushed an infantry brigade to their support. When it was over, Lieutenant Colonel Hyde found two dead enemy horses, and ruefully concluded that he had had "quite a lesson in the improper use of rapid-firing arms."[1]

The first "rapid firing arms" issued in any quantity in the Civil War were Colt's revolving rifles. Colt's repeating longarms had seen sporadic service in the U.S. army since 1838, when issues of the early Paterson model to the Second U.S. Dragoons during the Seminole War produced mixed results. The Model 1855 sidehammer .56-caliber five-shot Colt revolving rifle issued during the Civil War received much more positive reviews, but has been largely dismissed by modern writers as a failed and obsolete system. In fact, the truth of the matter is somewhat different.

In an 1859 U.S. Navy test, the Model 1855 was fired at a target of unspecified size at a range of 500 yards and only recorded seven misses

---

out of 250 shots fired. The officer in charge reported that, during the test, the Colts "were not cleaned, and sufficient time only allowed for them to cool when hot. They worked smoothly and easy. None failed to go off, and the cylinders showed less [fouling] deposit than usual."[2]

Skeptical of the accuracy of the Colt repeaters they were initially issued, Berdan's sharpshooters "thought at first that these Colts would not shoot true, but this proved not exactly the case, as they were pretty good line shooters." Unit historian Charles A. Stevens recalled that sharpshooter "Andrew J. Pierce...while on the way down the Potomac made a trial shot of the five chambers...at a buoy bobbing up in the river some 400 yards distant," and hit it twice.[3]

Some Colt repeaters, purchased on the open market, were in the hands of troops as early as the fall of 1861. Between November 1861 and February 1863, the Federal government purchased a total of 4,613 .56-caliber revolving rifles directly from Colt. Major General William S. Rosecrans thought highly of the Colt, and called for as many as he could get.

The Thirty-seventh Illinois Infantry ("Fremont Rifles") equipped its "two flanking companies and all non-commissioned officers with Colt's repeating rifle." One soldier declared the outfit's Colts "the prettiest guns I ever saw." They were effective as well. After a year of use the regiment reported that "the Colt's revolving rifles...are of the best quality." A significant number of Colts were still in use by the Thirty-seventh during the final quarter of 1864. Two remained in service with the regiment through 1865. Colts were also issued to some members of the Forty-second Illinois Infantry, and that regiment still carried two of them on its ordnance report for the fourth quarter of 1864. Historian John D. MacAulay lists twenty-six Union cavalry and twenty-nine Federal infantry outfits armed, in whole or in part, at one time or another during the war, with Colt revolving rifles. The overwhelming majority of these units served in the west.[4]

The Second Michigan Cavalry, General Phil Sheridan's first command, used Colt revolving rifles, most likely the ones turned in by Berdan's men, quite effectively in a number of actions, and the Colt armed Twenty-first Ohio Infantry added its firepower to the Spencers of General Wilder's "Lightning Brigade" at Chickamauga. Although ultimately in a losing cause, the Twenty-first fired over forty-three thousand rounds of ammunition before being overrun by Rebels armed with rifle-muskets.

The Federal government purchased 765 Colt revolving carbines and rifles before the outbreak of hostilities. Many of these guns were shipped to state arsenals in the South and were subsequently issued to Rebel units, along with captured Yankee Colts. North Carolina began the war with sixty Colt carbines and 120 Colt rifles, which were issued to state troops. Among other Rebel units armed with at least some Colt repeating long arms were the First Virginia, Third Texas and Thirteenth Tennessee Cavalry, as well as the Eighth Virginia and Eleventh Mississippi Infantry.[5]

There were some drawbacks to the Colt revolving longarms, however. The historian of the Ninth Illinois Cavalry remembered that: "the Colt's revolving rifle was an excellent arm, and had served us well on many an occasion; but there was one serious objection to them; when being discharged they would shoot splinters of lead into the wrist and hand of the man firing." Colonel Berdan's men feared the "danger of all the chambers exploding at once," although this fear seems to have been largely exaggerated. One veteran, who thought there was "but little to choose between" the Sharps and Spencer, and considered the Henry a "magnificent weapon" and "very accurate," believed the Colt revolving rifle "as good or better than any, in the hands of men who are cool and know how to use it." He also noted, however, that the Colt's "loading must be done without flurrying" and it was "a poor weapon to give to green troops on this account."[6]

Outside of the early issue to Berdan's sharpshooters as a stop-gap measure while their Sharps rifles were being made, Colt revolving rifles were rare among Union soldiers in the east. The instrument of Lieutenant Colonel Hyde's instruction was the .44-caliber Henry rifle. The Henry, with its fifteen shot spring-loaded magazine (a sixteenth round could be carried in the chamber) slung under a twenty-four-inch blued barrel, was the fastest shooting small arm used in the Civil War. A lever, actuating a toggle link mechanism housed in a brass-framed action, (some early guns had iron frames) extracted and ejected fired cartridge cases, cocked the Henry's hammer and reloaded its chamber with a simple flick of the wrist.

The Henry evolved out of the earlier "Volcanic" repeating rifles and pistols. The Volcanic arms fired a "rocket ball" bullet with a hollow base containing powder and priming compound. Produced between 1855 and 1860, Volcanic guns, costly, prone to malfunctions and limited in power, never achieved popularity.

Captain Allen L. Fahnestock, 7th Illinois Infantry, poses with his .44 rim-fire Henry rifle. Most Henrys, like those of the 7th, were privately purchased arms. They were the finest short-range combat weapons of the Civil War. *(USAMHI)*

The Volcanic company went bankrupt in 1857, and was reorganized as the New Haven Arms Company by Oliver Winchester.

In 1860, B. Tyler Henry, New Haven's plant superintendent, redesigned the Volcanic action to fire a .44-caliber rim-fire copper cartridge loaded with twenty-five grains of powder behind a 216-grain bullet. (A load with a 210-grain bullet and thirty grains of powder is also recorded.) The rim-fire cartridge, to that date only available in the anemic .22-caliber, carried its priming compound in the outer rim at the base of the cartridge case. When the rim was hit by the firing pin (the Henry had dual firing pins for surer ignition) it ignited the priming compound and the powder in the cartridge. Thus was born the Henry rifle.

Although the outbreak of the Civil War brought with it the hope of contracts for New Haven Arms, Union Chief of Ordnance Ripley, besieged by firearms inventors, crackpot and otherwise, was not receptive

Major General James W. Ripley, Union Chief of Ordnance. Despised by many as an obstructionist of ordnance progress, Ripley actually did a creditable job arming the Union during his tenure. *(USAMHI)*

to new weapons. The general was particularly leery of repeaters, which he believed expensive, wasteful of ammunition and too delicate for active service.

Although Ripley has been pilloried down the years for his conservatism, he faced the Herculean task of equipping a rapidly-expanding army with acceptable small arms. Diversion of funds and manufacturing facilities to the production of unproven weapons was, to the general, simply out of the question. His assessments were often quite accurate. Despite all assurances, Ripley contended that the manufacture of Sharps rifles for Berdan's sharpshooters would shut down the Sharps plant's capacity to produce badly needed carbines for several months. He was right.

Like other armsmakers, Oliver Winchester was not above going over Ripley's head, however, and presentation guns were soon on the way to prominent politicians, including Navy Secretary Gideon Welles. In May of 1862, the navy tested the Henry for accuracy, rapidity of fire and endurance. The rifle performed well, firing 1,040 rounds without cleaning and hitting an eighteen inch square with fourteen of fifteen shots at a range of 348 feet. Following an earlier test, Captain Gustavus A. De Russy of the Fourth Artillery commented that the Henry would be "a most useful addition to the weapons we now have in service." The Ordnance chief of the Army of the Potomac, who believed the "Henry rifle appears to be quite equal to any in service, in the compactness of its machinery and the accuracy of its fire," recommended that the government "purchase a number sufficient for one regiment." Despite the favorable reports, military contracts were not forthcoming.[7]

Had they come, it is doubtful they could have been filled. The first Henry rifles did not appear on the market until the summer of 1862, and by October only 900 guns had been manufactured. In late 1864, production peaked at 290 rifles a month, and a total of only 13,000 were manufactured through 1866. At a list price of $42 with sling when a private soldier's salary ranged from $13 to $16 a month, the Henry was expensive protection. For many it was well worth the price, however, and New Haven Arms sold every gun it made. Although dealers from New York to San Francisco were soon advertising Henrys, most of the first lot went to Kentucky, where the Unionist *Louisville Journal* thought Henrys "the simplest, surest and most effective" way to deal with Rebel guerrillas.[8]

Kentucky armed Company M of its Twelfth Cavalry regiment with the repeaters. Company M's Captain James Wilson allegedly killed seven bushwackers with eight shots from his Henry. Wilson's escapade was widely circulated in promotional literature, but Oliver Winchester admitted privately that although he had heard "some marvelous stories" about Wilson, he did not "feel confidence in their accuracy." Wilson and his troopers apparently did use their Henrys effectively on a number of occasions, however.[9]

Although Federal ordnance officers largely ignored the Henry, soldiers, mostly in the western armies, bought large numbers of the guns at their own expense. In January of 1863, Oliver Winchester reported that most of the 1,500 guns he had produced to date were "sold to individual officers of the Army and Navy." Gil Harbison of the Seventy-third Illinois "sent for a Henry rifle" after his buddy was shot carrying water on the picket line at Kennesaw Mountain. Harbison used his Henry with deadly effect "on or beyond the picket line" to revenge his friend until he also was killed at the battle of Franklin.[10]

Among units wholly or partially armed with privately purchased Henrys were the Seventh, Sixteenth, Twenty-third, Fifty-first, Sixty-fourth, Sixty-sixth and Eightieth Illinois, the Fifty-eighth, Ninety-third and Ninety-seventh Indiana and the Seventh West Virginia, all infantry outfits. Many individual soldiers from other regiments also carried Henrys. One surviving gun was owned by Michael G. Buzard, a member of the First Missouri Engineers.

Seeking replacements to fill the ranks of his Thirty-fifth New Jersey Infantry, which fought in the west with Sherman, Colonel John J. Cladek visited the offices of the Trenton, New Jersey *State Gazette* with Henry rifle in hand. The impressed editor reported: "we have been shown, by Colonel Cladek, of the 35th New Jersey Regiment, a new rifle (Henry's Patent) which he has received authority to purchase for the use of his command." Cladek did not, however, intend to buy Henrys out his own pocket. The colonel advised that a recruit could pay for his Henry with $50 out of his $250 enlistment bounty. Considering that the price of a Henry was $42, it appears that the colonel was not above making a buck on the deal! How many, if any, Jerseymen actually bought Henrys from the colonel is unknown.[11]

Relenting a bit from official policy, the Ordnance Department purchased Henrys for the First District of Columbia Cavalry. The First D.C., a special provost and counter-guerrilla battalion commanded by the mercurial Colonel Lafayette Baker, was issued 240 Henrys in 1863. The unit was later augmented by 800 Maine recruits, who also received Henrys. When the Maine men were transferred to the First Maine Cavalry, they brought their Henrys with them. Individuals in a few other units operating in the eastern theater, most notably the Twenty-third Illinois and the Seventh West Virginia, purchased their own Henrys.

Major General Winfield Scott Hancock assumed command of the First Veteran Volunteer Corps in late 1864. This unit, which only enlisted men with prior service, performed occupation duty in the Shenandoah Valley in 1865. Although never committed to large scale combat, the Veteran Volunteers were considered an elite organization and were issued their choice of arms. Many of these experienced soldiers requested Sharps, Spencer and Henry rifles, some of which had been turned in by soldiers who mustered out of other regiments, like Berdan's sharpshooters and the First D.C. Cavalry, and some of which were new government purchases. The Henry rifle of one Veteran Volunteer, Archibald McAlister, formerly of the Thirty-first Pennsylvania, survived the war and is pictured in John Parsons' book, *The First Winchester*. A total of 681 Veteran Volunteers purchased their Henrys upon discharge.

Old and new Civil War guns photographed at an N-SSA regional skirmish. *Left to right:* Belgian copy of the French Minie rifle, Navy Arms iron-frame Henry reproduction, Austrian Jaeger rifle, reproduction Sharps carbine and Saxon rifle-musket. *(Bill Goble)*

No one who bought or was issued a Henry ever regretted it. Robert L. Mountjoy of the Seventh Illinois pronounced his regiment's Henrys "the nicest guns I ever seen & the handiest to load." Contrary to ordnance worries about the weapon's delicacy, Mountjoy declared "there is not much rigging about them & I don't think they will get out of fix easy." Lieutenant W.S. Coner of the First. D.C. Cavalry reported that his unit's Henrys "carry well, do not get out of order easily, that the lever and spiral [magazine] spring breaks most often, that he prefers small calibers and considers it the best arm in the service." Soldiers of the Sixty-fourth Illinois proudly carried their Henrys in the Grand Review of Sherman's army in Washington after the end of the war: "Being armed with the deadly Henry sixteen-shooters (at their own expense), the men attracted special attention and received frequent cheers."[12]

As with most items of Federal issue, Confederate soldiers issued themselves Henrys by capturing them. Despite the First D.C.'s claim that "with this rifle and plenty of ammunition they could safely meet four to one men with any other arm," during Wade Hampton's cattle raid at Petersburg in September 1864 Rebel horsemen captured 230 members of the First D.C., and presumably their Henrys as well. At Chickamauga, Sergeant Christopher C. Cowan, a Henry-armed soldier in the Ninety-sixth Illinois Infantry, "kept up his firing until the rebel line was but ten or fifteen feet from him, when he was struck by a bullet and fell." Cowan's Henry entered Confederate service, and was recaptured at the fall of Atlanta the following year. Jefferson Davis' bodyguard carried Henrys and Private William E. Bevans of the First Arkansas' Company G recalled that "the commissioned officers of Company G carried captured Henry rifles in place of swords." A surviving Henry is identified as having once belonged to R.H. Bates, Twenty-ninth Texas Cavalry. Henry cartridges, which could not be manufactured in the south, limited the arms' usefulness to the Rebels, however.[13]

Although the Henry won no major battles for the Union, it proved quite useful on a number of tactical occasions. Fife Major Alason P. Webber of the Eighty-sixth Illinois borrowed his regimental commander's Henry to participate in a doomed charge at Kennesaw Mountain on June 27, 1864. Although Webber's Henry did not turn the tide of battle, "his rapid firing in the face of the enemy enabled many of the wounded to return to the Federal lines," and won him a Medal of Honor. The Seventh Illinois' Henrys helped hold the line at Allatoona Pass, Georgia in October, 1864. Despite its apparent effectiveness, no formal tactical doctrine ever evolved for the use of the Henry. Tactics were ad hoc and dependent upon the creativity of field commanders, many of whom had no idea of how to employ rifle-muskets appropriately, much less rapid firing arms.[14]

One wonders what today's politicians, eager to ban "assault rifles," would have made of the Henry, surely the assault rifle of its day. It certainly frightened Governor John Brough of Ohio, who, in 1864, fantasized an uprising by thousands of Henry-armed pro-Southern draft dodgers. Brough frantically telegraphed Secretary of War Stanton with a request to stop sales of the Henry for ninety days. Although Stanton replied that the government had no jurisdiction because the Henry was not a contract arm, the Henry salesman, who protested he only sold to loyal men, agreed to store his unsold weapons in an armory.

Although it terrified Governor Brough, the Henry scared more than a few Rebels as well, like the patrol Thomas Hyde's D.C. boys sent

A Yankee trooper from the 4th New York Cavalry proudly displays his Spencer carbine in this 1864 photo. As the year of 1864 progressed, more and more Federal cavalry regiments were rearmed with Spencers. *(Michael J. McAfee)*

skedaddling. Hyde's concern about ammunition wastage by soldiers armed with rapid-firing weapons, however, was shared by many officers in the postwar years, and the Henry and its successor Winchester arms made more of a mark in civilian (and Indian) than military hands. The United States did not formally adopt a repeating rifle, the bolt-action Krag-Jorgensen, until 1892.

In contrast to the Henry's limited availability, the Spencer became the most used and praised repeating rifle of the Civil War. Christopher Miner Spencer, inventor, manufacturer and salesman extraordinaire, was aptly described by John Hay, Abraham Lincoln's secretary, as a "splendid little Yankee." Spencer, a Connecticut native, embodied all the best aspects of nineteenth-century entrepreneurial capitalism.

Born in 1833, Spencer, who had little formal education, began working in a silk mill at the age of fourteen, where he demonstrated a particular genius for designing machinery. His lifelong interest in fire-arms led to employment with Colt and then Robbins and Lawrence, contractor for the famed Sharps. Spencer also worked on his own ideas and, on March 6, 1860, was awarded a patent on a new type of breechloading repeating rifle.

As with the Henry, the introduction of the self-contained metallic rim-fire cartridge in the 1850s made the Spencer Model 1860 technically possible. The Spencer, with its tubular buttstock magazine, was a simpler and sturdier design than the competing Henry. Although the gun's seven round capacity was less than half that of the Henry, and it was slower to load, the Spencer's .56-56 rim-fire cartridge packed a much heavier wallop than the Henry's .44 rim-fire.

A lever-action gun like its competitor, the Spencer's lever actuated a rolling block that fed cartridges from the magazine into the chamber. Unlike the Henry, however, its hammer had to be manually cocked for each shot. The advent of the Civil War promised a big market to Spencer as well as a legion of other firearms inventors. In the summer of 1861 the inventor secured manufacturing space in the Chickering Piano factory in Boston, and pressed the government to test his prototypes.

Like almost all "patent arms" purveyors, Spencer used any influence available to promote his repeater. Fortunately for him, a former neighbor, who was a personal friend of Navy Secretary Gideon Welles, secured a trial for the new gun. Although the Henry was also tested and both weapons received favorable reports, the Navy ordered 700 Spencer rifles with thirty-inch barrels and sword bayonets.

The army also tested the Spencer and preferred it to the Henry. Ordnance people liked the Spencer's sturdiness, heavy caliber, and relative ease of manufacture, and placed an order for 10,000 (later reduced to 7,500) rifles. Although the army wanted arms in the standard .58-caliber bore diameter, Spencer delivered his guns in .56-56, which was nominally .52-caliber.

There is a great deal of variation in .56-56 bore diameters, many of which are actually .54-caliber. In black powder days, bore tolerances were not considered as critical as today. The charcoal- based propellant "boosted" undersized bullets up to bore diameter, atoning for a multi-tude of machining sins. If a bore was undersized, a black powder driven bullet swaged down to bore size without undue pressure.

Deliveries of Spencer rifles began in December of 1862 and continued through June of 1863. The Commonwealth of Massachusetts also ordered

2,000 rifles, although other contracts delayed delivery of the Bay State guns until 1864. A total of 11,471 Spencer rifles were manufactured, and it is safe to say most made their way to the front during the war.

More numerous were the carbines, with orders beginning in the summer of 1863. Spencer's salesmanship was fully equal to his skills as an inventor and manufacturer, and he toured battlefronts and visited the White House promoting his gun. After a personal test by Abraham Lincoln, the Spencer's future was assured.

Carbine deliveries began in October of 1863, and a total of 64,685 were delivered through January, 1866. In addition, the government purchased 30,496 of the slightly different pattern .56-50-caliber Model 1865 Spencer carbines, made by the Burnside Rifle Company of Providence, Rhode Island. Unlike the Henry, virtually all of the Spencers manufactured during the war years were sold to the government.

Some writers have incorrectly assumed that all these guns saw service in the Civil War, which gives a skewed view of the Spencer's influence on the conflict. Including deliveries of 2,007 carbines on April 3 and April 12, 1865, as hostilities came to a close, 46,185 carbines were delivered by the April 12 date. Adding the 11,472 rifles gives a total of 57,656 Spencers which *possibly* saw combat. All of the Burnside-made guns were delivered after the close of hostilities.

The first Spencer was fired at Confederates in a skirmish near Cumberland, Maryland, on October 16, 1862. The prototype gun was in the hands of Sergeant Francis O. Lombard, a gunsmith friend of the inventor serving in Company F, First Massachusetts Cavalry. It was a while before others followed Lombard's example. Most, if not all, of the rifles purchased by the navy were issued to the Mississippi Marine Brigade. In January of 1863, the army issued Spencers to the Fifth, Sixth, Seventh and Eighth Independent Companies of Ohio Sharpshooters.

Spencers gained their greatest initial fame in the hands of men who didn't wait for the army to issue them. Colonel John T. Wilder traveled east to purchase Henry rifles for his Mounted Infantry Brigade. When the New Haven Arms Company couldn't supply the number of guns he wanted, Wilder, armed with a promissary note for $50,000 from his men, attempted to buy Spencer rifles directly from the factory. In the end, Wilder's men didn't have to pay for their guns, which were issued out of stocks delivered to the Federal government under contract. Eventually Wilder's regiments, including the Seventeenth, Seventy-second, and Ninety-second Indiana and the Ninety-eighth Illinois (the Ninety-second

Illinois joined the brigade later) were armed with a mixture of Spencer rifles and carbines along with Burnside single-shot breech-loading carbines.

On June 24, 1863, Wilder's brigade cleared Hoover's Gap, Tennessee, of Confederates and then held it successfully against a counterattack. Although often cited as a prime example of the efficacy of the Spencer's firepower, the fight at Hoover's Gap is as much a tribute to Wilder's speed of movement and tactical abilities as his men's armament. His brigade overran the single Rebel regiment in the gap and then, supported by an artillery battery, deployed on critical high ground and prepared for a Confederate counterattack. The Spencer-armed midwesterners carried guns loaded with seven rounds and another forty-two rounds in their cartridge boxes. An additional 100 rounds per man carried in saddle bags was not immediately available to the men on the firing line.

Confederate Brigadier General William Bate's counterattack was not long in coming. The Southerners charged the Seventeenth Indiana, which

N-SSA Mid-Atlantic Regional Commander Charlie Smithgall levers a round into his Spencer carbine. The seven-round Spencer fed its cartridges into the action from a tubular magazine in the weapon's buttstock. *(Bill Goble)*

poured Spencer fire into them. The Seventeenth soon ran short of ammunition and was on the verge of being overrun. Fortunately, Wilder's tactical deployment was sound, and the Rebels were raked by flanking fire from the 185 Spencers of the Ninety-eighth Illinois and canister from Captain Eli Lilly's artillery battery. The 650 Grayback attackers lost nineteen men killed and 126 wounded, a fairly heavy percentage, but hardly a massacre. Chickamauga provided a better test of the effects of rapid fire. There is no doubt that Wilder's fast-firing Spencers, along with the Colt revolving rifles of the Twenty-first Ohio, caused General Longstreet to believe he was confronting a much larger force, and helped to save the defeated Union army.

Spencer rifles were first carried into battle in the east by the Fifth Michigan Cavalry at Hanover Station and were later used at Gettysburg in the drawn cavalry battle behind the Union lines on July 3, 1863. General Custer credited the Spencers of the dismounted Fifth with enabling the regiment to hold a crucial fence line against the Rebels. In fact, the Fifth was never directly attacked, although its rapid flanking fire wrecked one of several Rebel charges before the regiment shot away its ammunition. Mounted saber charges by other Union horsemen, the superior accuracy and ammunition of the Federal horse artillery and the fact that some of Stuart's men had to withdraw when they ran out of ammunition were also factors in the fight, however.

Some have credited the handful of Spencers issued to the Seventeenth Pennsylvania Cavalry of Colonel Thomas C. Devin's brigade of General John Buford's division for the stand taken by the Federal cavalry on Gettysburg's first day. This seems doubtful, however. Despite the claims of participants, the Yankee cavalry does not seem to have been heavily engaged with Confederate infantry on McPherson's Ridge, and Colonel William Gamble's brigade took the brunt of the fighting. With 1,600 troopers engaged, Gamble lost only thirteen men killed and fifty-eight wounded. This casualty total includes losses suffered in later fighting, when Gamble's brigade protected the left flank of retreating Union I Corps infantrymen.

Henry enthusiasts might question General Custer's assessment of the Spencer as "the most effective firearm our cavalry can adopt." He was probably correct, however, since the Henry, although a superior rapid-fire weapon, could not be produced in the same quantity as the Spencer. Over the winter of 1863-1864, Spencer carbines began to flow into the field on a regular basis and were issued to a number of cavalry units. A number of infantry regiments were issued Spencer rifles as well. One such unit was the Forty-sixth Ohio Volunteers. In his monograph on the Spencer, John C. McQueen has reprinted, in its entirety, his original copy of a Spencer manual written by the Forty-sixth's Colonel Charles C. Walcutt.

Massachusetts infantry regiments began receiving their state purchased Spencer rifles in the summer of 1864. The sharpshooters of the Fifty-seventh Massachusetts regiment were not issued their Spencers, promised them at their January enlistment, until July. The men of the Thirty-seventh Massachusetts regiment were issued Spencer rifles on their way to the Shenandoah Valley the same month.

Other units received Spencers during the 1864 Valley campaign, including the sharpshooter detachment of the First New Jersey Brigade. Some Yankee soldiers issued Spencers to themselves. When Adjutant Edmund Halsey of the Fifteenth New Jersey took an inventory of his unit's weapons on August 19, 1864, he found one of his infantrymen armed with a Spencer carbine.

Colonel Rhodes of the Second Rhode Island, a featured character in the Public Broadcasting System's documentary on the Civil War, was a Spencer fan. On July 18, 1864, Rhodes borrowed forty Spencer rifles from the Thirty-Seventh Massachusetts to surprise some Rebel pickets who were picking off his men.

On September 19, 1864, at the battle of Opequon, the men of Rhodes' regiment filled their pockets with .56-56 rounds and ran to the support of the Bay State boys of the Thirty-seventh, who had, as General Ripley feared, shot away all their ammunition and were lying helpless under enemy fire. Resupplied, the Massachusetts men rejoined the attack, which was ultimately successful. Rhodes, a gun buff who was president of the Rhode Island Rifle Association in the 1890s, was impressed enough with the Spencer, however, to carry a Spencer carbine as his personal weapon in the closing months of the war.

According to Earl J. Coates and Dean S. Thomas in their *An Introduction to Civil War Small Arms*, thirty-six Union infantry and fifteen cavalry outfits were armed in whole or in part with Spencer rifles and thirty with Spencer carbines during the "1863-1864 time period." By 1865, many more regiments, primarily cavalry, were equipped with the repeaters.[15]

With good reason, aside from its wide issue, the durable Spencer became the most popular carbine of the Civil War. Although they liked their Colt revolving rifles, the men of the Ninth Illinois Cavalry did not complain when they turned their Colts in for Spencers, "a better arm for mounted service." Likewise, the troopers of the Second Michigan Cavalry, who had used their Colts to good effect, were happy to exchange them for Spencers, which the regiment's historian later pronounced "the newest and most effective weapon in the service." An officer of the Ninety-second Illinois of Wilder's brigade pronounced the Spencer "the best arm I have ever seen." Captain Oscar F. Bane of the 123rd Illinois declared the Spencer "superior to any weapon now made," and as august a personage as Lieutenant General Ulysses S. Grant felt the Spencers were "the best breech-loading arms now in the hands of troops." Like all firearms, however, the Spencer had its weak points. Some soldiers considered it too heavy for cavalry service, while others complained that

Although the Spencer Model 1865 carbine, chambered for the .56-50 cartridge, and specifically requested by General Wilson for his massive 1865 raid, was not issued during the Civil War, it remained in active service through the early 1870s, as evidenced by these soldiers in the Lava Beds during the Modoc war of 1870. *(National Archives)*

the rear sight and magazine springs, as well as the mainsprings, had a tendency to break.[16]

These defects were minor and easily overlooked or repaired, however, and Brigadier General Benjamin Grierson requested Spencers for all of his regiments in May of 1864. When Major General Wilson planned his Alabama raid, he specifically requested that all the regiments designated for the campaign be issued new Spencer Model 1865 carbines and Blakeslee quick-loading cartridge boxes. The leather-covered wooden Blakeslee box, invented by Erastus Blakeslee of the First Connecticut Cavalry, originally contained forty-two Spencer rounds in six seven-shot quick-loading tubes, not unlike the old loading tubes used in shooting galleries. Wilson wanted the seventy-shot ten-tube version and believed: "It is with this box as it is with the Spencer carbine, all bad by comparison." When the new Model Spencers were not available in time for the raid, Wilson stripped Model 1860 Spencers from his other regiments to arm the raiders.[17]

Like Henrys, Spencers were effective weapons and, perhaps as important, were great morale boosters. Corporal Zacheus Chase, Colonel Rhodes' orderly, borrowed the colonel's Spencer to go hunting on one occasion and ran into four Rebel stragglers. When Chase covered the Confederates and informed them "that he had seven cartridges in his carbine...they came in quietly." Like the Henry, however, the Spencer, although it may have dominated a skirmish, was not a war winner, or even necessarily a battle winner.[18]

Spencers in the hands of the Seventh Connecticut Infantry repulsed a Confederate assault at Olustee, Florida, in February of 1864, but did not save the battle for the Union. Although Spencers helped cover the Union retreat at Chickamauga, they did not turn defeat into victory.

The men of the Ninth New Jersey encountered "a western regiment, armed with sixteen-shooting rifles" on May 13, 1864 during Major General Benjamin Butler's advance on Drewry's Bluff. Moving in front of the Ninth's skirmish line, this regiment halted, faced to the front, opened its terrible fire for a few minutes and retired," leaving the advance to the Jerseymen and their rifle-muskets.[19]

The Ninth's historian, J. Madison Drake, remembered that his regiment's skirmishers had a quiet night and believed that: "The rapidity of the fire delivered from the [Thirteenth] Indiana regiment just before we moved into the forest must have frightened the Confederates, as neither they nor ourselves had ever before heard anything like it."[20]

In actuality the Hoosiers of the Thirteenth carried Spencers rather than "sixteen shooting rifles" that day. The Indianans and their repeaters failed to turn the tide four days later, however, when Butler's Army of the James was defeated and then "bottled up" in the Bermuda Hundred, where it remained until the capture of Petersburg in April, 1865.

Perhaps the most striking failure of the Spencer to save the day was illustrated by Blazer's Scouts. Frustrated by John Singleton Mosby's constant guerilla attacks on his supply lines in the Shenandoah Valley in September, 1864, Major General Philip Sheridan called for a volunteer force to hunt Mosby's 43rd Virginia Battalion down. Convinced of the efficacy of the Spencer, Sheridan wrote General Christopher Augur: "I have 100 men who will take the contract to clean out Mosby's gang. I want 100 Spencer Rifles for them."[21]

Captain Richard Blazer assumed command of the unit, which immediately began to pick off Mosby's men and guerrillas from other commands. The captain surprised and routed one of Mosby's companies at Myer's Ford. Although Blazer claimed "the seven shooters proved too much for them," his success at Myer's Ford was determined more by his swift movements and mastery of surprise than his men's Spencers. Several days prior to Myer's Ford affair, the Partisan Rangers had wrecked a company of the Spencer-armed Sixth New York Cavalry.[22]

As good a counter-guerrilla warrior as he was, Blazer was facing masters of the art in Mosby's men. His undoing came in an ambush where Company A of the 43rd feigned flight from the dismounted Yankees' rapid-fire repeaters. When Blazer's scouts mounted up to pursue, Mosby's Company B charged them, sixguns blazing. As Company B hit the Federals, Company A wheeled around and attacked their flank. Within minutes, Blazer's Scouts effectively ceased to exist and the captain himself was wounded and captured. Their Spencers could not save them.

By 1864, an increasing number of Confederates, including men of the Second North Carolina Cavalry, the Eighth Texas Cavalry and General Joseph Wheeler's escort guard, were carrying "galvanized" Spencers. Braxton Bragg's army culled seventy Spencer rifles from the Chicamauga battlefield in September, 1863. South Carolina sharpshooter Berry Benson was issued a Spencer on his return from convalescent leave in early 1865. In the final fighting around Petersburg, however, he quickly shot away his forty rounds of ammunition and could find no more. Benson picked up a discarded Enfield to carry during his few remaining days in Confederate service.

Nathan Bedford Forrest was one of several Rebel cavalry leaders whose men captured a number of Spencers which were, no doubt, used with great effect on their former owners as long as captured ammunition held out. In November of 1864 seventy-three men of Brigadier General Lawrence S."Sull" Ross' brigade of Texas Cavalry in Forrest's command carried Spencers. That same month every brigade in the Army of Northern Virginia's cavalry save one reported Spencers in service. One Rebel commander who didn't have much of a resupply problem for his Spencers was Mosby, whose guerrillas captured more than enough ammunition to keep their captured Spencers in action. Even though Mosby's men captured all the Spencers they could use, the men of the 43rd Virginia Battalion still preferred revolvers as their main offensive weapons.[23]

Although some have contended that repeating rifles caused a revolution in tactics, there is no solid evidence to buttress the allegation. Civil War "tactics" manuals were essentially drill manuals, not unlike the old army standby FM-22-5 I carried in my ROTC days. Like men armed with Henrys, Spencer-armed soldiers developed ad-hoc local tactics. The effectiveness of these tactics depended on the creativity of small unit leaders and were never committed to doctrine.

Colonel Walcutt's work details a new manual of arms for the Spencer, but offers no tactical suggestions for the weapon's employment. It does, however, stress fire control. If followed to the letter, Walcutt's drill, in which soldiers return to the "ready" position before levering another round into the chamber, negates to a degree the Spencer's prime virtue—rapid fire. Considering the situation the Thirty-seventh Massachusetts found itself in at Winchester, fears that men armed with repeaters might blaze away all their ammunition to little effect doesn't seem so far off the mark. One Confederate commander recalled that his men didn't mind fighting Spencer-armed Yankees for precisely that reason.

At longer ranges, the Rebels, with their Enfield muzzle loaders, often had an advantage over Spencer-armed Yankees. One Federal officer requested that "the [Spencer] cartridges should be filled with the very best powder—we cannot compete with some of the rebel guns at long range." His request demonstrates a basic lack of ballistic knowledge, which was far from unusual in Civil War officers. No matter what the quality of its powder, the Spencer round was a short-range proposition, for its relatively small capacity case could never hold the amount of powder necessary for long-range performance. In addition, the round's bullet weight and diameter/length relationship further contributed to its inability to perform accurately beyond a maximum range of about 200 yards. The claim of a Captain Barber of the Ohio Sharpshooters that his men armed with Spencers "seldom missed at 700 yards," is, quite simply, absurd.[24]

Some commanders may have exercised considerable fire discipline. The number of relatively heavy Spencer rounds a man could carry, (especially an infantryman) was necessarily limited. In General Wilson's massive cavalry raid in the final weeks of the war, troopers were issued 100 rounds each, with another eighty-five per man in reserve. Considering that a Spencer magazine can (conservatively) be emptied in under ten seconds and reloaded in well under a minute, Wilson's horsemen could have, in theory, expended their whole ammunition supply in half an hour of fighting. Yet a veteran commander considered 185 rounds enough for a whole campaign, and, in the event, it proved sufficient.

Traces of specific Spencer tactics can be found in Wilson's raid, as well as at the battle of Nashville in December 1864. Had the war lasted another year, a true tactical doctrine might well have evolved. Doctrine or no, the growing number of Spencers in the hands of Federal troops would probably have played a decisive role in the Union victory.

The realities and possibilities of the Spencer were soon forgotten, however, and the gun Brigadier General George D. Ramsay, General Ripley's successor as Chief of Ordnance, accurately called "the cheapest, most durable and most efficient" repeating rifle available was eventually replaced in the service by a single shot weapon. Despite its lack of long-range accuracy, the Spencer, like the Henry, was at its best in a rough and tumble close-range fight against superior numbers. a fact that apparently failed to penetrate the military mind of the era. General Custer no doubt rued the day his "most effective firearm" was dropped from the army inventory.

Collecting and Shooting Repeaters Today

Few, if any, people shoot Colt revolving rifles today, but it is not inordinately difficult to pull a trigger on a Henry or a Spencer. Oliver Winchester's factory ceased production of the Henry rifle in 1866, when

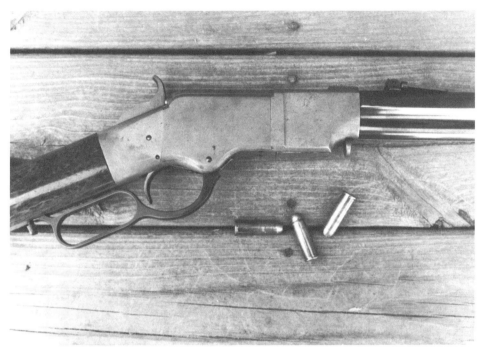

Uberti Henry rifle with .44-40 cartridges. The modern Henry rifle uses center-fire ammunition. The original gun, which this weapon emulates in all aspects save caliber, was chambered for a .44 rim-fire cartridge. *(Joseph G. Bilby)*

the gun was replaced by his namesake model of that year. The Model 1866 Winchester was chambered for the same .44 rim-fire cartridge as the Henry, but had an improved sidegate loading system and a wooden forestock.

Production of .44 rim-fire ammunition ended in the 1920s and by the centennial of the war in which it gained its fame, the Henry was relegated to an expensive collector's curio. The grand old gun gained a second lease on life, however, when it was reintroduced in 1979 by Val Forgett, who has made many old guns new again. Today Forgett's Navy Arms, Dixie Gun Works and other dealers offer Henrys for sale. All are made by Aldo Uberti, the Italian gunmaker known as the "king of replicas."

Anyone planning to use a Henry in authentic reenactments or in the N-SSA breech-loading rifle competition category should buy the military version of the gun, sporting a twenty-four-inch barrel and sling swivels, rather than the short-barreled carbine or "trapper" versions occasionally encountered. Winchester offered a multitude of barrel lengths on its later lever guns, but original Henrys, except for a few factory test samples, only came with twenty-four-inch tubes. Although most modern Henrys have brass frames, Navy Arms catalogs both brass and iron frame versions, the latter a rarity among original guns.

A Uberti Henry buyer has a choice of two barrel and magazine tube finishes, modern dark phosphate blue, or, for a small premium, a beautiful iridescent heat blue. Although historically correct, the latter is much more susceptible to wear and rust.

If I recall correctly, some of the early Navy Arms Henrys were chambered for the .44 rim-fire cartridge, no doubt for collectors who couldn't ante up the cash for an original rifle. I believe there was a limited run of .44 rim-fire cartridges as well, for those collectors who wanted to try out their Henrys or simply—and more likely—to display ammunition with their guns. Once fired, a rim-fire case is useless, for it cannot be practically reloaded. Although Native Americans short on loaded ammunition managed to reload .44 rim-fires by using a solution made from match heads and water, such a practice is extremely dangerous and should not be attempted.

Current Henrys are chambered for the .44-40 centerfire cartridge, a reloadable round introduced for the Winchester Model 1873. The .44-40, with a 200-grain bullet backed by forty grains of powder, was a more powerful round than its rim-fire predecessor. Although not strictly "authentic," this chambering provides modern Henrys with readily available shootable ammunition. Current .44-40 cartridges produced by Remington and Winchester are loaded with smokeless powder and jacketed bullets. Modern factory ammunition is safe to fire in a reproduction Henry, but cannot be used in N-SSA competition, which mandates black powder and lead bullets.

Should you come across any old "High Speed" .44-40 cartridges from the 1920s at a gun show, do not use them in your Henry. This ammunition, which when unboxed cannot be distinguished from ordinary .44-40 ammo, is designed for the much stronger 1892 Winchester. Its use in a firearm of older design like the Henry can wreck both gun and shooter.

Fired factory rounds can be reloaded with lead bullets and black powder to comply with N-SSA regulations. New, unfired brass cases are available from a number of sources, including Midway and Dillon. Bullet molds specifically designed for the .44-40 are produced by Lee, Lyman, Rapine and RCBS. The mold I am currently using is a two cavity Rapine, which throws beautiful bullets.

Bullets for the .44-40 should be flat-nosed, as the primer of a cartridge loaded in a tubular magazine rests on the bullet of the cartridge loaded behind it. Theoretically, recoil of the gun, especially with a primer not fully seated, could cause a chain fire, turning your Henry into a roman candle! This consideration is less critical in the mild recoiling .44-40 than with other cartridges, but the Henry's loading method creates a different problem. A round with a high primer sliding down the magazine tube from the muzzle might go off if it hit a pointed or even round nosed bullet at the bottom. I know of one such incident. Fortunately, no one was injured and the gun was not damaged, but the individual loading the magazine got quite a shock! Because of these possibilities, the N-SSA requires that only flat-nosed bullets be used in competition.

When actually shooting a Henry, be careful to keep your finger out of the trigger guard when chambering another cartridge. If the gun's trigger is inadvertantly pulled, it is possible to fire a round before it is fully chambered. This, in turn, can lead to an unsupported case splitting and segments of brass flying hither and yon, with unpleasant consequences.

Interestingly, most original Henry cartridges were loaded with pointed bullets for better long-range ballistics. With priming compound "spun" into the outer rim of the case during the loading process, the possibility of bullet point detonation was largely obviated.

Casting bullets for the .44-40 is a lot easier than molding minie balls, and, since they are less than half the weight of a musket slug, your lead supply will last a lot longer. A multiple cavity mold increases casting speed dramatically. Once bullets are cast, they must be sized and lubricated. Most people who cast a lot of bullets have a Lyman or RCBS lubricator/sizer. For those who don't, Rapine sells a simple sizer and Lee has an inexpensive lubricator/sizer which works on a reloading press. I size my .44-40 bullets to .427 diameter and lubricate them with SPG lubricant.

The best way to reload cartridges is with a bench-mounted reloading press and reloading dies made by Lee, Lyman, RCBS or one of the other leading manufacturers. A powder scale for weighing charges is also a must. For those with space problems, the Lee hand press, which uses standard dies, does a dandy job.

The fastest .44-40 loading tool in the market is the Dillon "Square Deal" progressive press. A progressive press is like a miniature ammu-

Sutler Bill Osborne of Lodge-wood Manufacturing holds a reproduction Spencer carbine, which was introduced and approved for N-SSA use in 1996. Although original Spencer cartridges used a rim-fire priming system, the Spencer reproduction is chambered for a center-fire version of the .56-50 cartridge, which can be reloaded after being fired. *(Joseph Bilby)*

nition factory, with cartridges automatically rotating through the loading process with each pull on the handle.

The reloading process involves depriming and resizing the fired cartridge case, repriming, neck expansion, powder charging, bullet seating and crimping. A solid crimp assures complete combustion and uniform bullet "pull" and prevents bullets from moving in the cartridge during recoil or the feeding process. With the Dillon progressive press, the reloader only inserts a cartridge case at the press' first station, and inserts a bullet in the case at the third station.

Loaded .44-40s should not exceed 1.592 inches in length. Consistant overall length is important in a lever-action rifle, as a cartridge which is too long or too short can cause feeding problems. Cartridge cases, which stretch on firing, should not become overlong either and should be periodically trimmed. Many reloaders have a special tool for case trimming, but an inexpensive Lee .44-40 case trimming kit, which includes a pilot, shell holder and cutter, works as well.

Although the .44-40 can be satisfactorily loaded with a number of

Author's rifle-musket. A Model 1863 Springfield, with original lock, barrel bands, trigger, guard and buttplate. Barrel and stock are custom reproductions by Mike Yeck. Below are N-SSA style plastic cartridge tubes. One is disassembled to show the simplicity of loading. *(Joseph G. Bilby)*

smokeless powders, for tradition's sake and because the N-SSA requires it, we'll only deal with black powder loads here. If you use a progressive press like the Dillon, *do not* use the integral powder measure for black powder loads! Friction created by the movement of the measure dropping a powder charge might result in an explosion of the volatile black powder. Remove the powder measure, then take each cartridge case off the press at the second station, insert the powder charge manually, then return it to the cycle. When loading rounds with smokeless powder, of course, the measure should be used.

Original folded head .44-40 cartridges were loaded with forty grains of black powder, but modern solid head cases will not hold that much propellant. Although the slightly greater capacity of the balloon head cases accounts for some of this difference, the unglazed black powder generally available today may be more of a factor. Glazed powder, now available again through GOI as their "cartridge" grade, settles better in a cartridge case, increases capacity and leaves less residual fouling after firing. Although slightly more expensive than the normal F grades, it is a good choice for black powder cartridge shooters.

Case capacity doesn't matter as much to target shooters, who generally fire less than maximum loads, most Henry shooters load .44-40s with twenty to twenty-five grains (weight) of FFFG, FFG or Cartridge black powder. This load does not quite fill up the case to the base of the bullet, and needs a filler, like cornmeal or a wad, to ensure proper powder compression and combustion. I use Ox-Yoke dry lubricated or "Wonder Lube" impregnated "Wonder Wads," as they help sweep fouling out the bore. Wads also protect the base of the bullet from gas cutting when the powder charge explodes. The .45-caliber Wonder Wads have to be squeezed into the .44-40 cases, while the .36-caliber wads fit easily and seem to expand to fit the bore on firing. Another type of wadding material, which I have not yet tried, but looks promising, is the "soft check" wax sheet. Thumb pressing the sheet over a cartridge case loaded with powder creates a custom fitted wad.

My own favorite load of a CCI large pistol magnum primer, twenty-five grains of GOEX FFG black powder, .36-caliber Wonder Wad and Rapine bullet lubricated with SPG. It produces benchrest groups which hover around one and a half inches at fifty yards. Magnum primers provide better combustion with black powder, reducing fouling in both gun and cartridge case. Cartridge cases fired with black powder must be washed with soapy water after firing, or they will rapidly corrode and deteriorate.

Although I have never used blank ammo in my Henry, blanks, either plastic or brass, are available from several sources, including Dixie Gun Works and The Old Western Scrounger. One reenactor I know reloads brass blanks, but I imagine he loses a lot in high grass while running around the battlefield.

A fact of black powder life, when shooting muzzle loaders, breech loaders or both, is powder fouling. The black residue may be cleaned by a number of methods, including the old army standby of water as well as a number of modern solvents, all more or less effective. A Henry barrel has to be swabbed from the muzzle, and it is advisable to open the action and stick a rag in the breech when cleaning, otherwise water, solvent and gunk may end up in the action. The use of Magnum primers, Cartridge black powder, SPG lube and Wonder Wads makes cleaning a

Henry less of a task than scrubbing out a muzzle loader. Blanks, no doubt, leave a gun a lot dirtier.

The sights on reproduction Henrys are true to the originals, and the sight picture is just as wretched for those of us whose eyesight leaves a bit to be desired. The rear sight notch, may, however, be opened up and dressed up a bit with a file or a new blank may be fitted, then filed to whatever sight picture seems most effective. Unlike those on muskets, Henry rear sights are dovetailed into the barrel and readily adjustable for windage, easing the sighting in process. The rear sight is drifted in its dovetail to adjust windage, and a ladder provides elevation for longer ranges.

My own Henry shot six inches high at fifty yards with its sight at the lowest elevation, so I levered the pressed in front sight blade up a bit to drop the point of impact. This sufficed for a while, but I eventually

Skirmisher Bob Wierski takes aim with a Spencer carbine. Short barrels and sight radius, combined with underpowered ammunition and improper tactical use, caused the Spencers to be less effective than they might have been in the field. *(Bill Goble)*

replaced the blade with a higher one soldered in place, then filed it down to raise the bullet's point of impact.

Making today's Henrys shoot well the old-fashioned way is both challenging and interesting, even if you can't really "load on Sunday and shoot all week." The rebirth of Henry shooting has just begun, and industrious N-SSA shooters will no doubt pioneer a number of advances in the years to come. Interestingly, the same may be true, on a more limited basis, with the Spencer.[25]

Christopher Spencer's success in the repeating-rifle field proved his own undoing. In the years following the Civil War, the world firearms market was flooded with guns. This led to the curious situation of the Spencer Company competing with itself, as efforts to sell new guns were undermined by the availability of cheap surplus Spencers. Other competition, from the more streamlined, large-capacity magazine Winchester (heir to the Henry) hastened the end of Spencer production. Although some regular army cavalry outfits were issued Spencers following the war, the repeaters were turned in for single-shot carbines with the advent of the Model 1873 .45-70 Springfield.

The Spencer's virtues as an affordable, durable, reasonably powerful repeater, however, made it popular among budget-minded civilians for many years after its military demise. Spencers were still dropping deer east and west into the early years of the twentieth century. For a long time, civilian Spencer shooters were amply supplied with surplus and commercially produced ammunition for their .56-56 and .56-50 guns. The sun began to set on the Spencer with the obsolete cartridge purge conducted by American ammunition manufacturers in the wake of World War I, however. Like the Henry, the rim-fire Spencer was limited to factory-produced ammunition. As the years slipped by, existing stocks were largely expended or deteriorated and by the Civil War Centennial, there were few Spencers firing salutes.

While other Civil War breechloading small arms, including the Henry, Sharps, Gallager, Maynard and Smith carbines have returned to production, at least temporarily, and are seen on firing lines at skirmishes and reenactments across America, the Spencer was not resurrected. American and European replica makers are no doubt capable of reproducing the Spencer, but have not chosen to do so. This writer examined a prototype American-made custom reproduction of the Model 1860 Spencer chambered for a proprietary 56.50 centerfire cartridge at Bill Osborne's Lodgewood Mfg. sutler booth at the N-SSA 1995 Fall Nation-

Skirmisher Robert Myers of the 69th New York also reenacts as a cavalry-man. He is portrayed here in cavalry gear holding his Spencer carbine. The carbine is fitted with an S&S Firearms reproduction center fire-breech block, which allows the rim-fire Spencer to speak again with both blanks and live ammunition. His Blakeslee cartridge box holds a number of tubes, each of which contains a full load of seven cartridges, ready to drop into the Spencer's buttstock magazine. *(Joseph Bilby)*

als. It was subsequently approved for N-SSA use. The gun, which retails for around $1,600, is also available in rifle configuration and chambered for the .44-40 and .45 Colt-calibers. The latter two chamberings will never be eligible for N-SSA competition, but may be of interest to the reenactor, who could fire his Spencer with relatively inexpensive blank ammunition. The .56-50 brass is available from the gun's manufacturer. Those interested in further information should contact Mr. Osborne.

It seems unlikely we'll see a new relatively inexpensive seven shooter from a major replica producer or importer anytime soon, however. Probably the most important reason the Spencer has not joined the replica mainstream is the unavailability of a satisfactory ammunition supply. The Gallager, Maynard, Smith and Sharps are externally primed breech loaders; cartridge-making material and cases, bullet molds and percussion caps for these arms are readily available from sutlers and ammunition is easily fabricated by shooters. The modern Henry can be fed .44-40 cartridges and remain true to its original bore diameter and ballistics, and reloading the .44-40 is a relatively painless procedure. Some shooters have even brought original Ballard carbines back to life by rechambering them for the .45 Colt revolver cartidge and relocating the gun's firing pin from rim to center fire. The Spencer, on the other hand, cannot be chambered for a readily available contemporary car- tridge which even approximates its original caliber.

There is hope, however, for owners of original Spencers who wish to blaze away with blanks at reenactments, participate in N-SSA breechloading rifle competition or simply bust tin cans in the spirit of the 1860s. Dixie Gun Works has long sold brass stock .56-50 cartridges cases, which may work in a .56-56. as well. The Dixie cases are primed with a .22 caliber short *blank* or a .22 short case with the powder and bullet removed, then loaded with black powder and a Spencer bullet. The priming blank must be aligned properly with the Spencer's rim-fire firing pin, however, effectively rendering the repeater into a single-shot.

For those who want to use their Spencers as repeaters, there is another solution. As early as 1967, an article on Spencer centerfire conversions by E. V. Hathaway appeared in the December issue of *Shooting Times*. Hathaway's conversion involved modifying an original upper breechblock. While relatively common when the article was published, spare Spencer breechblocks have grown scarce since. This problem was solved when S&S Firearms introduced a newly manufac- tured Spencer center fire upper breechblock. The hardened steel block, no doubt stronger than the original, is N-SSA approved, comes complete with spring-loaded firing pin (an improvement on the original) and sells for $100. It is available for all Spencer models, although minor fitting may be required for some guns. Since installation of the S&S breechblock does not require any firearm modification, a Spencer owner who wishes to shoot his rifle or carbine may retain his original breechblock and the collectible value of his gun.

I have never subscribed to the belief that all original antique guns are too fragile or valuable to shoot. As long as reasonable care and common sense are exercised, shooting original guns will not degrade their value, unless they are in "factory new" condition. Each gun is an individual case, however, and should be evaluated for safety by a good gunsmith before firing.

Once he installs a centerfire breechblock in his rifle or carbine, the potential Spencer shooter has to craft serviceable ammunition. Cartridges are usually made from .50-70 cartridge cases, although John C. McQueen reports using 11mm Spanish cases successfully. The major American ammunition makers have long since ceased production of .50-70 cartridges, but Dixie Gun Works sells new .50-70 brass at a reasonable price. Before discussing the creation of modern Spencer cartridges, however, a brief word on original ammunition is in order.

Civil War Spencers were chambered for the "Number 56" or .56-56 rim-fire cartridge, developed by the inventor, Christopher Spencer. Unlike many nineteenth century cartridge designations, the numbers do not indicate bullet or bore diameter or powder charge. They represent the outside dimensions, in hundreths of an inch, of the cartridge case's base and mouth. The diameter of the .56-56's 350 grain bullet was a nominal .52-caliber (most are actually around .54-caliber) and, like a modern .22 rim-fire, was held in the case by a "heel" at the bullet base. Most of the bullet's length, including the lubrications grooves, was exposed. A charge of forty-five grains of black powder gave the round a muzzle velocity of around 1,200 feet a second.

In 1864, Springfield Armory developed a new cartridge for the Model 1865 Spencer, a lighter gun than the Model 1860. This slightly tapered, heavily crimped round was dubbed the .56-50. A nominal .50-caliber, the .56-50 was shorter overall than the .56-56, but had a longer case, which protected the bullet's lubrication grooves. The .56-50's bullet weight and powder charge were identical to the .56-56, although the armory-designed round had a slightly higher velocity.

To complicate things, Christopher Spencer, who felt the .56-50 had an excessive crimp, designed his own somewhat bottlenecked version of the cartridge, and called it the .56-52. In addition, after the war a number of .56-56 carbines had their barrels sleeved for the .56-50/.56-52 cartridge. Both the .56-50 and the .56-52 are interchangeable with each other but, theoretically, not with the .56-56.

To further complicate matters, commercial .56-52 ammunition can be fired in .56-56-caliber guns. Neal Friedenthal of the N-SSA's Fifteenth New Jersey Infantry reports buying twenty rounds of commercially manufactured .56-52 cartridges (at collector's prices) in the early 1980s and shooting them in his .56-.56 carbine. Although the undersized cases, manufactured around 1920, split on firing, Friedenthal recalls that the ammunition gave reasonably good accuracy in his gun at fifty yards. I can categorically state that any attempts to shoot nineteenth century ammunition in a Spencer are not only prohibitively expensive, they are doomed to failure. Priming compounds have deteriorated over the years and they will not fire. If you want to shoot a Spencer today, conversion is the way to go.

To make Spencer centerfire ammunition, .50-70 brass must be shortened. Case dimensions for an individual gun may have to be calculated by having a gunsmith make a sulphur chamber cast. Another alternative is to cut and try the .50-70 case a little at a time until it fits the chamber. Once proper length is established, succeeding cases can be cut to match. According to Phil Siess of S&S, cases may be trimmed on a lathe or by sliding them over a half inch dowel and using a tubing cutter. A sheet provided by S&S with their breechblock details dimensions and provides instructions concerning trim and overall length for .56-56 and .56-50 guns. Overall cartridge length is critical in the Spencer, as incorrect length often leads to feeding problems.

Interior dimension of an individual gun's barrel may be obtained by "slugging" the bore, or driving a slightly oversize piece of soft lead down the barrel with a brass rod. The resultant slug mirrors the bore and should be measured with a micrometer. Rapine, Inc. makes Spencer molds in three different bullet diameters: .520, .535 and .546, and six different bullet weights. Two of the Rapine designs are "heeled" like the original .56-56 slug and, when loaded, expose most of their bearing surface beyond the cartridge case.

Most shooters prefer bullets .001 to .002 over groove diameter. If you can't find a Rapine mold that throws the exact diameter you want, then choose one slightly oversize. The bullets, cast from lead, may then be sized to the proper diameter with sizing dies available from Rapine or S&S. They should also be lubricated. A good choice is SPG lubricant. Rapine designs differ in one notable respect from original bullets; they are flat nosed. As with the Henry, original Spencer rounds were loaded with pointed bullets which rested on the center of preceding cartridges in the gun's tubular magazine. With the volatile priming compound contained in the rim of the Spencer's rim-fire ammunition, this was not normally a problem. There is, however, at least one recorded incident of a Spencer exploding shortly after the Civil War when recoil set off a cartridge and detonated the whole magazine. No doubt some priming compound slopped over to the center of the cartridge when it was loaded at the factory.

Such an incident is far more serious than a similar one with the Henry rifle, as the Spencer magazine rests alongside the shooter's head. Oliver Winchester was quick to point this fact out in a letter to then chief of Ordnance Brigadier General Alexander B. Dyer in 1865: "On this point we claim that our rifle is superior. No accident to life or limb has ever occurred to those using it; while the contrary has been the fact in regard to the 'Spencer.' If a charge should explode in the magazine, it would pass out in the direction of the muzzle of the gun without injury; whereas, in the 'Spencer,' there is constant danger, if such an accident should happen, the person using the rifle would receive the injury."[26]

Because of such a possibility, heightened with centerfire primers, flat nosed bullets and flat-nosed magazine followers are required for Spencers used in N-SSA competition. Along with centerfire breech-blocks, S&S Firearms stocks flat-nosed Spencer followers and a wide variety of original and reproduction parts. The company is a veritable one stop shop for everything needed to repair, rebuild or shoot a Spencer.

The easiest part of crafting Spencer ammunition is the assembling of the components into finished cartridges. Empty cases should be primed with a standard large rifle primer, using a .50-70 shell holder in a reloading press or priming tool. Centerfire Spencer cartridges will not hold a full forty-five grains of unglazed FFG powder, although they will probably take a full load of GOI glazed cartridge-grade black powder. Most shooters load thirty to thirty-five grains of FFG and fill any void between the base of the bullet and the powder charge with a filler like cornmeal. Wads cut from old milk cartons will provide the same function and help sweep fouling from the barrel. The original-style Rapine "heeled" bullet can be hand seated but should be secured in the case with silicone adhesive or a similar cement.

Spencer cartridge cases expand to fit the chamber of the gun they were fired in, and, as long as they are fired again in the same gun, do not need to be resized. They should be washed with soap and water after firing and before reloading to remove corrosive black powder residue. The amount of this residue is significantly reduced by the use of GOI cartridge grade powder. A quick wash and a trip through a tumbler will polish the cases like new.

For an in-depth look at Spencer centerfire cartridge creation, see Stephen F. Blancard's "Christopher Spencer's Horizontal Shot Tower," which appeared in the late and much lamented *Black Powder Report* magazine in September of 1985. Written before the availability of the

The N-SSA boasts a wealth of historical knowledge in its ranks. N-SSA commander Earl J. Coates *(left)*, a uniform and small arms expert, confers with the organization's artillery officer Charles Smithgall on the set of the movie *Gettysburg*. Smithgall coordinated the artillery for the film. *(Joseph Bilby)*

new Rapine "heeled" bullets, Blancard's case length dimensions are based on use of the old .50-70 slug. Case length will be different when bullets cast with a Rapine mold are used.

The reenactor who just wants to shoot blanks in his centerfire conversion has a much easier task. Easily reloadable brass and plastic blank cartridge cases are available, complete with loading instructions, from Lodgewood Mfg., S&S Firearms and other dealers.

You'd be hard put to find a Civil War veteran to talk to today but, with a little time and effort, you can make a veteran Spencer, mute for generations, speak with authority and accuracy. If for no other reason than to atavistically return to those heady days of the 1860s—shoot that Spencer!

Supply and Information Sources for Civil War Shooters

Battlefield Video Productions, PO Box 239, East Texas, PA 18046. The source for "Guns That Shaped a Nation," a forty-seven minute video which provides an excellent introduction to Civil War weapons, the men who made them and the men who used them. Video is $29.95 postpaid.

Ball Accuracy Inc., RD #1, Box 241, Millville, PA 17846. Custom gunsmith work on percussion revolvers, rebarreling and uniform chamber reaming on Remington and Rogers and Spencer revolvers. Complete gunsmithing services for all kinds of firearms. (717) 458-5197.

Nick Brevoort, 607 Eversole Rd., Cincinnatti, Ohio 45230. Custom rifle-musket parts for assembling custom guns, including Confederate models.

F. Burgess & Co., 200 Pine Place, Red Bank, NJ 07701. Top quality leather goods, specializing in holsters and other cavalry gear. Catalog $3.

The Civil War News, Rte. 1, Box 36, Tunbridge, VT 05077. The only national publication with two columns, by Joseph Bilby and Tom Kelley, devoted to Civil War firearms and shooting. The *News* also covers every conceivable aspect of interest to today's Civil War enthusiast, including book reviews, reenactments, living history and battlefield preservation. Subscriptions: $24 per year. 1-800-222-1861.

The Cavalry Shop, 9700 Royerton Rd., Richmond, VA 23228. Civil War leather goods, shooting and cleaning supplies. GI-style cleaning patches at reasonable prices are highly recommended. Catalog $1. (804) 266-0898.

Dillon Precision Products, 7442 E. Butherus Dr., Scottsdale, AZ 85260. Source of the .44-40 "Square Deal" progressive reloading machine, which makes life a lot easier for a Henry shooter, as well as .44-40 bullets and cartridge cases. 1-800-223-4570.

Dixie Gun Works, Gunpowder Lane, Union City, TN 38261. Reproduction imported rifles, rifle-muskets and muskets of all types and manufacturers, including the Dixie Sharps rifles and carbines, bullet molds, spare parts, cartridge tubes, leather goods and much more. Catalog (600 pages with 8,000 items) $4. Dixie has a large retail store selling all catalog items as well as original antique arms at the above address. Toll free order line 1-800-238-6785.

R.A. Hoyt, Freishutz Shop, 700 Fairfield Station Rd., Fairfield, PA 17320. Custom barrels for muskets and rifles, relining and rerifling original barrels, extension and relining of cut down original barrels. Also relining of breech-loading carbines, round-ball and cartridge rifles.

C&D Jarnigan Company, Historical Supply, Route 3, Box 217, Corinth, MS 38834. Authentic cartridge boxes, slings and other leather goods, as well as a complete range of uniforms. Catalog $3. (601) 287-4977 / (601) 287-6033. (FAX)

C.S. Arsenal Works, Rt. 1, Box 418, Clarksburg, WV 26301. Combustible .36 and .44-caliber revolver cartridge kits, including a turned and tapered cartridge former, cartridge template, glue stick, enough nitrated paper to make 100 cartridges and an instructional manual. Kit is $9.95 postpaid.

Larry Gollahon, 5725 Wayside Ave., Cincinnatti, OH 45230. Reproduction Smith and Maynard carbine parts. List SASE.

Jensco Restorations, Inc., 1611 Granger Road, Garfield Heights, Ohio

44125. Original and reproduction parts, 33" replacement barrels for "Zouave" rifles and "artillery model" rifle-muskets.

J&J Limited, 4 Summer Street, Scituate, MA 02066. SPG lubricant, reproduction Henry slings and cleaning rods, wax wads and other shooting supplies.

Lodgewood Mfg. William Osborne, Proprietor, 494 Ventura Lane, Whitewater, WI 53190. Original and reproduction parts for all U.S. Martial arms, 1780-1898, cartridges for caplock breech-loading carbines, Agent for reproduction Spencer rifles and carbines, and more. (414) 473-5444 / (414) 473-8970 (FAX)

Lyman, Rte. 147, Middlefield, CT 06455. The original source for minie-ball molds, Lyman still catalogs a number of styles, as well as other black powder shooting products. Catalog $2. Toll free information 1-800-22-LYMAN.

Midway, 5875 C. W. Van Horn Tavern Road, Columbia, MO 65203. Source for .44-40 cases for Henry shooters, Lee and other reloading products. Catalog free. 1-800-243-3220.

Navy Arms Company, 689 Bergen Blvd., Ridgefield, NJ 07657. Reproduction revolvers, rifle-muskets, Henry rifles, Sharps rifles and carbines, including the double set trigger "Berdan" Model, Smith carbines and Lemat revolvers, as well as a complete line of surplus military and modern sporting firearms. Catalog $2. Navy Arms has a retail establishment at the New Jersey address as well as on Hoffman Rd., Martinsburg, WV (right off Rte. #81) (201) 945-2500 (NJ) / (304) 274-0308 (WV)

National Muzzle-loading Rifle Association, PO Box 67, Friendship, IN 47021. The largest organization catering to the needs of muzzle-loading shooters. Rifle-musket shooting is part of the association's match program. Monthly magazine, *Muzzle Blasts*. Annual dues $30.

North-South Skirmish Association. The organization that started it all. For information on joining an N-SSA unit or forming one of your own, write Phil Spaugy, 501 N. Dixie Drive, Vandalia, Ohio 45377.

October Country, PO Box 969, Hayden Lake, ID. While primarily a "buckskinner" source, October Country sells a wide variety of cleaning rods and attachments useful for the rifle-musket shooter. The company is also a source for round balls in various sizes up to .690, for those with a yen to shoot a Civil War smoothbore musket. Catalog $3. (208) 772-2608.

Old Sutler John, PO Box 174, Westview Station, Binghamton, NY 13905. Rifle-muskets, shooting supplies, bayonets, leather goods, uniforms and more. Catalog and price list $2. (607) 775-4434.

Rapine Bullet Mold Company, Box 1119, Rd. #1, East Greenville, PA 18041. Various styles of molds for rifle-muskets, rifled muskets, smooth-bores, Henry and Spencer rifles, revolvers, caplock breech-loading carbines as well as incremental sizing dies. Catalog $2.

Regimental Quartermaster, Box 533, Hatboro, PA 19040. Reproduction (and some original) guns of all types, carbine cartridge cases, cartridge tubes, molds and other shooting supplies and accoutrements as well as books, uniforms, tentage and other Civil War reproduction goods. Catalog $2. (215) 672-6891 / (215) 672-9020 FAX.

S&S Firearms, 74-11 Myrtle Ave., Glendale, NY 11385. Original and reproduction parts for U.S. firearms 1795-1903, lockplates, barrels and stocks for custom guns, shooting supplies, sizing dies, Spencer conversion breechblocks, Euroarms rifle-muskets and the S&S Model 1855 Springfield rifle-musket and Richmond carbine.

Gerhardt P. Vikar, 50261 Bower, New Baltimore, MI 48047. Quality custom-made Civil War rifles and rifle-muskets. Reproduction of rare and unavailable parts if customer has broken part or dimensions.

Dan Whitacre, 519 Turtle Meadow Dr., Winchester, VA 22602. Custom barrels for .58-caliber rifle-muskets, .69-caliber Model 1842 rifled muskets and .69-caliber Model 1842 smoothbores. (540) 877-1468

Winchester Sutler, 4154 Hunting Ridge Rd., Winchester, VA 22603. Rifle-muskets, carbines, revolvers, full line of cartridge tubes, bullet molds, shooting and cleaning supplies. Catalog $3. (703) 888-3595 (noon to 10:00 PM).

Wolf's Western Traders, HC 59, Box 65, Edgemont, SD 57735. Source for *Loading Cartridges for the Original .45-70 Springfield*, which is $16.95 plus $1.95 shipping. Book is an excellent source of ballistic lore for rifle-musket and Civil War carbine shooters as well as .45-70 buffs. Wolf's also catalogs a number of goodies for black powder cartridge shooters.

Notes

In order to avoid clutter, notes have been restricted to those identifying the sources of direct quotes and information which, while pertinent, would be out of place in the text. Citations have been abbreviated. For full titles of sources, please see the bibliography.

CHAPTER I

1. Blackmore, *British Military Firearms*, p. 226; Lewis, *Small Arms and Ammunition*, p. 113; Blackmore, p. 226.
2. Willard, *Rifled and Smooth-Bored Arms*, p. 4.
3. Peterson, *Book of the Continental Soldier*, pps. 60-61.
4. Roberts, *Muzzleloading Caplock Rifle*, p. 185.
5. Baumann, *Arming the Suckers*, p. 83.
6. Ibid, p. 72. As late as the end of 1862, the Eighth carried a wide variety of arms, including smoothbore and rifled .69-caliber muskets.
7. Ibid, p. 89.
8. Willard, *Rifled and Smoothbore Arms*, p. 3.
9. *Sussex* (NJ) *Register*, May 15, 1863.
10. Newark (NJ) *Advertiser*, May 21, 1862; Willard, *Rifled and Smooth-Bored Arms*, p. 13.
11. Mulholland, *116th Pennsylvania*, p. 33.
12. Longacre, *To Gettysburg and Beyond*, p. 57.
13. Roe, *Monocacy*, p. 14; O'Grady, "88th Regiment," *New York at Gettysburg*. p. 513.
14. Statistics from Griffith, *Battle Tactics*, p. 76, and Daniel, *Soldiering in the Army of Tennessee*. pp. 45, 47.
15. Ladd, ed. *The Bachelder Papers*, Vol. III, p. 1402.

16. Starr, *Union Cavalry*, Vol. I, p. 219.

17. Brown, ed., *One of Cleburne's Command*, p. 13.

18. Oates, *Confederate Cavalry West of the River*, p. 66, 71; *OR*, Ser. I, Vol. XIII, p. 898.

19. Edwards, *Noted Guerrillas*, p. 62.

20. Peter W. McDaniel to L. P. Walker, August 23, 1861, possession of Martin J. Anton Jr.

21. Lewis, *Small Arms and Ammunition*, p. 126; Mallet's assignment may have been related to the production of guard cartridges rather than ammunition intended for combat. The smaller bore of the .577 Enfield would have accommodated fewer buckshot than the smoothbore.

22. Bruce, *Lincoln and the Tools of War*. p. 53.

23. Lewis, *Small Arms and Ammunition*, p. 149.

24. A "cook off" is a premature explosion of a powder charge dropped down the muzzle of a muzzle-loading gun.

25. Baumann, *Arming the Suckers*, p. 142; Paterson (NJ) *Guardian*, May 16, 1862.

CHAPTER II

1. Boatner, *Encyclopedia of the Revolution*, p. 935.

2. According to the *Oxford English Dictionary* (*OED*), the term "sniping" was used in India as early as 1773. In 1821, British troops complained that they were subjected to "a sniping fire from neighbouring walls." The *OED* defines a sniper as: "One who snipes, or shoots from concealment." The term was not widely used, however, until the latter part of the nineteenth century. Although not used during the Civil War, "sniper" will be used in this work to distinguish soldiers who were detailed to pick off enemy soldiers at long range from those who were "sharpshooters" who served as skirmishers.

3. Myatt, *19th Century Firearms*, p. 52.

4. To avoid confusion, for the purposes of this study the conical hollow-based projectiles fired in rifle-muskets will be referred to in the future as "minie balls."

5. The Model 1841 rifle gained the popular name "Mississippi" because of its deft use by Colonel Jefferson Davis' Mississippi rifle regiment in the Mexican War.

6. Philip H. Smith to uncle, [Frederick Canfield] July 20, 1862, Canfield Pickerson Family Papers NJHS.

7. Mallet, "Work of the Ordnance Bureau," SHSP, p. 1; Ripley, *Annual Report*.

8. As might be expected, there were a number of cases of incompetence and some of outright fraud among the contractors. For details see Edwards, *Civil War Guns*, pp. 25 - 64.

9. Mallet, "Work of the Ordnance Bureau" p. 13.

10. *Warren* (NJ) *Journal*, May 3, 1861; Bellard, *Gone for a Soldier*, p. 7.

11. Crow, *Storm in the Mountains*, p. 7.

12. Baird, ed., *Creek Warrior*, p. 102.

13. Baumann, *Arming the Suckers*. p. 75. It is possible that the problem lay with bad percussion caps, rather than weak mainsprings.

14. Penrose to Major General John Sedgwick, June 24, 1863, Regimental Correspondence Book, Fifteenth NJ Infantry, NA.

15. Ibid. Enfields are marked "25" or "24" on their barrels to differentiate gauge.

16. *OR*, Ser. I, Vol. XXX, Pt. 2, p. 277.

17. Vandiver, *Ploughshares into Swords*, p. 190.

18. *Hunterdon* (NJ) *Republican*, July 24, 1863.

19. Ryerson to sister, May 3, 1864, NJHS.

20. Colby, "Memoirs of Military Service"; Haines, *Fifteenth New Jersey*, p. 94.

21. Neff, "The Enfield Rifle," *Muzzle Blasts*, July, 1979; Brown, *Morgan's Raiders*, p. 69.

22. Edwards, *Civil War Guns*, p. 262.

23. Vandiver, *Ploughshares into Swords*, p. 93.

24. Bellard, *Gone for a Soldier*, p. 38; Davis, *History of the 104th Pennsylvania*, p. 36; *History of the Twenty-Third Pennsylvania*, p. 127; Baumann, *Arming the Suckers*, p. 147.

25. Baumann, *Arming the Suckers*, pp. 181, 189, 197 and 211.

26. Ibid, pp. 216, 221.

27. Doylestown (Pennsylvania) *Democrat*, July 12, 1863. Copy courtesy Bill Adams.

28. Baumann, *Arming the Suckers*, p. 98.

29. Ibid, p. 107.

30. Ibid, p. 176. Woodruff's memoir, dating from 1876, so thoroughly trashes the Austrian weapon that it may well be suspect as an "old soldier" yarn.

31. Statistics from Daniel, *Soldiering in the Army of Tennessee*, pp. 46-47.

32. Mallet, "Work of the Ordnance Bureau," pps. 7-8.

33. New Jersey *Quartermaster General's Report* for 1862, p. 10.

34. Ibid.

35. Robertson, *Soldiers Blue and Gray*, p. 55.

36. New Jersey *Quartermaster General's Report* for 1862, p. 11.

37. Robertson, *Soldiers Blue and Gray*, p. 56; Colby, "Memoirs of Military Service." Colby may have forgotten the type of musket his regiment was issued as well. Ordnance reports list the Ninety-seventh with American smoothbores.

38. Robertson, *Soldiers Blue and Gray* p. 56. As with stories of exploding and overweight muskets, there may well be some exaggeration here.

39. Marbaker, *History of the Eleventh New Jersey*, p. 175.

40. Benson, *Civil War Book*, p. 33.

41. Gibbon, *Artillerist's Manual*, pp. 221-222.

42. DeForest, *Volunteer's Adventures*, p. 64

43. Foster, *New Jersey in the Rebellion*, p. 168.

44. Casey, *Infantry Tactics*, p. 47.

45. In fact, the Austrians had more rifle-muskets in the ranks than did the French, who still armed many line outfits with smoothbores.

46. Casey, *Infantry Tactics*, p. 6.

47. Robert McAllister to wife, September 19, 1862, *McAllister Letters*, p. 209.

48. *OR*, Ser. I, Vol. X, Pt. II, pp. 368-369.

49. Maryniak, "Shooting Practice."

50. Ryerson to sister, August 20, 1861, NJHS.

51. Neff, "The Enfield Rifle; Ich B? to dear parents, May 1, 1862, copy courtesy Bill Adams; Quoted in Wiley, *Billy Yank*, p. 63.

52. Beaudot & Herdegen, eds., *An Irishman in the Iron Brigade*, p. 95.

53. O'Grady, "88th New York," *New York at Gettysburg*, p. 513.

54. Newark (NJ) *Journal*, November 30, 1863.

55. Benjamin D. Coley Diary, NJHS.

56. Letter and Correspondence Book, Fifteenth New Jersey Infantry, NA.

57. William C. Clark Diary, John Kuhl Collection; Nelson & Onstad, eds., *A Webfoot Volunteer*, p. 53.

58. Willard, *Rifled and Smooth-Bored Arms*, pp. 5, 12.

59. War Department, *A System of Target Practice*.

60. Scribner, *How Soldiers Were Made*, p. 227. The men of Scribner's regiment and the 24th Illinois, also part of the brigade he commanded, were largely armed with Enfields, which were sighted up to 900 yards.

61. British army "Annual Target Practice Return" form, Bill Adams collection.

62. Purdue, *Pat Cleburne*, p. 187.

63. *OR*, Ser. I, Vol. XXIII, p. 490.

64. Alberts, ed. *Rebels on the Rio Grande*, p. 44.

65. Drake, *Ninth New Jersey*, p. 10.

66. *OR*, Ser. I, Vol., Pt. P. 205.

67. Edwards, *Civil War Guns*, p. 264.

CHAPTER III

1. Sword, *Sharpshooter*, p. 28.

2. Ibid.

3. The Andrews Sharpshooters were named after Massachusetts Governor John A. Andrews.

4. Stevens, *Berdan's Sharpshooters*, pp. 3-4. Theoretically, at least, a shooter could put all of his bullets in the same hole and still have a ten-inch string, providing the hole was ten inches from the center of the bull.

5. White, *Civil War Diary*, pp. 323-324.

6. For an excellent account of the Dimick rifles in service with the 66th Illinois, see Fagan, " The Dimick Rifles of the 66th Illinois Infantry."

7. Baumann, *Arming the Suckers*, p. 152.

8. Stevens, *Berdan's Sharpshooters*, p.205; Carter, *Four Brothers in Blue*, p. 112.

9. White, *Civil War Diary*, p. 250.

10. Regimental Order No. 8, April 22, 1864, *Regimental Correspondence Book*, 15th NJ Infantry, NA.

11. For a complete list of these units and the number of Sharps rifles they inventoried, see Coates and McAulay, *Civil War Sharps Carbines and Rifles*, pp. 22-23.

12. Ibid, p. 25.

13. Dunlop, *Lee's Sharpshooters*, p. 18.

14. Young, "A Campaign with Sharpshooters," *Annals of the War*, p. 270; Benson, *Civil War Book*, p. 60.

15. For a comprehensive account of the Whitworth in Confederate service, see Morrow, *Confederate Whitworth Sharpshooters*.

16. Interview with Bill Adams, October 7, 1995.

17. Shannon, "Sharpshooters with Hood's Army." *Confederate Veteran*, Vol. p. 127.

18. Morrow, *Whitworth Sharpshooters*, p. 24.

19. *Scientific American*, August 13, 1864.

20. Ibid.

21. *OR*, Ser. I, Vol.XXIII, Pt. I, pp. 586-587.

22. Davis, *The Orphan Brigade*, p. 216.

23. *OR* Ser. I, Vol. XXVIII, Pt. I, p. 273.

24. Ibid; p. 323.

25. *OR*, Ser. I, Vol XXXV, p. 295.

26. Martin, *Gettysburg, July 1*, p. 149. For details of Reynolds' death and the various claimants, see pp. 140-149.

27. Tom Conroy to author, September 28, 1995.

CHAPTER IV

1. Starr, *Union Cavalry*, Vol. I, p. 126.

2. For a complete breakdown of Federal cavalry arms at Gettysburg, including revolvers and sabers,see Coates & McAulay, *Sharps Carbines & Rifles*, p. 21.

3. Baumann, *Arming the Suckers*, p. 39.

4. McAulay, *Civil War Carbines: The Early Years*, p. 44.

5. Webb, *Texas Rangers*, p. 215.

6. McAulay, *Civil War Pistols*, p. 63.

7. Forrest's men reported 482 Asheville rifles, 1,475 Mississippis and 725 Sharps carbines. For a full breakdown, see Coates & McAulay, *Sharps Carbines & Rifles*, p. 24. One authority gives the entire production of Asheville rifles as "estimated at about 300." Forrest's report would, therefore, indicate that Asheville production was higher than previously believed. It is also possible that his command received the entire production of Asheville Armory, which lasted from 1862-1863. Flayderman, *Antique Firearms*, p. 530.

8. McAulay, *Carbines of the Civil War*, p. 49.

9. Starr, *Union Cavalry*, Vol. II, p. 79; McAulay, *Carbines of the Civil War*, p. 74.

10. McAulay, *Carbines of the Civil War*, p. 106.

11. Strayer & Baumgartner, *Echoes of Battle*, p. 270.

12. Ware, *Indian War of 1864*, p. 6.

13. Starr, *Union Cavalry*, Vol. II, p. 78. Sargeant may have been using a bad lot of caps as an excuse to obtain the coveted Sharps.

14. McAulay, *Carbines of the Civil War*, p. 38.

15. Quoted in Coates & McAulay, *Sharps Carbines & Rifles*, p. 23.

16. Baumann, *Arming the Suckers*, p. 60.

17. McAulay, *Carbines of the Civil War*, p. 29.

18. Starr, *Union Cavalry*, Vol. II, p. 78.

19. Ibid, p. 412.

20. Ibid, Vol. I, p. 137.

21. Hyde, *Greek Cross*, p. 209.

22. Allen, *Down in Dixie*, p. 366; DeForest, *Volunteer's Adventures*, p. 196.

23. For a complete guide to shooting the Merrill, including what to look for when buying one, see Beck, "Shooting Merrill's Carbine."

CHAPTER V

1. Although there is a technical difference between revolvers, which carry their loads in a cylinder which revolves a chamber into battery behind the gun's single barrel for firing, and pistols, which are either single shot or semiautomatic guns fed from a magazine, the term "pistol" was used interchangeably with "revolver" in the mid-nineteenth century. For the purposes of this chapter, the nineteenth-century terms will be retained. When necessary, the term pistol will be modified by the term "single shot."

2. McAulay, *Civil War Pistols*, p. 64.

3. Starr, *Union Cavalry*, Vol. I, p. 198.

4. Strayer & Baumgartner, eds., *Echoes of Battle*, pp. 216, 218.

5. DeForest, *Volunteer's Adventures*, p. 2; Rhodes, *All For the Union*, p. 217.

6. Oates, *Confederate Cavalry West of the River*, p.70; McAulay, *Civil War Pistols*, p. 43.

7. Smith, *Frontier Defense in the Civil War*, p. 31.

8. Hale, *Third Texas Cavalry*, p. 49.

9. Baumann, *Arming the Suckers*, p. 41

10. Wiggins, ed. *Journals of Josiah Gorgas*, p. 128.

11. Starr, "Cold Steel," p. 154.

12. Brown, *Morgan's Raiders*, p. 50.

13. Ibid, p. 152.

14. Ibid, p. 159.

15. Mosby, *Reminiscences*, p. 30; Williamson, *Mosby's Rangers*, p. 21.

16. Starr, "Cold Steel," pp. 155, 156.

17. Edwards, *Noted Guerrillas*, pp. 144, 51. Younger's revolvers were most likely *not* the large pre-war Colt Dragoons. The term "dragoon" was often used to describe a .44-caliber as "navy" was used to describe any .36-caliber revolver. Younger's guns were probably Model 1860 Army Colts. Joseph Edwards' guns remained in the family until the 1930s when they were, unfortunately, sold. Interview with Steve DesMarais, April 30, 1995.

18. *OR* Ser I, Vol. XLI, Pt. III, p. 348; Pt. IV, pps. 727, 608.

19. Deeks, "Civil War Images."

20. Hilleary, *A Webfoot Volunteer*, p. 119.

21. Edwards, *Noted Guerrillas*, p. 15.

22. See, for example, Burch, *A True Story of Chas. W. Quantrell*.

23. Edwards, *Noted Guerrillas*, p. 83.

24. Ibid, pp. 134, 123.

25. Tobie, *First Maine Cavalry*, p. 124.

26. Mosby, *Memoirs.*, p. 285.

27. Stelle and Harrison, *The Gunsmith's Manual*, p. 39.

28. Robert W. Fisch to author, April 10, 1995.

29. Edwards, *Civil War Guns*, p. 321.

30. Ibid.

31. Keith, *Sixguns*, p. 210

32. Robert W. Fisch to author, April 10, 1995.

33. Ibid.

34. Robert Meinecke to author, May 2, 1995.

35. Charles G. Worman to author, July 27, 1992; Charles R. Howard to author, August 1, 1992.

CHAPTER VI

1. Hyde, *Following the Greek Cross*, p. 205.

2. McAulay, *Civil War Breech-loading Rifles*, p. 14.

3. Stevens, *Berdan's Sharpshooters*, p. 27.

4. Baumann, *Arming the Suckers*, p. 115; for a list of these regiments, see MacAulay, *Civil War Breechloading Rifles*, p. 18.

5. Todd, *American Military Equipage*, pp. 943, 1195, 1217. Model 1855 carbines were available in .56, .44, and .36-calibers. The smaller caliber cylinders held six shots.

6. Baumann, *Arming the Suckers*, p. 53; Stevens, *Berdan's Sharpshooters*, p. 27; Parsons, *The First Winchester*, p. 35.

7. McAulay, *Civil War Breechloading Rifles*, p. 41.

8. Parsons, *The First Winchester*, p. 13.

9. Ibid, p. 17.

10. Parsons *The First Winchester*, p. 17; Baumann, *Arming the Suckers*, p. 156.

11. Trenton (NJ) *State Gazette*, September 19, 1864.

12. Baumann, *Arming the Suckers*, p. 71; McAulay, *Civil War Breechloading Rifles*, p. 45; Baumann, p. 150.

13. McAulay, *Civil War Breechloading Rifles*, p. 46; Baumann, *Arming the Suckers*, p. 184; Strayer & Baumgartner, eds., *Echoes of Battle*, p. 233.

14. Strayer & Baumgartner, *Echoes of Battle*, p. 179.

15. Coates & Thomas, *An Introduction to Civil War Small Arms* pp.93-94.

16. Baumann, *Arming the Suckers*, p. 53; Thatcher, *A Hundred Battles in the West*, p. 181; McAulay, *Civil War Breechloading Rifles*, p. 104.

17. Baumann, *Arming the Suckers*, p. 179; *OR*, Ser. I, Vol. XLIX, Pt. I, p. 737.

18. Rhodes, *All For the Union*, p. 187.

19. Drake, *Ninth New Jersey*, p. 184.

20. Ibid.

21. *OR*, Vol XLIII, pt. I, p. 860.

22. Ibid, p. 616

23. For a regimental breakdown of Ross' brigade & the ANV, see Coates & McAulay, *Sharps Carbines & Rifles*, p. 24.

24. Baumann, *Arming the Suckers*, p. 179; McAulay, *Civil War Breechloading Rifles*, p. 101.

25. According to several sources, Confederate soldiers referred to the Henry and Spencer as rifles that the Yankees could "load on Sunday and shoot all week." Interestingly, all of these sources are Federal!

26. Oliver Winchester to Dyer, June 14, 1865, RG 156, NA. Copy courtesy Earl J. Coates.

Bibliography

Adams, William O. *A Brief Introduction to the P53 Long Enfield*. Scotland, CT: Author, 1994.

Albaugh, William A. III, Benet, Hugh Jr. and Simmons, Edward N.. *Confederate Handguns: Concerning the Guns, the Men Who Used Them and the Times of Their Use*. New York: Bonanza Books, 1963.

Alberts, Don E. ed. *Rebels on the Rio Grande: The Civil War Diary of A. B. Peticolas*. Albuquerque, NM; Merit Press, 1993.

Allan, Stanton B. *Down in Dixie: Life in a Cavalry Regiment in the Civil War Days from the Wilderness to Appomattox*. Boston: D. Lathrop and Co., 1888.

Bailey, D. W. *British Military Longarms: 1715-1865*. New York: Arms and Armour Press, 1986.

Baird, W. David, ed. *A Creek Warrior for the Confederacy: The Autobiography of Chief G. W. Grayson*. Norman OK: U. of Oklahoma Press, 1988.

Barnes, Franck C. *Cartridges of the World*. Chicago: Follet, 1965.

Baumann, Ken. *Arming the Suckers, 1861-1865: A Compilation of Illinois Civil War Weapons*. Dayton, OH: Morningside, 1989.

Beaudot, William J. K. and Lance J. Herdegen. *An Irishman in the Iron Brigade: The Civil War Memoirs of James P. Sullivan, Sergt.,Company K, 6th Wisconsin Volunteers*. New York: Fordam University Press, 1993.

Bellard, Alfred. (David Herbert Donald, ed.) *Gone For a Soldier: the Civil War Memoirs of Private Alfred Bellard*. New York: Little, Brown, 1975.

Benham, Calhoun. *A System for Conducting Musketry Instruction*

Prepared and Printed by Order of General Bragg for the Army of Tennessee. Richmond, VA: Enquirer Job Office, 1863.

Benson, Berry. (Susan Williams Benson, ed.) *Berry Benson's Civil War Book: Memoirs of a Confederate Scout and Sharpshooter.* Athens, GA: University of Georgia Press, 1992.

Bilby, Joseph G. *Three Rousing Cheers: A History of the Fifteenth New Jersey Infantry from Flemington to Appomattox.* Hightstown, NJ: Longstreet House, 1993.

_____. *Forgotten Warriors: New Jersey's African American Soldiers in the Civil War.* Hightstown, NJ: Longstreet House, 1994.

_____. *Remember Fontenoy: The 69th New York and the Irish Brigade in the Civil War.* Hightstown, NJ: Longstreet House, 1995.

Blackmore, Howard L. *British Military Firearms, 1650-1850.* Carlisle, PA; Stackpole.

Boatner, Mark M. III. *The Civil War Dictionary.* New York: David McKay Company, 1959.

_____ . *Encyclopedia of the American Revolution.* New York: David McKay Company, 1966.

Bowen, James L. *History of the Thity-Seventh Regiment, Mass. Volunteers in the Civil War of 1861-1865.* Holyoke, MA & New York: Clark W. Bryan & Company, 1884.

Brown, Dee. *Morgan's Raiders.* New York: Konecky & Konecky 1995 (reprint).

Brown, Norman D., ed. *One of Cleburne's Command: The Civil War Reminiscences and Diary of Capt. Samuel T. Foster, Granbury's Texas Brigade, CSA.* Austin: U. of Texas Press, 1980.

Bruce, Robert V. *Lincoln and the Tools of War.* Indianapolis IN: Bobbs-Merrill Co., 1956.

Buckeridge, Justin O. *Lincoln's Choice.* Harrisburg, PA: Stackpole, 1956.

Buel, Clarence Clough and Robert Underwood Johnson, eds. *Battles and Leaders of the Civil War.* (4 vols.) New York: The Century Company, 1884-1887.

Burch, J. P. *A True Story of Chas. W. Quantrell and His Guerrilla Band.* Vega, TX: Author, 1923.

Busey, John W. and David G. Martin. *Regimental Strengths at Gettysburg.* Baltimore: Gateway Press, 1982.

Carley, Kenneth. *The Sioux Uprising of 1862.* St. Paul, MN: Minnesota Historical Society, 1976.

Carr, Caleb, *The Devil Soldier.* New York: Random House, 1992.

Casey, Silas. *Infantry Tactics....* Dayton, OH: Morningside, 1985. (reprint)

Cleveland, H. W. S.. *Practical Directions for the Use of the Rifle*. Salem, MA: Gazette and Mercury, 1861.

Cline, Walter. *The Muzzle-loading Rifle - Then and Now*. Huntington, W. VA: Standard Printing and Publishing, 1942.

Coates, Earl J. & John D. McAulay. *Civil War Sharps Carbines & Rifles*. Gettysburg, PA: Thomas Publications, 1996.

_____ & Dean Thomas. *An Introduction to Civil War Small Arms*. Gettysburg, PA: Thomas Publications, 1990.

Crow, Vernon H. *Storm in the Mountains: Thomas' Confederate Legion of Cherokee Indians and Mountaineers*. Cherokee, NC: Museum of the Cherokee Indian, 1982.

Cunningham, Eugene. *Triggernometry: A Gallery of Gunfighters*. Caldwell, CO: Caxton Printers, 1982.

Daniel, Larry J. *Soldiering in the Army of Tennessee: A Portrait of Life in a Confederate Army*. Chapel Hill, NC: UNC Press, 1991.

Davis, Carl L. *Arming the Union: Small Arms in the Union Army*. Port Washington, NY; Kennikat Press, 1973.

Davis, William C. *The Orphan Brigade: The Confederates Who Couldn't Go Home*. New York; Doubleday, 1980.

Davis, William H. *History of the One Hundred and Fourth Pennsylvania Regiment from August 22, 1861 to September 30, 1864*. Philadelphia, PA: J. B. Rodgers, 1866.

De Forest, John W. *A Volunteer's Adventures; A Union Captain's Records of the Civil War*. Hamden, CT: Archon, 1970.

Drake, J. Madison. *The History of the Ninth New Jersey Veteran Vols*. Elizabeth NJ: Journal Printing House, 1889.

Dunlop, William S. *Lee's Sharpshooters*. Dayton, OH: Morningside, 1988. (reprint)

Edwards, John N. *Noted Guerrillas, or the Warfare of the Border*. Dayton, OH: Morningside, 1976. (reprint)

Edwards, William B. *Civil War Guns*. Harrisburg, PA: Stackpole, 1962.

Fellman, Michael. *Inside War: The Guerrilla Conflict in Missouri During the American Civil War*. New York: Oxford U. Press, 1989.

Flayderman, Norm. *Flayderman's Guide to Antique American Firearms and Their Values, 6th Edition*. Northbrook, ILL; DBI Books, 1994.

Foster, John Y. *New Jersey and the Rebellion: A History of the Services of the Troops and People of New Jersey in Aid of the Union Cause*. Newark, NJ: Martin R. Dennis & Co., 1868.

Fuller, Claud. *The Rifled Musket*. New York: Bonanza Books, 1958.

Garavaglia, Louis A. and Charles G. Worman. *Firearms of the American West: 1803-1865*. Albuquerque, NM: U. of New Mexico Press, 1984.

Gibbon, John. The Artillerist's Manual. New York: D. Van Nostrand, 1860.

Griffith, Paddy. *Battle Tactics of the Civil War*. New Haven; Yale University Press, 1989.

Haines, Alanson. *History of the Fifteenth Regiment New Jersey Volunteers*. New York: Jenkins and Thomas, Printers, 1883.

Hale, Douglas. *The Third Texas Cavalry in the Civil War*. Norman, OK: U. of Oklahoma Press, 1993.

Hallahan, William H. *Misfire: The History of How America's Small Arms Have Failed Our Military*. New York: Charles Scribner's Sons, 1994.

Hicks, James E. *U.S. Military Firearms: 1776-1956*. Alhambra, CA: Borden Publishing, 1962.

Hyde, Thomas W. *Following the Greek Cross Or, Memories of the Sixth Army Corps*. Boston & New York: Houghton Mifflin and Co., 1895.

Keith, Elmer. *Sixguns by Keith*. New York: Bonanza Books, 1961.

Ladd, David L. & Audrey, eds. *The Bachelder Papers*. (3 vols.) Dayton, OH: Morningside, 1994-1995.

Lewis, Berkely R. *Small Arms and Ammunition in the United States Service*. Washington: Smithsonian Institution, 1956.

_____. *Notes on Cavalry Weapons of the American Civil War*. Washington, DC: American Ordnance Assn., 1961.

Longacre, Edward G. *To Gettysburg and Beyond: The Twelfth New Jersey Volunteer Infantry, II Corps, Army of the Potomac, 1862-1865*. Hightstown, NJ: Longstreet House, 1988.

_____. *Jersey Cavaliers: A History of the First New Jersey Volunteer Cavalry, 1861-1865*. Hightstown, NJ Longstreet House, 1992.

Marbaker, Thomas B. *History of the Eleventh New Jersey Volunteers*. Hightstown, NJ: Longstreet House, 1990 (reprint).

Martin, David G. *Gettysburg, July 1*. Conshohocken PA: Combined Books, 1995.

McAulay, John D. *Carbines of the Civil War*. Union City, TN: Pioneer Press, 1981.

_____. *Civil War Carbines, Volume II: The Early Years*. Lincoln, RI: Andrew Mobray Inc., 1991.

_____. *Civil War Pistols*. Lincoln, RI: Andrew Mobray Inc., 1992.

McQueen, John C. *Spencer: The First Effective and Widely Used Repeating Rifle—And Its Use in the Western Theater of the Civil War*. Marietta, GA: Author, 1989.

McWhiney, Grady and Perry D. Jamieson. *Attack and Die: Civil War Military Tactics and the Southern Heritage*. University, AL: U. of Alabama Press, 1982.

Morrow, John Anderson. *The Confederate Whitworth Sharpshooters*. Atlanta, GA: Author, 1989.

Mosby, John S. *Mosby's War Reminiscences and Stuart's Cavalry Campaigns*. Boston: Geo A. Jones & Co., 1887.

Mulholland, St. Clair A. *The Story of the 116th Regiment, Pennsylvania Infantry: War of Secession, 1862-1865*. Gaithersburg, MD: Old Soldier Books, 1992 (reprint).

Myatt, Frederick. *The Illustrated Encyclopedia of 19th Century Firearms*. London: Salamander Books, 1979.

Nelson, Herbert B. and Preston E. Onstad. *A Webfoot Volunteer: The Diary of William M. Hilleary, 1864-1866*. Corvallis: University of Oregon Press.

New York Commission for the Battlefields of Gettysburg and Chattanooga. *Final Report on the Battlefield of Gettysburg [New York at Gettysburg]* (3 vols.) Albany NY: J. B. Lyon Co., 1900, 1902.

Oates, Stephen B. *Confederate Cavalry West of the River*. Austin; University of Texas, 1961.

Parsons, John E. *The First Winchester*. New York: Winchester Press, 1969.

Perrine, Lewis. *Quartermaster General's Reports 1860-1866*. Trenton, NJ: State of New Jersey, 1861-1867.

Peterson, Harold L. *Book of the Continental Soldier*.

Philadelphia Weekly Times. *The Annals of the War, Written bv Leading Participants North and South*. Dayton, OH: Morningside, 1988 (reprint).

Purdue, Howell and Elizabeth. *Pat Cleburne: Confederate General*. Hillsboro, TX: Hillsboro Jr. College Press, 1973.

Rhodes, Robert Hunt, ed. *All for the Union: The Civil War Diary and Letters of Elisha Hunt Rhodes*. New York: Orion Books, 1991

Roads, C. H. *The British Soldier's Firearm, 1850-1864*. London; Herbert Jenkins Ltd., 1964.

Roberts, Ned. H. *The Muzzle-loading Cap Lock Rifle*. Harrisburg, PA: Stackpole, 1940.

Robertson, James I, Jr., ed. *The Civil War Letters of General Robert McAllister*. New Brunswick, NJ :Rutgers University Press, 1965.

_____. *Soldiers Blue and Gray*. Columbia, SC: U. of South Carolina Press, 1988.

Roe, Alfred Seely. *Monocacy: A Sketch of the Battle of Monocacy, Md, July 9th, 1864*. Worcester, MA; 9th New York Heavy Artillery Veterans Organization, 1894.

_____. *The Ninth New York Heavy Artillery*. Worcester, MA; Author, 1899.

Scribner, Benjamin F. *How Soldiers Were Made*. Huntington, WVA: Blue Acorn Press, 1995. (reprint)

Shannon, Fred A. *The Organization and Administration of the Union Army, 1861-1865.* (2 vols.) Cleveland OH: Arthur H. Clark Co., 1928.

Smith, David Paul. *Frontier Defense in the Civil War.* College Station, TX: Texas A&M, 1992.

Starr, Stephen Z. *The Union Cavalry in the Civil War.* (3 vols.) Baton Rouge LA: LSU Press, 1979, 1981, 1985.

Stelle, J. P. and William B. Harrison *The Gunsmith's Manual.* Highland Park, NJ: The Gun Room Press, 1972 (reprint).

Stevens, Charles A. *Berdan's United States Sharpshooters in the Army of the Potomac: 1861-1865.* Dayton OH; Morningside Books, 1984 (reprint).

Sword, Wiley. *Sharpshooter: Hiram Berdan, His Famous Sharpshooters and their Sharps Rifles.* Lincoln, RI; Andrew Mobray, 1988.

Strayer, Larry M. & Richard A. Baumgartner, eds. *Echoes of Battle: The Atlanta Campaign.* Huntington, W. VA; Blue Acorn Press, 1991.

Thatcher, Marshall P. *A Hundred Battles in the West; St Louis to Atlanta, 1861-1865: The Second Michigan Cavalry.* Detroit, MI; Author, 1884.

Thomas, Dean S. *Ready...Aim...Fire! Small-Arms Ammunition in the Battle of Gettysburg.* Gettysburg, PA: Thomas Publications, 1981.

U.S. War Department. *The War of the Rebellion: A Compilation of the Official Records of the Union and Confederate Armies.* (128 vols.) Washington: U.S. Government Printing Office, 1880-1901.

_____. *A System of Target Practice.* Washington: U.S. Government Printing Office, 1862.

Time Life Books Eds. *Arms and Equipment of the Confederacy.* Alexandria, VA: Time-Life Books, 1991

Tobie, Edward P. *History of the First Maine Cavalry, 1861-1865.* Boston: Emery, 1887.

Todd, Frederick P., et. al. *American Military Equipage, 1851-1871, Volume II, State Forces.* New York: Chatham Square Press, 1983

Tyler, Mason W. *Recollections of the Civil War.* New York: G. P. Putnam's Sons, 1912.

U.S. War Department. *Reports of Experiments with Small Arms for the Military Service by Officers of the Ordnance Department, U.S. Army.* Arendtsville, PA: Dean S. Thomas, 1984. (reprint of 1856 edition)

Vandiver, Frank E. *Ploughshares into Swords: Josiah Gorgas and Confederate Ordnance.* College Station, TX: U. of Texas Press, 1952.

Vickery, Max, et. al. *Muzzle-loading Shooting and Winning With the Champions.* Friendship, IN: Powder, Patch and Ball Publications, 1973.

Ware, Eugene F. *The Indian War of 1864.* Lincoln, NE: U. of Nebraska, 1994 (reprint).

Watkins, Samuel, R. *"Co. Aytch," Maury Grays, First Tennessee Regiment; or, A Side Show of the Big Show*. Dayton, OH: Morningside Press, 1982 (reprint)

Webb, Walter Prescott. *The Texas Rangers: A Century of Frontier Defense*. New York: Houghton Mifflin, 1935.

Wert, Jeffrey. *Mosby's Rangers*. New York: Simon & Shuster, 1990.

White, Russell C., ed. *The Civil War Diary of Wyman S. White, First Sergeant, Company F, 2nd United States Sharpshooters*. Baltimore: Butternut and Blue, 1993.

Wiggins, Sarah Woolfolk, ed. *The Journals of Josiah Gorgas, 1857-1878*. Tuscaloosa, AL: University of Alabama Press, 1995.

Wiley, Bell Irwin. *The Life of Johnny Reb: The Common Soldier of the Confederacy*. Baton Rouge LA: LSU Press, 1943.

Wilkinson, Warren. *Mother, May You Never See the Sights I Have Seen: The Fifty-Seventh Massachusetts Veteran Volunteers in the Army of the Potomac 1864-1865*. New York: Harper & Row, 1990.

Willard, George L. (William C. Goble, ed.) *Comparative Value of Rifled and Smoothbored Arms*. Hightstown, NJ, Longstreet House, 1995 (reprint).

Wolf, J.S. & Pat. *Loading Cartridges for the Original .45-70 Springfield Rifle and Carbine*. Hill City SD; Wolf's Western Traders, 1991.

Wray, William J. *History of the Twenty Third Pennsylvania Volunteer Infantry, Birney's Zouaves*. Philadelphia, PA: Regimental Assn., 1904.

ARTICLES

Austerman, Wayne, "'Blue Whistlers' and Colt Dragoons: The Arms of Terry's Texas Rangers," *Dixie Gun Works Black Powder Annual*, 1988.

_____, "Vulcan's Lieutenant: Lieutenant Colonel John W. Mallet and Confederate Ordnance, *Dixie Gun Works Black Powder Annual*, 1989.

Baenteli, John F.. "Production and Purchases of Civil War Revolvers," *American Rifleman,* December 1956.

Banks, Ron, "Death at a Distance," *Civil War Times Illustrated*, March/April, 1990.

Baumann, Ken, "Captain Newton's War," *The Gun Report*, December, 1991.

Beck, Tony, "An Introduction to Civil War Breech loaders," *Dixie Gun Works Black Powder Annual*, 1993.

_____, "Shooting Merrill's Carbine," *The Skirmish Line*, January-February, 1996.

Bellinger, Bill. "an Introduction to Collecting Confederate Firearms." *The Gun Report*, September, 1991.

Bilby, Joseph G., ed. "Memoirs of Carlos W. Colby." *Military Images Magazine*, September-October, 1981.

_____., "Prince of the Pistoleers," *Dixie Gun Works Black Powder Annual*, 1986.

_____, "Origins of the American Gunfighter," *Muzzle Blasts*, November, 1986.

_____, "The Keystone Travelers: A Regimental History of the 104th Pennsylvania," *Military Images Magazine*, March-April, 1992.

_____, "Some of Us Will Never Come Out: The Jersey Brigade at Gaines' Mill," *Military Images Magazine*, November-December, 1992.

_____, "'A Better Chance Ter Hit:' The Story of Buck and Ball." *American Rifleman*, May, 1993.

Blancard, Stephen F.,"Christopher Spencer's Horizontal Shot Tower," *The Black Powder Report*, September, 1985.

Burgess, James, "A Fast and Accurate Sharps Cartridge," *The Skirmish Line*, May-June, 1980.

Carlile, Richard, "The 1st District of Columbia Cavalry," *Military Images Magazine*, September-October, 1986.

Cleveland, H. W. S., "Rifle Shooting—Offhand." *Scientific American*, August 13, 1864.

Cooper, Jeff,"How Good Was Hickock," *Guns and Ammo*, March, 1960.

Deeks, Henry, "Civil War Images," *The Civil War News*, November, 1995.

Fagan, Dan P. "The Dimick Rifles of the 66th Illinois Infantry," *The Gun Report*, March, 1996.

Flores, Dan, "Sharpshooters in the Civil War," *Gun Digest*, 1977.

France, Dave, "How to Keep Your Sharps Shooting," *The Skirmish Line*, January-February, 1989.

Hacker, Rick, "Cap and Ball Revolvers," *American Rifleman*, August, 1988.

Howell, Cleves H., "The Whitworth Rifle." *American Rifleman*, January, 1952.

James, Gary, "The Reliable Remington," *Civil War Times Illustrated*, September-October, 1990.

Leinicke, Jim and Bill Weedman. "Skirmishing Ballistics: Civil War Smallbores—.54 Minies," *The Skirmish Line*, September-October, 1995.

_____. "Skirmishing Ballistics: The .69 Rifled Musket," *The Skirmish Line*, November-December, 1995.

_____. "Skirmishing Ballistics: The 505-Grain New Style Minie," *The Skirmish Line*, January-February, 1996.

Mallet, John W. "Work of the Ordnance Bureau," *Southern Historical Society Papers*, Vol XXXVII, January-December, 1909.

Maryniak, Ben R. "Shooting Practice." *Buffalo Civil War Round Table Newsletter*, May, 1990.

Meinecke, Robert, "Practical Tuning for the Percussion Revolver," *Muzzle Blasts*, April, 1991.

Neff, Robert O. "The Enfield Rifle," *Muzzle Blasts*, July, 1979.

Newman, Mark, "Arming the Privates," *Civil War*, September-October, 1990.

Rutledge, Lee A., "Uncle Sam's Multi-Shot Cartridges," *The Gun Report*, April, 1992.

Shannon, Isaac N., "Sharpshooters in Hood's Army," *Confederate Veteran*, Vol. XV, March 1897.

Spangenberger, Phil, "Overloaded Percussion Revolvers?" *Guns and Ammo*, January, 1986.

_____, "Uberti, King of the Replicas," *Dixie Gun Works Black Powder Annual*, 1989.

_____, "The Forgotten Versatility of Black Powder Sixguns," *Guns and Ammo*, August, 1990.

Spaugy, Phil, "Shooting the Henry Rifle." *The Skirmish Line*, May-June, 1990.

Starr, Stephen Z., "Cold Steel: The Saber and the Union Cavalry," *Civil War History*, Vol. XI, 1965.

Sword, Wiley, "The Guns at Ivy Mountain," *The Gun Report*, February, 1965.

Weller, Jac, "Shooting Confederate Infantry Arms," *The American Rifleman*, May, 1954.

_____, "Shooting Confederate Infantry Arms, Pt. II," *The American Rifleman*, June, 1954.

Wilson, R. L. "Genesis of the Winchester," *American Rifleman*, June, 1991

MANUSCRIPTS

"Annual Target Practice Form" Bill Adams Collection.

"Ich B. to Dear Parents," Bill Adams Collection.

William R. Clark Papers, John Kuhl collection

Benjamin D. Coley Diary, New Jersey Historical Society.

Phillip H. Smith to Uncle [Frederick Canfield], Canfield/ Pickering Papers, New Jersey Historical Society.

Dickerson Family papers, New Jersey Historical Society.

McDaniel Family papers, possession of Martin J. Anton Jr.

Regimental Letter and Correspondence Books, 15th New Jersey Infantry, National Archives.

Oliver Winchester to Brig. Gen. A. B. Dyer, June 14th, 1865, RG 156, National Archives.

NEWSPAPERS

Doylestown (PA) *Democrat*

Hunterdon (NJ) *Republican*

Newark (NJ) *Advertiser*
Newark, (NJ) *Journal*
New York Times
Paterson (NJ) *Guardian*
Sussex (NJ) *Register*
Trenton (NJ) *State Gazette*
Warren (NJ) *Journal*

General Index

Berdan, Hiram, 104-107, 110
Buford, John, 145-146, 200
Cameron, Simon, 55
Cleburne, Patrick R., 83-84, 119-120, 122
Dimick, Horace E., 112
Fayetteville Armory, 55
Forrest, Nathan B., 62, 118, 136, 144, 205
Fremont, John C., 66, 133
Gorgas, Josiah, 30, 54, 165
Griffith, Paddy, 24, 73-74
Harper's Ferry, WV, 27, 51, 52, 55
Hickock, James B., 172, 173
Holmes, Theophilus H., 29
Huse, Caleb, 57, 58, 62
Ivy Mountain, KY, 29
James, Jesse, 171, 172, 173
Kearny, Philip, 55
Lee, Robert E., 76
McCulloch, Ben, 56
Martin, David G., 123-124
Meagher, Thomas F., 15, 23, 79
Minie, Claude-Etienne, 43
Morgan, John H., 62, 118
Mosby, John S., 167, 204
North-South Skirmish Association, 87
Olden, Charles S., 55, 56
Posey, Carnot, 15
Post, Henry A., 107

Quantrill, William C., 29, 169, 171
Ramsay, George D., 206
Ripley, James W., 30, 54, 55, 108-109, 130, 137, 190-191, 206
Richmond Armory, 55, 94-95
Schuyler, George L., 58
Spencer, Christopher M., 196
Springfield, MA, 51
Terry, Benjamin F., 29

Units, Confederate
  Army of Northern Virginia, 67, 117, 205
  Army of Tennessee, 27, 63, 67, 83, 84, 122, 135
  Kentucky "Orphan" Brigade, 119, 122
  South Carolina Brigade (McGowan's), 117
  Thomas' Legion, 56
  2nd Creek Regiment, 57, 168
  Palmetto Sharpshooters, 116, 117
  10th Alabama, 106
  11th Alabama, 106-107
  1st Arkansas, 195
  2nd Florida Cavalry, 133
  44th Georgia, 77
  2nd Kentucky Cavalry, 62
  4th Kentucky Cavalry, 94
  Louisiana Tigers, 97

Firearms Index